CACTI & SUCCULENTS
FOR COLD CLIMATES

CACTI &
SUCCULENTS
FOR COLD CLIMATES

---

274 OUTSTANDING SPECIES FOR CHALLENGING CONDITIONS

LEO J. CHANCE

TIMBER PRESS

PORTLAND / LONDON

Published in 2012 by Timber Press, Inc.

The Haseltine Building
133 S.W. Second Avenue, Suite 450
Portland, Oregon 97204-3527
www.timberpress.com

2 The Quadrant
135 Salusbury Road
London NW6 6RJ
www.timberpress.co.uk

Printed in China

Chance, Leo J.
  Cacti and succulents for cold climates : 274 outstanding species for challenging conditions /
Leo J.
Chance. -- 1st ed.
       p. cm
  Includes bibliographical references and index.
  ISBN-13: 978-1-60469-264-8
  1. Cactus. 2. Succulent plants. 3. Gardens--Design. 4. Gardening. I. Title.

SB438.C36 2012
635.9'525--dc23
                                      2011045149

A catalog record for this book is also available from the British Library.

DEDICATION

To the memory of Charles Boissevain

and Carol Davidson, whose book

Colorado Cacti started me down a path

that has consumed me, but has

made my life much richer and has

brought me into contact with some

of my favorite people.

CONTENTS

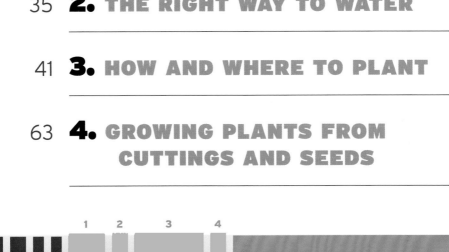

C acti, yuccas, and agaves practically constitute the brand for the southwestern United States: a cowboy on a pony, a cactus, and a red cliff—and presto, vintage Americana! In fact, one or another species of cactus and many another succulent can be found in virtually every one of the lower forty-eight states. On the flats, you can hardly be out of sight of a cactus anywhere west of the 100th meridian, except at higher, wetter elevations perhaps, and on the humid Pacific coastal strip. Both the Great Plains and the great Intermountain basins and plateaus have a significant succulent flora: *Yucca glauca* (common soapweed) grows in vast colonies on the Great Plains almost to the Canadian border, and *Escobaria vivipara* (Plains ball cactus) and several *Opuntia* species (prickly pears) rove far north into Canada, *O. fragilis* (brittle prickly pear) making it practically to arctic latitudes near Great Slave Lake.

Farmers and timid souls may find cactus to be a challenge, but for lovers of the American West, cacti are evocative and essential. True succulent aficionados prefer the gnarly, prickly stems and endlessly variable shapes, forms, and spination to the ephemeral, miracle flowers. A cactus in full bloom is truly one of Nature's loveliest spectacles. As you flip through this book, you can hardly resist the allure of glowing blossoms that come in an astonishing range of tints. Really, nothing can beat a blooming cactus: the iridescent, shimmering texture of the petals, the explosion of complex anthers, and usually a starkly contrasting stigma. Often as not a menagerie of insects is feeding, sleeping, or mating inside the blossom, and the stamens in many prickly pears perform an elaborate, frantic ballet when a bee perches on them, brushing the sipping insect with pollen, or when a person brushes them with a finger—a great trick to share with kids.

Although the flowers of some ball and columnar cacti may last a week, most cactus blooms last only a day or two at most, and some precious clones and plants rebloom repeatedly through the season. Like cherry blossoms, much of the magic of cactus flowers is their transience: you must stop everything, linger, and enjoy them because soon they will wither. Cactus blossoms are a metaphor for the fleeting nature of time and life itself. No wonder we love them so.

Many gardeners in the West have been captivated by cacti, and in most towns in the region, someone has a collection of the local sorts. Fifty or a hundred years ago the West was so untrammeled and cacti so abundant that no one thought twice when a rancher dug up a bunch of *Echinocactus texensis* (horse crippler) plants and stuck them into a rocky pile of soil studded with a few rocks, a so-called rock garden. As cities exploded across the West and cactus collecting became a popular hobby in parts of the country, more and more of the unusual native ball cacti were harvested by some entrepreneurs for resale, usually to die somewhere along the way. Many ball and barrel cacti were practically eliminated in accessible localities.

The Cactus and Succulent Society of America (CSSA) has taken a bold stand to discourage wild collecting of cacti: the spectacular cactus shows staged by CSSA affiliates ban the display of collected plants. Today, collecting hardy cacti is not only illegal in many states, it is unnecessary because of the availability of nursery-grown specimens.

The movement towards low-water gardening, sometimes labeled xeriscape or watersmart gardening, has also brought a renewed interest in succulents. People in hotter, drier areas have found that a container with cacti will survive a period of neglect, making cacti the perfect patio plants for busy professionals who do not have the time to spray and mist or water their houseplants or outdoor containers reliably.

More public gardens are featuring artistic succulent displays, from the extravaganzas of the Huntington Botanical Garden in Southern California or the Desert Botanic Garden in Phoenix, Arizona, to the imaginative "undersea" succulent garden at San Diego Botanic Garden, with its gnarly crested *Euphorbia* standing in for corals and sea urchin cacti. Hardy succulent gardens can be found across the colder and even moister states, and these too are being combined with drought-tolerant shrubs and wildflowers to create garden scenes rather than the prickly cactus ghetto of yore.

nnumerable books have been written over the last few centuries on succulents. Only two address hardy succulents, one of them written in Hungarian! *Télálló kaktuszok, agávék és pálmaliliomok* (Winter hardy cactus, *Agave*, and Palms) was written by Zsolt Debreczy in 1976. While cutting edge at the time, it includes only a fraction of the plants addressed in the present book. Gwen Kelaidis's lavishly illustrated *Hardy Succulents*, which came out in 2008, includes South African and Eurasian plants, with only the commonest American succulents. Although both books are classics of a sort, they barely scratch the surface of what's possible with American hardy succulents. So many keen gardeners have been growing such a wide spectrum of native American succulents that the time for a comprehensive handbook like this one written by Leo Chance is long overdue.

eo has spent three decades growing, studying, and researching a wide range of hardy succulents, the widest of anyone I know. He has acquired an exceptional private collection of plants and has designed outstanding gardens in which he has tested and observed many of these plants in various conditions and microclimates. Each time I visit his garden, I marvel to see his large assortment of South American succulents, the largest I know of in a Zone 5 (-20°F or -28°C) garden, and Leo never ceases to amaze me by pointing to a new species of *Escobaria* or *Echinocereus* thriving in his garden with a name that I have never heard of. He has been an enthusiastic promoter and salesman of hardy succulents for much of his professional life, educating customers at a leading garden center where he has a devoted following and at the Colorado Cactus and Succulent Society's annual succulent extravaganza where he has consistently provided the widest spectrum of hardy succulents for sale.

Leo has been the touchstone of the regional cactus and succulent renaissance, working closely with Steve and Linda Brack at Mesa Garden in Belen, New Mexico, and succulent growers up and down the Colorado Front Range, who have made this area a center of hardy succulent lore and experience. He has spent his vacations and spare time visiting hardy American succulents in their habitats and touring nurseries and gardens, applying what he has garnered to his exquisite private garden. Best of all, Leo has the gift of crystallizing his expertise into engaging and lucid expository prose to help anyone enchanted with these treasures grow them successfully in temperate gardens worldwide.

Growing hardy succulents has been a centerpiece of my professional work at Denver Botanic Gardens and indeed a source of great pleasure in my personal garden. I only wish I had Leo's book years ago to help guide me on my path. I am excited at the prospect of the extraordinary, beautiful, and water-wise gardens that will be enriched thanks to the cultural tips and design ideas included in this amazing resource. Finally, our bookshelves will have a fitting monument to honor this major and unique element of America's native flora.

Panayoti Kelaidis

The amazing demonstration garden at Mesa County Fairgrounds in western Colorado is as inspiring as the gardens in Southern California that made author Leo Chance want to garden with succulents in the first place.

PREFACE

My fascination and eventual passion for gardening with cacti and other succulent plants began over thirty years ago. At that time I took a trip with my wife, Ann, to Southern California, and everywhere we went my attention was drawn to cactus gardens. They decorated the grounds at hotels, restaurants, and parks, as well as many residential yards. Driving home through Arizona and New Mexico we saw many more cactus and succulent gardens. It was then the idea of creating a scaled-down cactus garden in zone 5 (-20°F or -28°C), using cacti and other desert plants, started to develop in my mind. The next obvious step, after deciding that I wanted such a garden, was to find out exactly what plants would be suitable and what kind of situation they would need to thrive.

Visiting garden centers almost everywhere I went, I sought both plants and advice. Very little correct information and still fewer plants seemed to be readily available. Even nurseries that specialized in cactus and succulent plants had little or no advice about what species would be capable of survival outdoors in colder climates. For the most part, the garden center professionals were discouraging. Often, *Sempervivum* plants (hens and chicks) and *Sedum* species (stonecrops or live-forevers) were offered as cacti. These can be valuable plants in water-wise gardens, but they are a long way from being cacti. On one occasion, a local garden center employee told me that *Vinca minor* (common periwinkle) might be a cactus, as it had somewhat thick leaves when compared to most garden perennials. Almost all of the authorities at the plant nurseries I visited in the area were in agreement: I was on the road to failure. According to the best understanding at the time, the plants I wanted to garden with simply could not survive Colorado's climate.

But I knew for a fact that some cacti were native to the region. I had grown up hiking in the prairies and various

parts of the foothills. I am sure I found out about cacti in the
same painful way that many kids in the western United States
do. But which ones would make suitable garden subjects?
Within a few weeks, I read every book our local library had
on the subject of cactus and other succulents. The treasure was
Colorado Cacti by Charles Boissevain and Carol Davidson.
With this book as my guide and inspiration, my wife and I
spent many weekends in search of cactus habitats. As we did
so, a hardy cactus garden started to seem more like a possibil-
ity. It could be done!

About thirty cactus species are native to Colorado and, as it
turned out, all of them were at least worth a try in the garden.
I found that some of them are as ornamental and desirable
as the plants that first caught my attention in Southern
California gardens a few years
earlier. And if my state had native
cacti, it seemed likely that the
surrounding states might also
offer some worthy candidates.
Sure enough, I discovered more
and more kinds of cacti. Now it
became a matter of how to
obtain them.

The western United States is
mostly privately held property,
where landowners do not always
allow trespassing. Collecting
plants or seed on public land is
often illegal and in many cases
is simply unethical. At the time
Colorado Cacti was written, nature
still was assumed to be able to
provide a never-ending source

of cactus plants to anyone with a shovel. As more land is constantly developed, that assumption has unfortunately been proved untrue. Many of the sites discussed in that book as prime cactus habitats are now covered with buildings or other types of development.

In the late 1970s I came across the mail-order nursery Mesa Garden in Belen, New Mexico. It had then, and still has, the largest selection of native succulents, including cacti and cactus seed, in the country. I arranged a visit to the nursery and have returned regularly. Eureka, I had found people that really cared and had great knowledge about all succulents, including cacti. They were even interested in the limits of cold that succulents could endure. Then and there I realized that although many cacti are native to regions that have cold winters, not many had been grown in gardens outside of their natural ranges. These plants had only been tested in places where cacti and succulents are supposed to grow. As it turned out, the relationship I developed with Steven Brack, the owner of Mesa Garden, put me in a position to try many species that might never have been found to be adaptable to gardens in cold climates.

In 1980, as my wife and I returned from Big Bend National Park in West Texas, I bought two small plants of *Agave havardiana* (Havard's century plant). At the time I had no idea what species they were, but they were growing in rusty, old, tin, coffee cans and were offered at a bargain price. These plants came from a roadside stand in the Davis Mountains and were labeled "Davis Mountains cactus." When we arrived home, I potted them into nice pots and kept them in our dining room window through the winter, taking them outside for the summer. After two or three years, the plants outgrew the space I had for them. I had no choice other than to leave them outside in the fall. I was sure that they would

Cacti and wildflowers bloom in early summer in a corner of the author's garden.

be dead by the middle of winter, but both were still alive, though a bit scarred, the following spring. By late spring, they were even showing signs of new growth. I planted them in the garden, where they grew and eventually bloomed, one in 2004 and the other in 2005. With their roots in the ground instead of in pots, the plants went through the winter without scarring. *Agave* species, also known as century plants, are an important part of the gardens that had given me the inspiration to try gardening with desert plants in the first place. At that time, I could not have been more excited. Finding this *Agave* species to be tolerant of cold winters sent me seeking and finding more plants to try.

In relatively little time, I was able to find native cacti and trunk-forming yuccas and agaves to create a dryland-looking garden. Also, I was able to find cacti from surrounding states that are able to adapt to harsh winters and unpredictable weather at all times of the year. My garden idea had become a reality. But it is hard to stop a search that has been fruitful, especially when a person is having such a good time. After all of the years that I have been on the hunt for new cacti and other desert plants to include in my garden, I still experience an unexplainable thrill when I find a new species. Over many years, I have found a growing number of both North and South American cacti that can survive several seasons in succession in my garden, not to mention the incredibly ornamental *Yucca* and *Agave* species. The numerous cacti and succulent species surviving in such a harsh environment prove them to be practical garden plants, especially in dry climates.

This well-maintained public cactus and succulent garden, part of the Western Colorado Botanical Gardens in Grand Junction, is a great place to learn about water-wise gardening.

ACKNOWLEDGMENTS

So many people should be thanked that I could probably fill a whole volume, but without the following people, I would never have been able to complete this project.

Panayoti Kelaidis, senior curator of Denver Botanic Gardens, not only helped with publishing, but also with advice and encouragement, as well as photographs and has been a good friend to me and anyone with an interest in gardening.

Zach Tice came to the rescue every time my minimal computer skills failed me. I couldn't have done it without him. He also provided many photographs.

I owe many thanks to Steven Brack, owner of Mesa Garden in Belen, New Mexico, who has been a valued friend for many years and has taught me much about cacti and other succulents, as well as providing countless plants for experimentation.

My wife, Ann, for companionship on this spiny adventure that I have taken, and for spending every one of her vacations for over thirty years on some kind of mission that was related to succulent plants.

Also I would like to acknowledge Mike Crump and Rita Auer, owners of Crump Greenhouse, Buena Vista, Colorado; Jeff Ottersberg, owner of Wild Things, a wholesale nursery in Pueblo, Colorado; and cactus expert Jeff Thompson, also of Pueblo.

Thanks to Bill Adams, owner of Sunscapes Rare Plant Nursery, Pueblo, for useful information and use of photos, also for many plants that have been donated to test the limits of cold and drought that they can endure.

I also need to thank Don and Donnie Barnett, a first-class father-and-son gardening team in Pueblo, for help with photos and information.

Many thanks go to Steve Miles of Boulder, Colorado, for his wonderful photos and helpful information.

Cold-hardy cacti and woody lilies fill Kelly Grummons's beautiful dry-land garden.

Thanks to Kelly Grummons of coldhardycactus.com and Timberline Gardens, Denver, Colorado, for help with photos and plant material.

I would also like to thank Edie Gibson and Stone Path Gardens, Colorado Springs, Colorado, for energetic support for this project.

Many other individuals and organizations provided photos or allowed me to photograph plants in their gardens including Bob Pennington, Agua Fria Nursery, Sante Fe, New Mexico; Chelsea Nursery, Grand Junction; Mesa County Arboretum and Gardens, Mesa County Fairgrounds, Grand Junction; the Conrad family, Pueblo; Greg Foreman, Evergreen; Ben Heitman, Colorado Springs; Paul and Lola Nafziger, Last Go Round Ranch, south of Colorado Springs; and Western Colorado Botanical Gardens, Grand Junction. To all of you, thank you.

Thanks go to Mountain States Wholesale Nursery in Glendale, Arizona, for plants that were donated to test their ability to withstand cold, not only to myself but also to growers throughout the western United States.

I also have to say thanks to the Denver Botanic Gardens, the Colorado Cactus and Succulent Society, and the Cactus and Succulent Society of America for everything that they do to promote my favorite pastime.

INTRODUCTION

Throughout the world, water becomes more precious every day. In fact, water rationing has become a part of life in many areas, whether in historically dry regions or not. People living in rural areas are often unable to tap into city water supplies and must rely on wells that are not bottomless. Many other areas suffer from water shortages. It is clear that as the human population grows, water will be in short supply. But as human beings we have a need to beautify and improve the world around us. For many of us that means gardening. Planting many traditional garden favorites without providing them with copious amounts of water is asking for frustration. It makes more sense to garden with a healthy respect for the environment in which we live.

Until recently, in dry climates with cold winters, cacti and other dryland plants were neither known nor understood by even some of the most experienced gardeners. That does not make them any less useful in the landscape. In fact, it makes it more exciting to use them. It is my sincere hope that this book will help encourage more interest in these vegetative wonders and that they will be more commonly used in gardens.

Many people are working longer hours and have less time and energy for yard work than was once the case. The need for attractive yet low-maintenance plants is real. Gardens that require additional water encourage weeds, which in turn demand attention. Keeping weeds under control can be time consuming or require the use of poisonous chemicals. Cacti and other New World succulents can get by on even less water than many weeds.

As urban sprawl continues, deer, rabbits, and other wildlife become common in the garden. Growing plants that can defend themselves from these hungry animals can be helpful.

The Barnett family's garden is a great example of how lush yet dry a well-planned cactus and succulent garden can be.

We are fortunate that plants as tough yet as structurally beautiful as cacti even exist. Few other forms of plant life can create such an impressive floral display with so little effort from the gardener. Few other plant groups can add as much interest to dry landscapes. No one can deny that there is something special about these plants. Almost anyone who pays any attention to flora will find cacti to be instantly recognizable.

Still, the fact remains that people in climates with adequate rainfall to grow large numbers of garden perennials are among the most avid collectors of cacti and other succulents as houseplants. And in warm climates where gardeners are not limited in the number of species that can survive their winter temperatures, succulents are also very popular. These plants have an esthetic quality that has interested people ever since the first cacti were introduced to Europe and Asia. Plants that have such practical qualities along with brightly colored, showy flowers and interesting, sculptural features deserve a place in modern gardens.

The exact definition of a succulent plant is not consistent in horticulture. For instance, genera such as *Yucca* and *Agave*, which are sometimes referred to as woody lilies, are considered by some to be true succulents, while others consider them to be nonsucculent xerophytes, that is, plants that have adapted to survival in dry situations.

All the plants discussed in this volume store water in their leaves, stems, or roots. They also all must receive adequate moisture during the growing season, and most need a dry resting period to maintain good health. The plants described in the following pages are thirsty in spring, and almost all of them need water in summer when they are active and growing, but then must have a dry period through the winter. Some species will go dormant in the heat of summer and are best kept on the dry side at that time. Those species will be pointed out as part of individual plant discussions. Again, it is important that night temperatures are cooler than those during the day for many succulent plants to truly thrive.

The term *succulent plant* does not imply that a genetic or family relationship exists. All cacti are related to each other, while they are only distantly, if at all, related to some of the other succulents. For instance, cacti are more closely related to *Dianthus caryophyllus* (carnations) than they are to the woody lilies or to the most familiar garden succulents such as sedums and sempervivums. What all these plants have in common is similar environmental pressures. Thus there is agreement that the definition of succulents includes the ability to store water for use during dry seasons. For gardeners, that is the most important thing to understand: succulents are plants that have the ability to survive predictable dry periods by using stored moisture.

1

UNDERSTANDING HARDINESS

A variety
of cacti
flourish with
wildflowers
and more
traditional
rock garden
plants
in the
author's
garden.

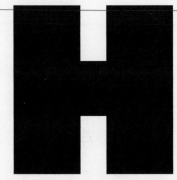ardiness, or the ability to endure extreme cold, is a lot more complicated than it might seem. All the plants described in this book have survived winters in USDA zone 5 (-20°F or -28°C), but many variables must be taken into account as all zone 5 winters are not the same, and all zone 5 climates are not alike. For example, temperatures that decline slowly in the fall are much easier on plants than a sudden deep freeze. Where I live, on the eastern plains of Colorado, we often have a mild autumn with a sudden arctic blast that results in temperatures of 10°F (-12°C) or colder. In the spring, a couple of mild weeks can encourage new growth that may be damaged by temperatures around 20°F (-7°C), after a winter in which periods of temperatures well below 0°F (-18°C) caused no harm.

Plants that are in less-than-the-best of health may not make it through a severe winter. That doesn't mean the species as a whole is not capable of withstanding the climate. Many plants have special soil requirements that must be met for the plants to be able to withstand the extremes of temperature that a plant in a more favorable situation may. It is important to give plants enough water during the first growing season, while they are establishing root systems. This will encourage healthy roots to develop and, if it is not done, even cacti may not be able to survive the stress of winter.

Plants also may have problems with the heat of summer. Wind exposure can be a major stress factor for succulent plants, especially in winter, and can even cause death. Winds can dehydrate dormant evergreen succulents. Though it is surprising to many people, cacti and succulents are easily sunburned, especially during spring and autumn freezes when they are halfway dormant. This is especially true at high altitudes where ultraviolet rays are stronger. Understanding and using microclimates will enable the gardener to include many more species.

In some cases plants will live for only a few years before they are lost, but that is part of gardening. Some species are short lived. All perennial gardens have plants that need to be replaced from time to time. I have tried and failed in my attempt to grow a few things in the garden more times than I would like to admit. In some cases, after killing numerous plants, I was able to find a more adaptable member of the species or the right location.

Growing Hardy Cacti and Succulents in Winter-Wet Climates

You don't have to live in the American West to be able to grow hardy cacti and succulents. Gardeners who live in parts of the world that experience wet winters with unreliable snowfall can grow many of these plants. *Opuntia humifusa* is native to the eastern states. *Escobaria vivipara* and *Opuntia fragilis* can be found growing naturally on the plains of Canada. Some of the *Yucca* species are more suited to wetter climates in the east than they are the dry western states. This means that in much of the continental United States, parts of Canada, the United Kingdom, and a good deal of continental Europe many of these species can be enjoyed in gardens. Even some gardeners in China are successfully growing cold-hardy cacti and succulents. Success can be achieved by observing the following cultural practices:

Make sure the planting site gets full sun in both summer *and* winter. In the Northern Hemisphere, this means a south- or southwest-facing site. If plants are in shade during the winter months, they will be much more likely to rot out.

Perfect drainage is essential, so give your plants fast-draining soil. Heavy clay soils and rich soils high in organic matter are not recommended. If possible, create raised beds or berms. Mix the native soil with one-half coarse sand. Do not add organic matter; add a trace mineral fertilizer at the recommended rate.

If possible, incorporate rocks into the plan, both to create pockets of soil for planting and to provide reflected sun and warmth.

During the hottest part of the summer, water plants every week to ten days if there is no rain.

Mulch the planting bed with a two-inch (5-cm) layer of crushed gravel. Replenish this when needed.

In autumn cut off all additional water to succulents to force dormancy ahead of freezing temperatures.

Any cactus species from the American plains can be easily grown in cold, wet climates. Several others have the ability to adapt to climates that are much colder and wetter than the ones in which they are native. The following species have been known to thrive in gardens in the eastern United States, and many of them have been reported to live for years in gardens in Germany.

Cylindropuntia davisii	*Echinocereus triglochidiatus*	*Opuntia basilaris*
Cylindropuntia imbricata	*Echinocereus viridiflorus*	*Opuntia compressa*
Cylindropuntia kleiniae	*Escobaria guadalupensis*	*Opuntia erinacea*
Cylindropuntia ×viridiflora	*Escobaria leei*	*Opuntia fragilis*
Cylindropuntia whipplei	*Escobaria missouriensis*	*Opuntia humifusa*
Echinocereus albispinus	*Escobaria sneedii*	*Opuntia macrorhiza*
Echinocereus baileyi	*Escobaria vivipara*	*Opuntia nicholii*
Echinocereus chloranthus	*Gymnocalycium bruchii*	*Opuntia phaeacantha*
Echinocereus coccineus	*Gymnocalycium gibbosum*	*Opuntia polyacantha*
Echinocereus fendleri	*Maihuenia poeppigii*	*Pediocactus knowltonii*
Echinocereus reichenbachii	*Opuntia arenaria*	*Pediocactus simpsonii*

These species are certainly not the only ones that can be expected to thrive in a winter-wet climate, but they may be a good place to start for beginners. Especially many of the *Escobaria*, *Echinocereus*, and *Gymnocalycium* species should be worth trying in cold and wet climates, as gardeners in several eastern states have reported success with them. Also, there are dozens of named *Opuntia* cultivars with showy flowers that have become available to gardeners in recent years, and almost all of them could be recommended to gardeners in climates where cacti are garden rarities.

The Influence of Provenance

Some individuals of any species are simply able to cope with certain difficulties more easily than others. For example, *Agave parryi* from Arizona has a large altitudinal range in nature; plants growing at lower elevations have to cope with extremes of heat in their native habitats but very little cold, while plants of the same species growing at higher elevations have to deal with wetter, colder winters but enjoy milder summer temperatures. Special adaptations such as this make some individuals of the species suitable to northern gardens. This principle is especially true of the many South American cacti species. Having an idea of where seed was collected in nature, or if a clone has proved its ability to survive in your climate may be important to know before buying a large, expensive specimen.

An amazing number of healthy cacti and other succulents fill a small area in the garden of Steve Miles, one of the pioneers of experimenting with succulents as garden plants in colder climates.

Cultural Practices
That Enhance Hardiness

Covering, or mulching, plants during the harshest months of winter can mean the difference between a plant that thrives for years and one that becomes a fading memory. Some plants can be left under a blanket of autumn leaves through the winter while they are dormant and will be fine. In fact, covering most plants can give them enough protection to increase a hardiness zone. It is a common practice in the nursery trade to cover garden perennials with cloth through the winter, to provide a little extra protection. Frost cloth, as it is called, is sold at garden centers and can be very effective. Many succulents, such as the *Pediocactus* species from the southwestern United States, are buried under snow in nature for brief periods each winter, but the snow always melts within a few days, or at most weeks. Except for *P. simpsonii* (mountain ball cactus), these plants seem to do best if they are not covered for long periods of time.

Almost all of the South American cacti do best buried under cloth, leaves, or snow for the entire winter season. Leaves from deciduous trees, falling on the garden, can offer some degree of protection when they cover plants in winter, but they also can cause problems by holding moisture for too long in spring. Plants that have been deprived of light through the winter can easily be sunburned if they are uncovered abruptly on a sunny day in spring. Also keep in mind that the hooked spines on some cacti can cause frost cloth to cling to the plants; care must be taken when removing the cloth to not disturb the plants.

Farmers that produce fruit such as apples and cherries will tell you that freezing temperatures in late spring will not injure crops, as long as they are able to thaw before the sun hits them directly. In my garden I have noticed that this also seems to be the case with some succulents, including cacti. The problem arises in autumn when plants are not dormant

and temperatures drop suddenly. Often, succulents that are exposed to strong sunshine in the morning, while their tissues are still frozen, will be scarred or even killed, while a plant of the same species growing a few feet away, but not in direct sunlight until temperatures have warmed and allowed tissues to thaw, will be unharmed.

This dynamic is a good part of the reason that plants buried under snow through the coldest part of winter show less signs of damage in spring. The other part is, of course, that they are protected from drying wind and the most frigid air. Gardeners at lower elevations may not face this problem. I have found that by placing plants on the north or west side of a rock that is large enough to provide shade in winter, this problem can often be avoided. The rock will absorb the sun's rays and provide a warmer microclimate. As the days grow longer in the spring, the sun is more overhead and the plant will no longer be shaded. Most dormant plants have no need for direct sunlight.

Purple wildflowers (*Penstemon* sp.) mingle with red cactus flowers (*Echinocereus triglochidiatus*) in a carefree corner of the author's garden.

2

THE RIGHT WAY TO WATER

Surviving
on natural
rainfall,
this area
of the
author's
garden
requires very
little
upkeep other
than some
deadheading.

The amount of water given any plant is important enough to make the difference between success and failure in growing that plant. With cacti and other fleshy, dryland plants, the timing of water becomes as crucial as any other factor.

Cacti and their garden companions are thirsty in the spring when they are breaking dormancy. They need water to encourage growth through the warmer months. These same plants have to be kept dry while they are resting during the cooler months. Sharp drainage is more important to fleshy plants than it is to most other forms of vegetation. Seedlings need water more often than they will when they are larger, and new introductions to the garden have to be watered more often than established plants of the same species. Some books claim that it is best not to water cacti at the time of planting because it will cause them to rot. I used to follow that advice, but have learned by experience that cacti that are not left dry the first few weeks after being planted will settle in much more quickly than those given no water at planting time.

Looking back at my losses with succulents and cacti, much of it was the result of a fear of water. This is not to say that getting carried away the other direction is a good idea, but a middle ground must be found.

When watering, give enough water to encourage deep, healthy root systems to develop and then let the surface of the soil dry completely before watering again. It is good to plant a few indicator plants that will let you know when it is time to water; wildflowers with thin leaves, such as penstemons or evening primroses, can be used for this purpose. While it is best to err on the dry side, it is best not to err, and that will come with time and experience. Many of these plants will continue to grow in autumn if temperatures are warm and moisture is available. By limiting water at that time to what nature provides, plants will be forced into dormancy and will be better prepared for sudden, dramatic drops in temperatures.

Cacti and succulents are most abundant in select climates in nature. What comes to mind for many people is the hot, dry desert of Arizona or West Texas, but even there moisture must be available for certain periods if the vegetation is to survive. Among the places where cacti are plentiful are the semiarid rolling grasslands that do not receive adequate moisture for forests to survive, the semidry situations where trees are broadly scattered, and on rocky hillsides where soils do not hold water well.

It is in the dry grasslands and rocky soils that do not hold moisture where we find many of the species that are suitable for winter-hardy cactus gardens. When wintering succulents, including cacti, many *Yucca* species, and all *Agave* species, outside in cold climates, it is best to keep them as dry as possible until warmer weather arrives. Many of these plants are able to withstand cold much easier than they can handle wet conditions when they are dormant, although when they do die, it is the cold that tends to be blamed. All succulent plants are native to climates that have enough rainfall to support plant growth through a season and to store moisture for a predictable dry season. Succulence in plants, including cacti, is about storing water during the growing season.

Heat is beneficial to almost all succulents and cacti. Tricks like placing plants close to a south-facing wall that reflects heat can be useful. Temperatures are sometimes surprisingly warmer when the sun is reflecting off of a light-colored surface. Cacti that are native to cool mountain climates high in the Andes can be grown to perfection by gardeners in Phoenix or Tucson, where heat is excessive for months, much hotter than their homes in the Andes. But very few of these same plants can be grown where winter temperatures are much colder than would be the case in their native habitats.

Plants that have had time to develop an adequate root system, which may take a couple of years, are more capable of withstanding extreme weather conditions. Some years are hotter, colder, wetter, or drier than others. A slow-growing plant that has only had one season to establish its root system may not be able to survive that extra-harsh winter that comes every twenty-five years or so, while a plant of the same species that has had a chance to become established over a longer period of time may be able to take such a winter in stride. Cacti and other dryland plants will often grow long, lateral roots slightly below the surface of the soil to take advantage of light, summer rainfall. I have sometimes planted "marginal" species in summers that were followed by a couple of mild winters; by the time a hard winter came, the plants were established enough to survive. A mild growing season can help plants become stronger and more likely to cope with the following winter, but the order of the seasons is beyond our control. Don't feel bad if you have to replace a few succulent plants or cacti after a harsh winter.

The Conrad family's cactus garden is only four years old. Many of these plants were in small containers when they were planted.

3

HOW AND WHERE
TO PLANT

Trays of
cacti at
a wholesale
nursery are
ready to
be shipped
to retail
nurseries.

o matter where you get your plants, it is important to treat them with a little extra care the first few weeks until they have had a chance to settle in. Planting early in the spring before the intense heat of summer is ideal for most species, but early spring is not always when the plant that you have always wanted becomes available to you. When planting during the hottest months, it may be worth waiting for a cloudy day or finding a way to provide temporary shade, such as a rock or a plant growing in a flowerpot that can be moved at a later time. Although it is not attractive, a small piece of paper tissue can provide temporary shade to the crown of a small plant.

It is especially essential to provide shade for plants that are shipped. New acquisitions that just came out of a small pot or were shipped bare root in a dark box need to be protected. It cannot be overstated how easily many succulents, including cacti, can sunburn when the level of light is increased abruptly.

Even the most drought tolerant species has to develop a good root system before it can withstand excessively dry conditions and long hours in direct sun without being damaged. In fact, some of the most xeric plants need deeper watering and more time to settle in, because it is necessary for them to build a larger underground storage system. These same plants will thrive in hot, dry sunny situations once they are established.

Feeding

A few years ago, the owner of the largest wholesale cactus and succulent greenhouse operation in the area told me that he had cut back on fertilizer for a whole season and hadn't seen much difference in the growth or flowering of the cacti. The truth is that these plants are for the most part light feeders. Most professional and successful hobby growers do use commercial soluble or organic fertilizers for containerized plants and believe that it is beneficial. For years now I have lightly spread nutrients in the form of composted manures through my garden. I use the kind of composted manure that comes in bags from the garden shop and has no odor. I do this at a rate of once a month through the growing season. This practice also helps to compensate for any erosion from raised beds or berms. Composted manures from any animal, kelp, fish emulsion, bone meal, or any other type of organic fertilizers feed the beneficial bacteria that help to create an ideal soil for plant growth. I also spot water using an organic fertilizer at half strength on recently planted areas of the garden.

Overuse of chemical fertilizers can be harmful to the good bacteria in the soil, which can be detrimental to long-term plant performance. This is a good place to err on the side of too little rather than too much. Succulent plants may grow quickly and flower more prolifically, but can become leggy and weak when gardeners get carried away with fertilizer. Nitrogen can burn the tips of any kind of plant roots when it is too abundant.

Many beneficial bacteria such as mycorrhizae have become readily available in garden centers. These bacteria and fungi help to break down the nutrients in organic fertilizers and make them useful to plants. The use of these bacteria when planting will help plants such as woody lilies and wildflowers to develop strong root systems more quickly and to use organic fertilizers efficiently. It is not a good idea to use chemical root stimulators when planting with beneficial bacteria.

If plants are purchased in containers, it may be necessary to remove the soil before planting. Plants that are grown in the nursery trade are almost always potted in an artificial soil mix that contains large amounts of peat or sphagnum moss, which dries, and more importantly absorbs water at a much different rate than loamy garden soil. This makes it difficult for healthy plant roots to develop. Peat moss will shrink when it dries and can damage roots in the process. The best way to remove the nursery soil is to let the root ball set in water for a few minutes, then wash it from the roots with a stream of water. After that, let plants dry in deep shade for a few hours until they are ready to be placed in the garden. This drying time allows any roots that are injured during the soil removal process to callus before they are planted. It is not necessary to remove all of the artificial soil, but most of the root system should be in contact with the soil in which the plant will be growing. If roots are tangled, care should be taken to tease them loose without tearing and breaking them excessively. Many plants purchased by mail order will be shipped bare root, in which case the nursery soil has already been removed before the plants were boxed.

Winter-hardy cacti and other succulents thrive in Don Campbell's garden at the foot of the Colorado National Monument.

Siting Your Plants

Understanding and using microclimates is a skill that any gardener will find helpful, but with yuccas or agaves, as well as many cacti and other succulents, it is even more important. For some of the marginal species, the use of favorable microclimates may be the difference between life and death for the plant and success and failure for the gardener. Watch the snow melt in spring; see where bulbs and other early season plants start growing first. Plants that are covered with snow for brief periods when air is coldest will often be unharmed by frigid temperatures while similar plants that are exposed will be injured or even killed.

Almost every garden has sites that offer a variety of wind, moisture, and sunlight exposures. Dig holes to see where the soil holds water longest and where it dries most rapidly; find out how deeply the water penetrates. If you are planting on berms, look to see how fast water is absorbed and where it runs off the berm. Plants positioned near heated buildings, especially on the south side, are more protected from cold, winter wind than those in the open. Cold air is heavier and settles at low points, so conditions at the top of a hill or berm may be slightly warmer. Even an artificial high point that is only a few feet in elevation may be slightly warmer.

Success with a garden is much like the value of real estate: a lot depends on location. A sunny spot where a berm or raised bed can be installed is a suitable garden site. If the soil in that spot is not appropriate for growing cacti and succulents, it can be amended. The amended soil should be neither overloaded with organic material nor too heavy with clay to absorb water. For almost any garden, adding humus is beneficial; however, most cacti and their garden companions perform best in gritty, sandy loams in dry climates, meaning that the soil should have only enough organic material in it to make its absorbent. Gravel is the best soil amendment for

cacti and succulents. It helps open soils to absorb water, chan-
neling it to the root zone where it is needed and away from
the surface where it can be a problem or run off. Any type
of gravel mixed into the top layer of soil will be helpful, but
pea-sized gravel works wells and will increase water drainage.

In wetter climates, humus-rich soils that allow air to penetrate may dry more quickly and therefore have an advantage.
Don't be afraid to experiment. You may learn something no
one else knows, and anyway, it's part of the fun of gardening.
Some cactus species will grow lush and plump and have more
flowers in deep, nutrient-rich soil but will not live long. The
same species may be long-lived though less impressive when
grown in drier conditions with gritty soil.

Preparing a Berm

For those not familiar with rock garden jargon, a berm, the
easiest place to successfully grow many succulent plants, is
essentially a mound that creates microclimates by improving
drainage and giving east, west, north, and south exposures.
Such a mound also draws interest to a chosen spot in the
garden. The best way to raise miniature plants to a position
where they can be easily seen is to put them on the upper
edge of a berm. Furthermore, if you are gardening where the
native soil is not the best for the plants you want to grow,
you can make islands of quality soil by bringing in topsoil to
create berms.

When creating a berm or raised bed, use the least expensive
stone material for the foundation or substrata layer. Large
gravel about half the size of an apple or orange or slightly
smaller works well. It can be smooth river rock or crushed
gravel with sharp edges—either type will help to hold soil
in place. The depth of rock should be at least six to eight

Cacti from both North and South America remain uncovered in winter in this part of Steve Miles's garden, because it is close to his house, which creates a slightly warmer microclimate.

inches (15 to 20 cm), but can be up to several feet, depending on what fits into your garden design. Gravel does not erode as easily as soil so you can create sharper hillsides for the berm without having them wash away as quickly. The other advantage to a thick layer of coarse rock is increased drainage. How important it is to increase drainage depends on how wet the climate is where you are gardening and what plants you are growing.

After laying down a base of rock, add a layer of topsoil that is neither too light with humus nor too heavy with clay. Landscape suppliers generally sell several kinds of garden soils and topsoils. Find the one that contains the least organic material. It is not necessary that it is without compost, but compost should not be the primary ingredient. You should be able to pour water on the soil and watch the water disappear without pooling first. Lighter soils that are full of humus tend to erode more quickly. The soil layer needs to be only a few inches thick, but deep enough to hold the root systems of container-grown plants. The topsoil can be amended with smaller gravel to create a gritty type of growing medium. I have found that plants that develop deep, fat, tuberous root systems grow better in a medium in which nothing larger than pea gravel is used for the first few inches directly under the plants. These plants also thrive next to a partially buried larger rock, which allows their roots to take advantage of moisture draining off the rock.

Once the raised area is shaped and sized, it can be covered with a decorative layer of stone. The type of stone is a matter of taste, affordability, and availability. In my gardens I generally use moss-covered sandstone or lava. For the sake of esthetics, the rocks in this top layer should be of the same type but variable in size and partially buried. This creates a more natural look and will encourage water to be absorbed

more deeply into the soil. Although this final layer of rock is
not essential for successful cultivation of succulent plants, it
does add favorably to the overall visual effect of a garden. It
will also slow erosion and have some insulation value, keeping
hot sunshine and cold air from having direct contact with the
soil. In hot, dry climates a layer of gravel will protect the soil
from the drying effects of the sun and will prevent water from
evaporating as quickly. A thick layer of rock mulch that is
three to four inches (7.5 to 10 cm) will also help to suppress
weeds. Using wood products, such as bark or other organic
mulches, for this decorative layer is not advisable as they
can absorb moisture, thus competing with thirsty plants for
limited rainfall. Also, they are lighter and more likely to be
moved by water and gravity.

Local rocks
and the
native loam
soil in which
many local
cacti and
wildflowers
grow provide
proper
drainage and
nutrients
for Jeff
Thompson's
dryland
garden.

Larger rocks or boulders set here and there in the berm will help to create further microclimates by providing shade and wind-blocks for small plants until they are able to grow large enough to store the water necessary to sit in hot sun for hours at a time. Decorative boulders will also help to hold the heat from the sun and add to the overall esthetics of the garden. Most well-designed cactus gardens on berms have many of the same appealing qualities that we find in traditional rock gardens. They just need less moisture.

To Backfill or Not

Many gardeners backfill planting holes with amended soil, thinking that plants prefer it to the surrounding soil. You should improve the entire bed if your garden soil is not suitable. By amending only small pockets you can create soils that vary in their ability to take up or hold moisture, which can stifle root growth. When plants are placed in small holes filled with ideal growing medium, it does not encourage their roots to spread into the less-than-ideal soil beyond that pocket. Healthy dryland plants need to develop large, spreading root systems to survive dry spells during the growing season. Healthy cacti and other succulents that can endure the stress of hot summers and frigid winters need vigorous root systems that often extend quite a distance from the plant. When plants are grown in berms, uneven soils are generally not a problem, as the soil is usually from a single source. When soil types differ and water is not absorbed evenly, some portions of a garden will dry more quickly than others, making the decision to water or not more difficult. Yes, in hot, dry conditions even high-desert plants including cacti will need to be given water or they may not flower.

Handling Cacti Safely

Once the site is chosen, the soil is prepared, and the plants are obtained, it is time to plant. I have had more than one guest to my garden ask how such spiny plants can be planted without harm to the plant or the gardener. The best answer is to handle this type of plant carefully!

There are several ways to remove cacti from containers, but the easiest is to gently squeeze the opposite corners of the pot while tilting it slightly. Let gravity take it from there. Of course, the plant should be held close to the surface where it will land!

Be especially careful to avoid the small spines on chollas and prickly pears known as glochids. The absence of longer, thicker spines may make some of these plants look harmless, but these tiny spines detach easily and can penetrate skin with the slightest touch. Wearing gloves can be helpful when handling these plants.

To remove a cactus from a container, first try squeezing the corners of the pot a few times to loosen the soil. If the plant is still not co-operating, simply cut the container.

Another method involves twisting a sheet of newspaper into a "rope" that can be wrapped around a plant's stem and used to easily move even the spiniest cacti. For larger, heavier plants, double or triple the number of sheets of paper.

TOP LEFT:
Twist a sheet of newspaper to make a disposable rope. Cactus spines are not likely to adhere to such a rope.

TOP RIGHT:
Wrap a newspaper rope around a cactus and use it as a handle to remove the plant from the pot and set it in the ground.

BOTTOM LEFT:
Any cactus can be handled with one hand using a disposable rope, no matter how the plant is shaped. This leaves the other hand free to hold the root ball.

BOTTOM RIGHT:
A spiny cholla is easily removed from its pot using a paper rope.

Often, cactus sellers will also sell suture clamps or other tools that can be useful for working with spiny plants. Likewise, kitchen tongs can be very useful for handling dangerous plants. Almost any thrift store has a selection of inexpensive kitchen tools that could be used for such purposes. The tongs I use were ready to be tossed out of our kitchen at home.

Generally, spiny plants can be handled with heavy-duty, preferably thick, leather gloves; however, some species, such as many of the chollas or prickly pears, have needle-sharp spines that can penetrate even leather, as can the tips of *Agave* leaves, so care should be taken. Having the planting hole ready before removing a plant from its pot will make the project go more smoothly. This is especially true with larger plants.

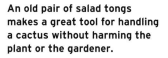

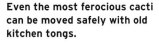

Usually used to control bleeding in surgeries, a long, straight-tipped hemostat is useful in the cactus garden for removing weeds near the base of a spiny plant, pulling spines that become embedded in flesh, or even separating offsets from a mother plant.

An old pair of salad tongs makes a great tool for handling a cactus without harming the plant or the gardener.

Even the most ferocious cacti can be moved safely with old kitchen tongs.

Rock Gardens

Some of the most interesting and attractive members of the cactus family are miniatures with ornate flowers that cannot be appreciated fully unless they can be inspected closely. If some of these gems are included in a rock garden, it is important that the garden also include safe and easy access for viewing the plants up close. In a garden that includes fiercely spined plants, planning is important.

It is not fun to make contact with most cacti, yuccas, and agaves. I once heard of a woman who took out a cactus garden weeks after lovingly planting it, because she had poorly planned the placement of a cholla. As you plan your rock garden, consider the ultimate size and, in some cases, the dangerous qualities of the plants you are using. Plants grow while you are doing other things and they don't always take long to outgrow the space you have provided for them. In a few years, a century plant with dagger-like leaf tips or a spine-covered cholla in a four-inch (10-cm) pot can grow to more than a foot (30 cm) across and become very painful to come into contact with. Depending on the species, in several years that same plant can be three or four feet (90 to 120 cm) across.

Thankfully, most cacti and century plants can be moved easily without stress to the plant, so don't be overly afraid of mistakes in plant placement. Although errors can be corrected, it is still best that they are avoided. *Yucca* species are the exception here and they are generally resentful of having their roots disturbed.

The Garden Potential of Cacti and Succulents

Many cacti are real show-offs when in bloom. It is not uncommon for these ferocious-looking plants to provide incredible displays of delicate, colorful flowers that can rival anything in the plant kingdom. The rosette shape of the woody lilies is after all, the same basic form as that of the much loved rose. The silhouettes of many cacti, such as chollas and some of the larger prickly pears, can be very attractive from a distance.

For size, we are bit limited in colder climates by the fact that species of *Yucca* and *Agave* are expensive if purchased as specimen-sized plants and will take some time to become an impressive focal point when purchased as small plants. But, there are still the large-stemmed prickly pears and chollas that are reasonably inexpensive, even as specimen-sized plants. Some chollas become tall or bushy plants that can create an interesting focal point in relatively little time. There are grasses and drought-tolerant trees, shrubs or bushes that can also serve this purpose, as well as adding textural interest. Several of these plants are described at the end of this book in a separate chapter on companion plants. Well-placed, decorative boulders can do the trick of drawing the eye from a distance. Cactus gardens can be outstanding with backlighting at night.

As for the small plants that keep you looking at a garden, cacti and other succulents really can't be beaten. Some of the miniature cacti and succulents that will grow in cold climates are among the most interesting members of the entire plant kingdom.

When my garden began to fill in and become established, many visitors in winter started to make comments about how green it was. While most traditional garden perennials die to the ground or turn into clumps of dry leaves in winter, most of the dryland succulents shrink down a bit but remain

Agave neomexicana (New Mexico mescal) in the author's garden looks as nice after a snowstorm in late winter as it does in summer.

quite attractive. At this time of year the woody lilies look no different than they do in the warmer months. During the coldest months of the year, a cold-hardy cactus garden is better looking than most other perennial gardens. Certainly not all, but many of the western wildflowers are also evergreen or semievergreen.

All the members of the cactus family that can be grown in cold climates have the ability to expand and contract. In spring, cacti swell up by taking in water and in the fall they will shrink, sometimes becoming a bit shriveled and wrinkly by cutting off water intake. It is best not to argue with your plants if you want them to do their best for you. When growth begins in spring, encourage it by giving extra water if there is no natural rainfall. In autumn, as plants begin to dehydrate, the wise gardener will cut off all irrigation to them, except what is provided by nature.

Like many cacti, *Echinocereus triglochidiatus* (claret cup hedgehog, king's crown cactus) dehydrates and shrivels in winter but still remains attractive.

Cacti in Containers

Some gardeners find it advantageous to grow cacti and succulents in containers or troughs as opposed to garden beds. Plants can be moved to cover during extreme periods of wet or cold. For those who rent or move often and have a passion for gardening, using containers is a way to create a mobile garden. Tall containers can keep dangerous plants above the reach of small children. They can also keep valuable plants out of the reach of squirrels or other pests.

Miniature plants can be more effectively displayed at close range. Panayoti Kelaidis, the senior curator of Denver Botanic Gardens, successfully grows a large variety of cacti and other succulents in colorful ceramic containers at the edge of his garden path and he believes that many of them benefit from being potted. Attention can be brought to small plants that might be lost in a larger setting by such staging. Microclimates can be created by placing containers in sunnier or shadier spots, or into positions protected or exposed to wind. Containers can be moved under building eaves during wet periods. Water can be more easily controlled in pots as large containers will dry more slowly than smaller ones.

At Denver Botanic Gardens, containers filled with tender succulents are taken outside for the summer to complement cold-hardy succulents in the garden.

Commercial cactus and succulent soil mixes for containers can be found at most garden centers, but any planter box mix that is not overly full of humus will provide an adequate growing medium if pea gravel is blended into it. How much pea gravel is used depends on the plants being grown and how wet the climate is.

Other succulents can benefit from container culture as well. Many people have been more successful with *Lewisia* species (bitterroots) and other crevice dwellers that need extremely sharp drainage, when growing them in containers, such as troughs, instead of garden beds. Plants with special soil needs can be cared for more easily in containers. Colorful, ceramic pots or moss-covered troughs can make a valuable addition to many garden settings, or give the opportunity to garden for those with limited space. Keep in mind that the growing media used in containers must be gritty and provide adequate drainage. Generally speaking, larger containers are more useful outside, as the soil mass will not freeze and thaw as readily.

Bright containers filled with healthy, colorful cacti and other succulents decorate the edge of a path in Panayoti Kelaidis's garden.

Cacti in Cold Frames

All the plants described in this book can easily be grown in properly designed, unheated greenhouses or cold frames. In such settings, plants are protected from rain, wind, and cold air in winter. In climates with excessively wet winters, this may be the only way to grow more than a handful of species. Care must be taken to ensure that plants are not directly exposed to direct, strong sunlight through glass. Sun shining through glass will almost be certain to burn plants that are frozen at the time.

Without a doubt, Jeff Thompson in Pueblo, Colorado, has built the most effective cold frame that I have ever seen. Jeff's walk-in cold frame is about ten feet (3 m) tall and has a clear, acrylic roof, which allows maximum solar heating, but does not allow the sun to shine directly on the plants. The south-facing, front panels, which are removed in summer, are frosted and filter the sunlight that could damage frozen plants. Literally hundreds of succulents are grown to perfection in this structure, and Jeff doesn't pay a heating bill for them in winter. A little protection from the elements can make all the difference in the world.

LEFT:
Plastic sheeting covers an area of Steve Miles's garden in winter.

RIGHT:
An amazing assortment of succulents, including many cacti, thrives in Jeff Thompson's well-designed cold frame.

Troubleshooting

With proper preparation and plant placement, gardens with cacti and succulent plants are unlikely to create problems for the gardeners. A few simple steps will help to avoid troubles in most situations. Soil that drains well is essential and will minimize plant losses. The best advice is to introduce only clean, healthy plants into your garden. Succulent plants can be damaged by abrupt changes in culture. Full shade is not going to encourage healthy growth. Constant moisture will encourage rotting.

It is not a good idea to expose succulents to full sun until they have been acclimated to strong light conditions. If the plant is in a container, let the pot set where it will be placed in the garden for a few days. This allows the plant to adjust to its environment, before it is removed from the container and set in the soil. Provide light shade for a few days after planting if the weather is hot and sunny.

Most problems with disease can be avoided by following these few simple rules, but if a cactus shows signs of rot at the base, remove the top of the stem and leave it in the shade on a dry surface. Often new roots will form, at which time the plant can be placed in a new location in the garden.

Pests

Few critters are tempted to graze on cacti other than insects and beetles. Deer and rabbits will sometimes be a problem for the other succulents, but usually only for a few weeks while the plants are establishing in the garden. Most garden centers will have a variety of foul-smelling sprays to keep plants safe while they are settling in.

Any *Opuntia* plant (prickly pear) that appears to have patches of cotton attached to the stems should be discarded. This symptom indicates the presence of a type of scale insect known as cochineal (*Dactylopius* sp.), which will spread to other prickly pears and is almost impossible to wipe out. For years cochineals were used in southern Europe to produce red dye, and when they are squashed, a red liquid can be seen in the cottony mass. Nothing controls the insects effectively, and plants infested with them should be removed from the garden.

Though they are not fatal to the plants, cactus bugs (*Chelinidea vittiger*) leave unattractive, circular, yellowish green scars on prickly pear pads. These flat, gray and yellow bugs look like chinch bugs. In the juvenile form these bugs are green and have rounded bodies.

LEFT:
Cochineal (*Dactylopius* sp.), a type of scale insect, on a prickly pear pad.

RIGHT:
This cactus bug (*Chelinidea vittiger*) was sprayed with insecticidal soap and is no longer a problem.

Other succulent pests are beetles, the worst of which is the black longhorned cactus beetle (*Moneilema* sp.), which will kill *Echinocereus* and *Opuntia*. Fortunately, these flightless beetles are unlikely to be encountered in the garden unless there are infected populations of cacti nearby.

Another unwanted garden visitor is a small beetle with a black and brownish, banded body. It is sometimes referred to as a yucca beetle or tiny cactus beetle (*Carpophilus melanopterus*). This little pest appears in large numbers in the heat of summer and will destroy the flowers of prickly pears and yuccas.

Fortunately, readily available (and relatively environmentally benign) plant sprays, such as neem oil or insecticidal soaps, will usually destroy these infestations. I have read that neem oil will harm cacti, but I have used it for years without ever seeing damage. Systemic insecticides are not effective with succulents and can be fatal to bees and other pollinators when they are absorbed by wildflowers growing near the treated plants.

LEFT:
The black longhorn cactus beetle (*Moneilema* sp.) can kill cacti but thankfully cannot fly.

RIGHT:
Tiny cactus beetles (*Carpophilus melanopterus*) can quickly shear the petals from prickly pear flowers.

4

GROWING PLANTS FROM CUTTINGS AND SEEDS

Only a few weeks old, these cacti seedlings are about the size of an apple seed.

Many cacti, yuccas, and
agaves can be propagated with little effort. This is a way of
obtaining plants to fill in or expand gardens, experiment with,
or use for gifts or trade.

Depending on the species, new plants can be obtained
from stem cuttings, offsets, or seed. Plants grown from
cuttings or offsets will be genetically identical to the original
plant, while seed-grown plants will show variability, the
way siblings differ from their parents and from each other.
By collecting seed or taking cuttings from your own garden
plants you will be assured that the plants you grow are suited
to your climate. This is positively the least expensive source of
new plants.

Most plants benefit from an occasional pruning, and in the
case of many cacti almost anything removed in the process
can be rooted. Rosette-forming plants such as agaves or
yuccas are usually much more attractive if the rosettes are not
crowded. Removing extra offsets will make the plants more
esthetic and in most cases these can be propagated quite easily. Also, cactus sellers sometimes offer cuttings of chollas and
prickly pears at a fraction of the price that plants are sold for.

Some species are rarely offered and seed may be the only
means of acquiring these plants for your garden. By practicing
with seed from your garden you can learn what works for you
and what doesn't at almost no cost.

Propagation by Cuttings

Cuttings from cacti such as *Opuntia* (prickly pear), *Maihueniopsis*, and *Cylindropuntia* (cholla) species root quickly, especially early in the growing season but can be taken any time during the warm months. Simply cut at the narrow point between joints or stems, and then let cuttings dry in the shade for a day or two. At that time, place the cutting into the smallest pot that will hold it, or plant it directly into the garden and keep the soil reasonably moist for a couple of weeks, or until new growth appears. It is not advisable to use too large of a container for cuttings, as the soil may stay overly moist for too long when water is applied and the cuttings may rot instead of rooting. Using sharp, clean tools when taking cuttings will help to insure success. At planting time, be certain that the growing medium is firm around the cuttings, assuring that they have good soil contact. Cuttings should be placed deeply enough in the soil that they are secure.

When watering, it is best to not disturb the soil with the water flow. For this purpose, misting hose-nozzles and spray bottles are helpful. Even slight movements can break tiny roots that are beginning to develop. Pots can also be placed in pans and moistened from the bottom, letting the soil absorb water through capillary action. Initially, these pots should be given a light watering when the soil is dry. The amount of water should be increased as signs of growth are visible. Light shade will reduce stress and help cuttings root more quickly.

Clustering, barrel cacti can be divided by removing entire stems. Cut the stems as close to the base of the plant as possible. After the cuttings have been left to callous in the shade for several days, they can be planted anywhere that they can be watered when the soil surface is dry. Cuttings of all types will root more quickly if they are protected from intense sunlight until signs of growth are visible. It is best if shading is not removed abruptly.

By removing extra rosettes or offsets, which are also referred to as pups or suckers, you can reproduce rosette-forming species such as yuccas or agaves and their relatives. This is best done in spring through summer. Keep the offsets in dry shade for a couple of days before planting them where they are wanted. Often, rosettes can be removed with some root; they can be given water whenever the soil is dry through the growing season.

Seed Propagation

Growing plants from seed takes a little longer than growing plants from cuttings, but it is fun and truly amazing to see how quickly many succulents will grow. Seed is relatively cheap and can provide an abundance of plants at little expense. Garden centers have a large assortment of containers designed for this purpose. A number of everyday household items will work just as well. For instance, paper cups, fast food containers, or Styrofoam egg cartons with holes punched at the bottom will do the job. Be sure that any container used has adequate drainage holes at the lowest point and is clean.

Several readily available, sterile soil mixes are designed especially for growing seedlings. Most of these growing media are useful for any type of seed, but plants such as cacti should not be kept in this type mix when they are large enough to be transplanted. If the seedlings have outgrown their original containers, but are not ready to go into the garden, they should be moved into a more succulent-friendly soil mix. Any soil that drains well and does not hold moisture for more than a day after water is applied will be fine. Because seedlings will remain fairly small for the first season, coarse sand is a better soil amendment than pea gravel at this stage.

When planting seed, moisten the soil thoroughly and then fill containers with soil, firmly pressing the mix into place until it is level. Sprinkle the seed over the surface as evenly as possible. Seedlings that are overcrowded will be more likely to fail than those that are not.

It is important that the seed has good soil contact. This can easily be achieved by covering the seed very lightly with a thin layer of the seed starter mix and then applying a slight amount of pressure evenly to the surface, pressing the seed firmly into the soil mix. A block of wood is often recommended for this purpose.

After seed has been sown, the pot can be placed in a tray that will hold water. This set-up allows the soil to absorb moisture from below and avoids disturbing tiny seedlings when watering them. Always place the pots into a dry tray and then fill the tray with water. Placing pots into trays that are already full of water can cause the soil to be pushed up in the pot. Don't let seed containers sit in a constant pool of water. It is not a bad idea to wash the tray from time to time to avoid salt build up. Add only enough water that it will be absorbed in a half hour or so, but be sure that moisture is reaching the surface. Check trays daily, adding water when needed. The soil mix should not be allowed to become dry on the surface for at least four to six weeks, depending on the growth rate of the seedlings, which in turn depends on temperatures.

Heat speeds the rate of germination, and most seeds will sprout at any time of the year if warmth can be provided. Garden centers sometimes recommend heat mats to speed germination and the growth rate of small seedlings. This can be effective, but remember that the soil will dry much more quickly, especially at the bottom of the pot.

Seedlings must have strong light for long periods of the day to grow strong and be healthy. Except during the shortest days in winter, windows provide sufficient light for indoor germination of cactus seed, but grow lights also can be helpful if that is more practical.

Seed pots can be covered with clear plastic or glass, to create high humidity until germination has occurred, but coverings should be removed as soon as green sprouts are seen. Temporary humidity will speed the germination period for most seeds, including the seed of desert plants. It is best to remove the covering in the evening or on a gray day, so that sensitive seedlings have a chance to adjust to the lower

Young cactus plants at Agua Fria Nursery are acclimatized to outdoor conditions in full shade before gradually being moved into stronger sun.

humidity levels more easily. Spray bottles can be useful for misting seedlings at this time.

When temperatures allow, tender young plants can be taken outside, placed in full shade, and then moved gradually into stronger sun. Seedlings can be lost when changes of any kind are too abrupt. I plant all of my seed outside in the middle of winter and it will typically sprout in midspring, but many times it will wait until monsoon rains occur in summer.

Many seeds need stratification to germinate, which means they must go through a period of freezing temperatures. At Mesa Garden, where thousands of seed pots are planted each year, Steven Brack has noticed that some cactus seeds will not germinate evenly unless the barometric pressure drops suddenly. That is a weather indicator that says heavy rains are on the way.

5

COLD-HARDY CACTI

Various types of cacti and succulents on display in the demonstration garden at Mesa County Fairgrounds.

o most people, the largest and most instantly recognizable family composed entirely of succulents is the cactus family, or Cactaceae. Certainly, it is the most diverse family of succulent plants in the New World. With few exceptions, members of the Cactaceae grow naturally only in North and South America, having been introduced to most of the dry, subtropical regions of the world.

Even people who are not fans of these spiny organisms can't help but appreciate the flabbergasting beauty of the flowers that many of these plants produce. Most of these flowers open during the day and close in late afternoon. However, it is not only the flowers that make cacti so attractive but also the endless variety of patterns and colors created by the spines.

For gardeners with harsh winters the cactus family can logically be divided into four groups. The first group consists of the upright chollas, commonly referred to as pencil or walking stick cactus, which become shrubs or bushes. The second group, one of the most recognizable groups, is the prickly pears, with flat, pancake-shaped segments known as pads, joints, or stems. The next group is the globular plants—the barrels, balls, hedgehogs, or pincushions. These cacti have stems that are more or less rounded at the top. What remains in the cactus family are the oddballs, cacti that simply don't fit neatly into the other three categories, but make some very interesting and garden-worthy plants.

Many relationships in the Cactaceae are not yet thoroughly understood by science, and researchers, working independently around the world, are not always in agreement. Sometimes their studies result in reassigning plants from one genus or species to another, or reducing them from species status to a variety or subspecies. Such moves create new names for familiar plants and often create disagreements among taxonomists that may take years to settle, if they are resolved at all. One day DNA studies will bring clarity to these disagreements, but it will take years for many plant sellers to change the names of their offerings. Keep in mind that taxonomy is an important science; though it can sometimes create confusion for gardeners and cactus hobbyists, it is not necessary that you change your labels every time a species is reassigned. Furthermore, as you search for new plants for your garden or collection, remember that if your quest cannot be found by one name, it might be available with a different one.

The Chollas:
High-Desert Walking Sticks

Even in climates with cold winters and short growing seasons, some of the upright chollas can become massive shrubs or bushes in a few years, easily reaching six to eight feet (1.8 m to 2.4 m) tall and several feet in diameter. Fortunately, all chollas respond nicely to pruning or shaping. Removing new lateral growth causes plants to grow taller and cutting the main, central, upright stem creates a bushier plant.

All chollas have easily detachable spines that can be seriously painful. These are interesting and beautiful plants, often with showy flowers, but if you choose to use them, please take warning as to their possible dangerous nature.

Stems of any size from all chollas root quickly when they are planted directly in the garden during warm weather. Before planting the stems, however, allow them to callous in

Cholla spines glisten in the morning sun in the Conrad family's garden. These chollas were in small pots only three years ago.

the shade for a few days. Often the stems root where they fall when they become detached from the plant.

Most chollas are now separated into the genus *Cylindropuntia*, but some continue to use the genus name *Opuntia* for these plants. *Opuntia imbricata* and *Cylindropuntia imbricata*, for example, refer to the same plant and either name is fine to use, although recent DNA studies favor *Cylindropuntia*. The few chollas from South America, which are included in the genus *Austrocylindropuntia*, are not able to withstand real winters and thus are not described here.

Like prickly pears, chollas have temporary, short, green, cylindrical leaves on new stems. These small leaves die and drop from the stem as new growth reaches maturity and spines are formed. The main stem, or trunk, of chollas becomes thick and woody and is covered with bark at maturity. The flowers are almost always more abundant at the tips of the stems. The lateral stems of upright chollas are often referred to as joints or arms.

The upright chollas have no special soil requirements, as long as drainage is adequate, and are not prone to insect or disease problems. Because they are sun lovers, they are more attractive if given the hottest exposure available. This is a great group of plants for gardens that are backlit at night. The silhouettes of these cacti are very effective in such settings.

Cylindropuntia acanthocarpa (syn. *Opuntia acanthocarpa*) (buckhorn cholla) grows over much of western Arizona and usually has yellow flowers when found at higher elevations and reddish flowers in the low desert. Cactus hobbyist Jeff Thompson has discovered an eye-catching, thick-stemmed form in an isolated colony on a ranch. The outstanding flowers, unlike any other cactus flower that I have seen, are yellow with random, orange streaks on the petals. The plant has proved cold hardy, having survived several years in Jeff's zone 5 (-20°F or -28°C) garden and two winters in mine. Jeff has named his find "parrot tulip cholla." It will be a true gift to those who garden with cacti when it becomes available in the trade.

Cylindropuntia davisii (syn. *Opuntia davisii*) (Davis' cholla) is found in nature scattered though West Texas and eastern New Mexico, growing in dry grasslands. It has flat, golden spines that are over an inch (2.5 cm) long and point in all directions away from the stem, but primarily downward. It is a beautiful plant when sunlight strikes the spines at sunrise or sunset. Even for a cactus, this cholla is a ferocious plant and it is more painful to tangle with than most. If you want to discourage people or animals from cutting through an area, this cactus is your best choice. It grows to about three or four feet (90 to 120 cm) tall. In winter, its branches drape down and it looks quite dehydrated, but it springs back quickly when the temperature warms. The flowers are a coppery, greenish yellow and a little over an inch (2.5 cm) across. The tan colored fruits are hard and dry. The northern form of this species is reliable in cold, dry climates and has been in my garden for over twenty years without problems.

TOP:
Close-up of a flower of *Cylindropuntia davisii* (Davis' cholla).

BOTTOM:
A young plant of the most northern form of *Cylindropuntia davisii* (Davis' cholla) growing in the author's garden. In very little time it will become a thick bush.

A large, bushy example of the silver form of *Cylindropuntia echinocarpa* (silver cholla) in a high-desert garden.

Cylindropuntia echinocarpa (syn. *Opuntia echinocarpa*) (silver cholla, golden cholla) is a densely spined cactus that can be found in two color variations. One form has silver spines, the other has golden; therefore the two common names. The abundant spines are arranged neatly on the stems, making both forms highly decorative. The plant is medium sized, reaching four or five feet (1.2 or 1.5 m) in height, and is slow to become bushy in colder climates, but in time can be almost half as wide as it is tall. In winter, when it is dormant, it is a nicer looking plant than many of the other cold-climate chollas because its arms do not droop as dramatically as many of the others do. The greenish yellow flowers are more interesting than showy. As a whole, this is a very attractive plant and will remain that way year-round. This species is native to much of Arizona, including high altitudes on the Mogollon Rim where it lives on gravelly hillsides and dry flatlands. It also can be found growing naturally in parts of southern Utah, Nevada, and California.

Cylindropuntia imbricata (syn. *Opuntia imbricata*) (tree cholla) is probably the most

An example of the golden form of *Cylindropuntia echinocarpa* (golden cholla) with an open flower, at Agua Fria Nursery.

tolerant of this group to cold and wet conditions. It is also the fastest growing and becomes the largest plant in this section. The flowers are over two inches (5 cm) in diameter, numerous, and very pretty, typically bright reddish purple to light pink. Showy, plump, yellow fruits follow the flowers in late summer. This cholla can become a large landscape specimen, reaching well over six feet (1.8 m) tall. It turns into a dense, three- to four-foot (90- to 120-cm) wide shrub with a thick, woody trunk, supporting lateral stems that can be more than an inch (2.5 cm) thick and several inches long. The arms, or stems, flop down during winter dormancy, making this cholla look dehydrated, but not unattractive. The

spines are about three-quarters of an inch (2 cm) long and will vary somewhat in color, but are usually yellow to gray, with a pinkish to brown base. 'Alba' has white flowers and does not grow as quickly or as large as the typical form. A second, slow-growing and rare spineless form in cultivation makes an interesting and unique contribution to the garden; it was collected from nature in New Mexico. *Cylindropuntia imbricata* is the common cholla from southeastern Colorado into eastern New Mexico and West Texas, sometimes growing at impressively high altitudes in the western part of its range.

TOP: *Cylindropuntia imbricata* (tree cholla) in the author's garden with flowers that are lighter in color than is typical for the species.

BOTTOM: The unique, spineless form of *Cylindropuntia imbricata* (tree cholla) is becoming more widely distributed in horticulture.

In addition to the typical species (var. *imbricata*), two varieties are recognized from West Texas: var. *argentea* with silvery spines, and var. *arborescens*, which is taller. Both varieties are also tolerant of cold climates and have wintered in zone 5 (-20°F or -28°C) gardens. Nurseries sometimes sell plants with the label "*C. arborescens.*"

Cylindropuntia kleiniae (syn. *Opuntia kleiniae*) (Klein's pencil cholla) grows naturally in mountainous central Arizona and can be a very useful cholla in the garden. It grows to over six feet (1.8) in height and can become a dense bush, but may be trimmed into a narrow upright shape. This makes it a reasonable choice for a small garden. Individual stems, or joints, are pencil thick, from half an inch to several inches (13 mm to 8 cm) long, and turn from green to purple in winter. The silver spines are about an inch (2.5 cm) long and point mostly down and away from the stem. The flowers are rose colored, about an inch and a half (4 cm) in diameter, and are very pretty. In late summer, bright red fruits appear, which are fleshy and quite eye-catching well into autumn. The stems of this cholla do not droop as much as the stems of some of the other chollas do in winter. Some botanists believe this cholla is an ancient natural hybrid involving *C. imbricata* and *C. leptocaulis*. It is a very cold tolerant and adaptable cactus that remains attractive

Cylindropuntia kleiniae (Klein's pencil cholla) with an open flower in the author's garden.

year-round. A recently studied form of this species from West Texas is somewhat smaller and has been named var. *riograndensis*.

Cylindropuntia kleiniae × **C. imbricata**, a hybrid between Klein's pencil cholla and tree cholla, has stems shaped more like *C. imbricata* but is intermediate in size between the two parents, and has spines more like *C. kleiniae*. General growth habit is more upright and open than either parent.

Cylindropuntia leptocaulis (syn. *Opuntia leptocaulis*) (desert Christmas cactus, pencil cactus) has, as its common names indicate, pencil-sized and -shaped stems, which are

Unique for its reddish flowers, *Cylindropuntia kleiniae* (Klein's pencil cholla) × *C. imbricata* (tree cholla) is one of several cold-hardy hybrid chollas in cultivation, some of which have very pretty flowers.

An interesting, less-bushy-than-usual form of *Cylindropuntia leptocaulis* (desert Christmas cactus) in Jeff Thompson's garden.

Close-up of the long-lasting fruits of *Cylindropuntia leptocaulis* (desert Christmas cactus).

Cylindropuntia ramosissima (diamond cholla) at Wild Things nursery.

green and hold on to showy, bright red fruits well into winter. The species is incredibly widespread in nature, with some clones much more tolerant of cold and winter moisture than others. This small to medium-sized cholla seldom reaches four feet (1.2 m) tall in cold climates, although it becomes a densely branched bush. In most cases, the stems are slightly thinner than a pencil and are decorated with a dark band running lengthwise. The yellow flowers are less than an inch (2.5 cm) in diameter. The silver spines are about an inch (2.5 cm) long and grow at almost a right angle to the stem, but pointing slightly downward. In nature, this species is found from Arizona, through New Mexico, into Texas and parts of Oklahoma. Throughout its natural range it is often used in gardens and is a carefree, attractive plant. The stems get thinner in winter but do not droop, making this cholla a good year-round garden subject.

Cylindropuntia ramosissima (syn. *Opuntia ramosissima*) (diamond cholla) grows very slowly and, as a true desert plant, resents moisture in winter, even more than the other plants in this group. In my garden, it is marginal. Almost every year my plants have a few scarred tips from winter temperatures on at least some branches, but they recover quickly in the spring. Because this cholla is such an interesting and ornamental species, it is still worth its space in the garden. As a young plant it is almost spineless but any spines it does have are silver, over an inch (2.5 cm) long, and grow at almost a right angle to the stem. Old plants become heavily spined. The pencil-thick stems have a decorative, diamond-shaped pattern that looks like it has been stamped into them, thus the plant's common name. The rust-red flowers are slightly less than an inch (2.5 cm) across. Because it is very slow growing in colder climates, this cholla would be a good choice for gardens where space is limited or for containers that could be moved to a protected position in winter. The species is native to western Arizona, as well as parts of Nevada, and California, where it favors sandy, desert flats. Late freezes, after a mild spell in early spring, can cause damage to the stem tips.

Cylindropuntia spinosior (syn. *Opuntia spinosior*) (cane cholla) does not become as bushy as some of the other chollas, but does reach over six (1.8 m) feet tall in just a few seasons. The stems are about as thick as a kitchen broom handle and vary from two to fifteen inches (5 to 38 cm) long. Its arms hang from the central stem in winter, when it is dormant but it is not unattractive. This species has one of the more manageable growth habits of any of the chollas in the garden, being very upright and not too broad. The unique, rose-colored flowers are about two inches (5 cm) in diameter and are quite ornamental. The spines are silver or gray, shorter than those of most chollas at less than half an inch (13 mm) long, and are arranged neatly in a spiral pattern. Though tall enough to be a focal point in any garden, this very attractive cholla has a narrow upright habit that makes it one of the best choices where space is limited. The species occurs naturally in the grasslands of eastern Arizona and western New Mexico, growing among scattered trees, sometimes at high altitudes. It has been growing in my garden for over twenty-five years and has never shown the slightest signs of winter damage, except the year when a freezing rainstorm with very cold temperatures arrived in early October. Plants at that time were not fully dormant.

Cylindropuntia ×viridiflora (syn. *Opuntia ×viridiflora*) (Santa Fe cholla) quickly makes a dense shrub to about four feet (1.2 m) tall

Uniquely colored flowers adorn the broomstick-thick stems of *Cylindropuntia spinosior* (cane cholla) in the author's garden.

and wide. Although *viridiflora* means "green flowers," the most commonly available plants of this species in cultivation have very pretty, peach-colored flowers. The flowers are about an inch (2.5 cm) in diameter. These plants are always sold as the "orange-flowering" Santa Fe cholla. Except for the flower color, this cholla looks and grows like a smaller version of the more common *C. imbricata* in almost every way. *Cylindropuntia* ×*viridiflora* is rare in nature, inhabiting only a limited area around Santa Fe, New Mexico, which of course gives the plant its common name.

This species has become somewhat readily available in horticulture due to its interest to gardeners and because it is very easy to grow. It is adaptable to a variety of soils and is among the most cold tolerant of all chollas. The spines are silvery gray and glisten in the sun. If you want a rare and attractive plant with which you have a good chance of being successful, this one fits the description. Many botanists believe this cholla is an ancient, natural hybrid between *C. whipplei*, which grows in western New Mexico, and *C. imbricata*, which is common around Santa Fe, New Mexico.

TOP:
The "orange-flowering" form of *Cylindropuntia* ×*viridiflora* (Santa Fe cholla) attracts a visitor in the author's garden.

BOTTOM:
Close-up of a flower of *Cylindropuntia* ×*viridiflora* (Santa Fe cholla).

Cylindropuntia whipplei (syn. *Opuntia whipplei*) (plateau cholla) grows naturally over a large portion of northern Arizona, southern

Utah, parts of Nevada, and into the Four Corners region where it enters southwestern Colorado. It can often be found growing with short grasses among pinyons and junipers. This cholla varies substantially in appearance throughout its natural range. The high-altitude form from Colorado has longer, thinner, less spiny stems than is usual for plants from northern Arizona, and almost creeps along the ground, seldom exceeding eighteen inches (45 cm) tall. Most of the plants from Arizona, Nevada, and Utah grow in a more upright manner, but this is a variable species with many unique colonies. The three-quarter-inch (2-cm) long spines are shining white and point down and away from the stem. The shiny, yellow-green flowers are over an inch (2.5 cm) wide and are usually abundant in early summer.

Some of the upright forms of *Cylindropuntia whipplei* are among the most attractive cacti of any type that can be grown outside in colder climates. Jeff Thompson, a dedicated and knowledgeable hobbyist, has recently found an exceptional form of the species on a ranch in northern Arizona. The form has thin, crowded spines that hide the short stems and is destined to become a garden favorite as it becomes more available.

Cylindropuntia whipplei hybridizes with several species. Its natural hybrid with *C. echinocarpa* is known as *C. ×multigeniculata* and is cold hardy in zone 5 (-20°F or -28°C).

Prickly Pears:
Iconic Plants of the Southwest

Prickly pears (*Opuntia* spp.) are the most widely distributed members of the cactus family in nature. They are also some of the easiest to grow, sometimes too easy. In general, all prickly pears have large, showy, brightly colored flowers and pancake-shaped stems. They are native from Canada to Patagonia in southern Argentina. Some of them become enormous, with stems, called pads, which grow larger than a dinner plate, while others are true miniatures. Certain prickly pears grow in some of the harshest desert environments in which vegetation exists, while others grow on frigid mountaintops.

For many people, prickly pear is the first plant that comes to mind when they hear the word *cactus*. The problem with prickly pears for the gardener in cold climates, besides their dangerous nature, is that there are too many choices. These plants add a unique charm and a definite Southwest desert feel to a garden.

In this section, we will look at a handful of the most obtainable, garden-worthy, and interesting prickly pears, as so many of these plants are similar from a gardener's perspective. Many of these plants naturalize in a garden and may, over time, wander from their original planting site. Many tested and named cultivars of prickly pears are available commercially and will prove to be good choices. The scientific names of plants in this group are confusing, even to experts in the field, so I am using familiar names for the reader's convenience.

For gardeners interested in growing prickly pears, the plants can be grouped according to four ornamental characteristics. The first division is based on stem size. Some prickly pears have smaller pads, others have larger pads. The second factor is spininess, ranging from very spiny to seemingly spineless. The third way of dividing this group is by flower color. From shades of yellow, sometimes with an orange throat, to pinks and reds, and among the named cultivars are even some white-flowering types. The fourth division is by type of fruit. Some plants have large, plump, showy, red or purplish fruits from summer into autumn. The fruits are sometimes referred to as tunas. Other plants have hard, dry fruits, which are essentially hard brown or tan seedpods.

Native Americans ate the juicy-type fruits, which are still used as a food source in Mexico, and which all kids growing up in the western United States have to try. The fruits have a sweet, fruity flavor. If you find yourself curious about tasting these fruits, be sure to remove all the tiny spines before sampling. Immature pads of prickly pears that are used as an ingredient in some Mexican food recipes are known as *nopales*.

Almost all prickly pears have extraordinarily large, brightly colored, eye-catching flowers equal to any fancy rose. Although individual blooms are not long lasting, some plants produce an abundance of flowers over a long period. This is another good reason for using named cultivars in the garden.

Like chollas, prickly pears can be started quite easily from cuttings during warm weather. In fact, large pads can be cut into several pieces, which can all be expected to root and grow.

Opuntia aurea (creeping beavertail) has become a popular garden prickly pear in climates with cold winters because of its unusually showy, three-inch (7.5-cm) wide, yellow or magenta flowers. The plant lacks long spines and thus looks safe to touch, but has tiny, painful spines that become attached to skin quite easily. Called glochids, these hairlike prickles are only found on chollas and prickly pears. The pads are sometimes

Prickly pears at the demonstration garden at Timberline Gardens.

Opuntia aurea (creeping beavertail) 'Golden Carpet' is an excellent yellow-flowering choice for a garden.

The depend-
able pink-
flowering
*Opuntia
aurea* (creep-
ing
beavertail)
'Coombe's
Winter Glow'
has proved
its value
in gardens.

Opuntia basilaris var.
brachyclada (beaver tail) is a
useful prickly pear for troughs
or gardens where miniatures
are grown.

over five inches (13 cm) long and turn a very pretty cranberry color in winter. The green fruits are not showy. In nature, this species can be found in parts of Utah, where it grows in sandy soils, but in the garden it is quite adaptable to any well-drained soil and it is easy to grow. In addition to var. *aurea*, the typical variety, two other varieties appear to be spineless and have large flowers, namely, var. *discolor* and var. *diplopurpurea*. Benson (1982) gave the name *O. basilaris* var. *aurea* to what is generally considered to be a variety of *O. erinacea*. This name has caused some confusion and some sellers use that name for this species.

Opuntia basilaris (beaver tail) grows throughout much of the Mojave Desert in interior Southern California, but also can be found in western Arizona, Nevada, and parts of Utah, as well as northern Mexico. The species is variable in its large range. The pads vary considerably in size and to some degree in shape from one area to another, as do flower colors. Not all plants tolerate cold, and some are very sensitive to moist conditions. The plants that have adapted best to my garden have blue-green, oval pads a little over four inches (10 cm) across and bright pink flowers close to three inches (7.5 cm) wide. Some cold-hardy clones have larger pads, but most are sensitive to winter moisture. Mesa Garden sells a dependable selection of the species (#SB1976) that I collected near

Tonopah, Nevada, several years ago. *Opuntia basilaris* is without long spines, but does have glochids and is more dangerous to handle than it may appear to be. It produces hard, brown fruits. Variety *brachyclada* has smaller, elongated pads that are the same blue-green as variety *basilaris* and is also hardy. Benson's

Opuntia basilaris (beaver tail) is among the most popular prickly pears with gardeners in hot climates, where choices are not limited.

(1982) "variety *aurea*" has bright yellow flowers; although this name is not generally accepted in taxonomy (see details under *O. aurea*), it is still used by some growers.

Opuntia compressa (Plains prickly pear) has flat, oval pads about four inches (10 cm) across with inch (2.5 cm) long spines on the upper third of the stem. The flowers are usually about two inches (5 cm) wide and can be many shades of yellow, sometimes with an orange center, but also may be pink or red. The juicy, red fruits are large and attractive in late summer and fall. This species, *O. macrorhiza*, and *O. humifusa* (sometimes sold as *O. rafinesquei*) are the common prickly pears in the eastern United States, where they are generally found growing in sandy soils or rocky outcrops. The three are more capable of dealing with wet and cold conditions than almost any other members of the cactus family. Still, the soil must drain well for these plants to thrive. All three species fit pretty much the same description and have the same basic growth habit. They will crawl along the ground in every direction, with the oldest pads dying off as new ones replace them. It is not uncommon for these prickly pears to become large, dense mats.

Opuntia compressa (Plains prickly pear) 'Gold Mine' survives cold, windy winters and hot, dry summers. Few plants can withstand the harsh weather conditions that this species takes in stride in its natural habitat.

In early autumn *Opuntia engelmannii* (Engelmann's prickly pear) bears showy red fruits, as seen on this plant at Denver Botanic Gardens.

Opuntia engelmannii (Engelmann's prickly pear) has the largest pads of any prickly pear that is cold hardy to zone 5 (-20°F or -28°C), as much as a foot (30 cm) across. This is another species with a huge natural range, in which individuals from some locations are exposed to much more cold and wet than others. Plants have a semierect growth habit and can become several feet tall. The flowers are yellow with fiery orange centers and are about three inches (7.5 cm) across. They are followed in late summer by plump, reddish purple fruits that persist into the colder months. This very subtropical looking prickly pear can make a strong focal point. Although most clones of this species do not adapt to colder climates, some plants have been living in gardens for decades and have proved themselves to be reliable. If you want to grow this one, try to find a clone that is known to be cold tolerant and plan some space for it, as it becomes huge in time. The dark brown spines have white tips, are about an inch (2.5 cm) long, and grow primarily along the upper edge of the pad. Variety *lindheimeri* is native to parts of New Mexico and Texas and enters into Oklahoma, making it more adaptable than var. *engelmannii* to colder and wetter situations.

The numerous dense spines of *Opuntia erinacea* (hedgehog prickly pear) in the cactus garden at Mesa County Fairgrounds obscure its relatively small pads.

Opuntia erinacea (hedgehog prickly pear) is a variable, low-growing cactus from the Great Basin with oblong pads that are four to six inches (10 to 15 cm) across. Because plants of this species vary so much, they have collected a large, confusing number of scientific names. The stems can be almost naked of spines, or be armed enough to almost hide the entire green to blue-green stems. The many named varieties of *O. erinacea* are based on the more-or-less spiny appearance or silver to reddish spine color. Spines can be thick and stiff to thin and pliable. The attractive flowers may be from intense yellow to hot pink and are normally close to three inches (7.5 cm) across. The fruits are dry and brown. This species, as with the *O. compressa* group, tends to travel as it grows. Many botanists consider plants sold as *O. basilaris* var. *aurea* to be a variety of *O. erinacea*, but others will place it as a variety of *O. polyacantha*. Some varieties of this prickly pear tend to be a little touchy about poor drainage. Recognized varieties of this species include, but are not limited to, var. *erinacea*, var. *hystricina*, var. *ursina*, and var. *utahensis*. Other botanists who have studied this group and most plant sellers recognize many of these varieties as separate species. There are some excellent named cultivars of this prickly pear, which may help the gardener avoid the confusion caused by the scientific names.

Opuntia fragilis (brittle prickly pear) has a huge natural range that includes much of the western and midwestern United States as well as parts of Canada. It is a variable prickly pear with so many named forms, cultivars, and varieties that some people collect only this species. It is one of the most tolerant cacti to cold and wet. The stems are generally oval and flat, but in some forms the pads are shaped like marbles. Stems easily break away from the plant to root wherever they fall. They are brittle during rainy periods. Each joint is only an inch (2.5 cm) or so around and may have no spines other than glochids,

TOP:
Almost spineless, the low-growing *Opuntia fragilis* (brittle prickly pear) 'Little Gray Mound' is a useful container or garden plant.

BOTTOM:
With a protective layer of spines, this plant is more typical of *Opuntia fragilis* (brittle prickly pear) than the spineless form.

Showy pink flowers and a manageable size contribute to the popularity of *Opuntia fragilis* (brittle prickly pear) 'Alberta Rose'.

This particularly decorative cactus is known as *Opuntia debreczeyi* (potato cactus) in horticulture and as *O. fragilis* (brittle prickly pear) f. *denuda* in science.

or may be covered in short to long spines that vary in thickness and color. The flowers are close to two inches (5 cm) in diameter and range in color from pastel to intense shades of yellow to pink. The fruits turn from reddish green to brown and dry by autumn.

This prickly pear has some of the smallest stems in the group and makes a nice rock garden, trough, or container plant. A closely related plant, or especially decorative form of this species, known as *Opuntia debreczeyi* (potato cactus) in horticulture and as *O. fragilis* f. *denuda* in science, has become popular with gardeners. Using my method of dividing the cactus family, this species fits into the oddball group because it is less typical of the prickly pears in general than any other species included here. I have had a plant of this species for many years that was collected in central Nevada; it grows flat pads when conditions are dry and marble-shaped pads when more moisture is present. There are several named cultivars of this species in cultivation and some have incredibly showy flowers.

Opuntia hystricina (syns. *O. erinacea* var. *hystricina*, *O. polyacantha* var. *hystricina*, *O. ursina*) (porcupine prickly pear) is a showy species that is densely covered with thin, three-and-three-quarter-inch (9.5-cm) long, stiff, but pliable, silver spines. The downward-pointing spines hide the green pads, which are generally less than four inches (10 cm) across. The flowers are about two and a half inches (6 cm) across and may be yellow, orange, or pink. The fruits are dry and brown.

In nature, this species is found over a vast area in the Four Corners region where Colorado, Arizona, Utah, and New Mexico meet. Usually it is growing with short grasses on hillsides, among scattered pinyons and junipers.

This cactus is very hardy and easy to grow. In time, it makes low mats of crowded, spiny stems that glow in the sun and are quite attractive. What helps to make it a good prickly pear for the garden is that it does not spread so fast that it becomes hard to control. Although the species may be marketed under any of its many synonyms, it really is easier to grow and enjoy these plants than it is to be sure what to call them.

Opuntia macrocentra (syn. *O. violacea* var. *macrocentra*) (black spine prickly pear) is one of the showiest prickly pears when it is flowering. It has a semiupright growth habit and large, six-inch plus (over 15 cm), blue-green pads that become violet-purple in autumn. From the middle of summer to autumn, showy, plump, purple fruits line the upper edge of the pads. Thick, black spines with white tips grow along the upper edge of each pad. The flowers are abundant, over three inches (7.5 cm) across, and are shiny yellow with a bright reddish orange interior. In nature, this species can be found growing in dry, flat, sandy sites from central New Mexico to central Arizona. During winter, the plant flops over and lies down. In summer when it is in full bloom, it receives as many rave comments from visitors as does any other plant in my garden. Some growers list this prickly pear as variety of *O. violacea*, a tender species that is popular in subtropical gardens. *Opuntia macrocentra* is cold hardy to zone 5 (-20°F or -28°C) as is its variety *minor*. It is best to keep this prickly pear as dry as possible in colder months.

Long spines crowd the tops of the pads of the appropriately named *Opuntia hystricina* (porcupine prickly pear) at Mesa County Fairgrounds.

When in flower, *Opuntia macrocentra* (black spine prickly pear) always attracts attention.

Opuntia microdisca (mat tunilla) has a large natural range in southern Argentina. In time, it makes dense mats of tiny, round or elongated, thin stems growing over each other. Each spiny, flat pad is only about an inch (2.5 cm) across and a quarter inch (6 mm) thick. The short, twisted spines are straw-colored to black, and flexible but painful to touch. The terracotta-colored flowers are less than an inch (2.5 cm) in diameter and are followed by small, bright red fruits. Because of its size, this prickly pear could be lost in a typical garden, but it works very well in a dry rock garden with other miniatures and certainly could be used effectively in containers or troughs. Clones of the species vary in their ability to withstand extreme cold, but some are capable of -15°F (-26°C) without harm. Like many South American cacti from cold regions, this prickly pear can be covered with snow or mulch for the entire winter season without harm. Edward Anderson includes the species in the genus *Tunilla* in his book *The Cactus Family*.

After a few years in the author's garden, this plant of *Opuntia microdisca* (mat tunilla) is still less than two inches (5 cm) across.

Opuntia nicholii (Nichol's prickly pear) is an exceptionally nice garden prickly pear that can be easily controlled. In early summer it is adorned with three-inch (7.5-cm) wide, stunning, bright yellow flowers that glow in the sun. The four- or five-inch (10- or 13-cm), gray-green, oblong pads have flat sides and are up to three-quarters of an inch (2 cm) thick. The stout spines give the plant a clean, white look and cover the pad uniformly but not densely. The fruits are dry and brown by the end of summer, and are not showy. *Opuntia nicholii* is native to the Grand Canyon region, where it grows on dry, rocky slopes and ledges. It is legally protected in habitat but is not rare in cultivation. Plants are slow growing but can make large, loosely formed mats over time. In the garden, soil should drain exceedingly well, as this prickly pear can be sensitive to prolonged periods of moisture at any time of the year, but particularly during cold months. It is a valuable plant in hot, dry, windy situations where most plants would suffer.

Opuntia phaeacantha (smooth fruit prickly pear) has large, flat pads up to eight inches (20 cm) across and may be almost round to somewhat diamond shaped. The flowers are nearly three inches (7.5 cm) across and are typically bright yellow with reddish orange centers, but may be entirely orange or other colors. The large, bright purplish red fruits provide interest into autumn. This plant grows upright to some degree, getting maybe thirty inches (75 cm) tall, but it is primarily a spreader and can take over a large area. Like all prickly pears, it is controllable by pruning. The pads lie down almost flat to the ground in winter. This species

is the most tolerant of the large-pad prickly pears to wet and cold, growing into the higher foothills along the Colorado Front Range where temperatures can be expected to drop well below 0°F (-18°C) during a typical winter. The brown and white spines are over an inch (2.5 cm) long and grow

TOP:
Once it is established, *Opuntia nicholii* (Nichol's prickly pear) is the perfect plant for the hottest and driest situations where most perennials would quickly fail.

MIDDLE:
A fairly typical, large plant of *Opuntia phaeacantha* (smooth fruit prickly pear) flowers at Mesa County Fairgrounds.

BOTTOM:
Opuntia phaeacantha var. *major* (smooth fruit prickly pear), seen here at Paul and Lola Nafziger's Last Go Round Ranch, has larger pads and a more upright habit than the typical species.

mostly along the upper edge of the pad. A desirable variety of this species grows from around Santa Fe, New Mexico, west into Arizona; known as var. *major*, it is much more upright in its growth habit than var. *phaeacantha* and has larger, more oval-shaped pads, giving the appearance of a slightly smaller form of *O. engelmannii*.

Opuntia polyacantha (starvation prickly pear) is commonly found at higher elevations throughout much of the U.S. Interior West (from Montana, Idaho, and Wyoming south to Nevada, Utah, Colorado, Arizona, and New Mexico). It is one of the most common prickly pears in eastern Colorado, as it is through much of the Great Plains. Like most plants with a large natural range, it is very variable. Its spines, for example, range from red to silver as well as in thickness, length, and pliability. Due to its variability, the species has many named forms and varieties, all of them cold hardy. The flowers are around two inches (5 cm) in diameter and may be many shades of pink or yellow. The fruits are the dry and brown type. The growth habit is low and spreading, like that of *O. compressa*, with four-inch (10-cm) pads, but it is a much spinier prickly pear. This very adaptable species is quite easy to grow and, as cacti go, it is tolerant of humid, rainy climates. Plants spread vigorously and can become good-sized specimens quickly. *Opuntia erinacea*, *O. hystricina*, and *O. arenaria* are sometimes included as varieties of this species, as is *O. rhodantha*. Some outstanding white-flowering cultivars of this prickly pear, such as 'Crystal Tide' and 'Snowball', are now available in cultivation.

TOP:
A yellow-flowered *Opuntia polyacantha* (starvation prickly pear) at Timberline Gardens.

BOTTOM:
Opuntia polyacantha (starvation prickly pear) 'Crystal Tide', one of the white-flowering cultivars available to gardeners.

Opuntia trichophora (hair spine prickly pear) is a ground-hugging prickly pear, with flat, greenish pads that grow to about four inches (10 cm) long. Long, hair-thick, shiny, white spines are longest on the lower portion of the stem hiding the plants. When the sun strikes this plant at the right angle, it glows. The flowers are shades of yellow or red, and are about two and a half inches (6 cm) across. The small, brown fruits are dry. The species spreads slowly but can make dense mats in time. In nature, it is present throughout the northern half of New Mexico, parts of southern Colorado, and much of northeastern Arizona, growing on rocky hillsides with short grasses. This adaptable prickly pear thrives in any fast-draining soil, but looks best if given full sun. Through the years, it has been included as a variety of several other species, including *O. polyacantha* and *O. erinacea*.

A small plant of *Opuntia trichophora* (hair spine prickly pear) with dry, brown fruits grows among grasses in the author's garden.

Opuntia ursina (grizzly bear cactus) grows on hot, dry, rocky hillsides, mostly at higher elevations within the Mojave Desert region in California, Arizona, and Utah. It is valued by gardeners for its dense covering of long, thin, glistening, silver spines, which are pliable and about as thick as coarse hair. The flowers are about two and a half inches (6 cm) across and may be pink or yellow, but are sometimes not able to fully open due to the numerous spines. The fruits are dry and brown. In time, this decorative prickly pear makes a good-sized mat of closely crowded stems. The plants need soil that drains well and is low in organic material. To look their best, they also need long periods of direct sun. This outstanding species is often used in frost-free gardens. Although plants are cold tolerant, they cannot be exposed to prolonged periods of moisture at any time of the year. Botanists

Opuntia ursina (grizzly bear cactus) in autumn in the Dryland Mesa Garden at Denver Botanic Gardens. This plant has a less spiny appearance than is typical for the species.

and growers often place this species as a variety of *O. erinacea* or *O. polyacantha*.

Opuntia hybrids

Opuntia hybrids often occur in gardens where many species are growing together if bees or other pollinators are present. Some of the flowers produced by these plants can be spectacular. A few years ago I noticed a plant that looked like a small beaver tail prickly pear (*O. basilaris*) in my garden. This little cactus produced flower buds when it was much smaller than I had ever seen a beaver tail bloom. It turned out to be a cross between the beaver tail I had collected in Tonopah, Nevada, and a plant from the mountains in Colorado. This hybrid, named 'Dazzler' after a friend made a remark about the striking, huge, pinkish purple flowers, now grows in hundreds of gardens. It is extremely adaptable, having inherited the ability to endure long, cold, wet winters from its high-altitude parent and the ability to survive a hot, dry climate from its other parent. Don't be surprised if such a treasure makes an appearance in your garden.

TOP:
Opuntia 'Dazzler', the best prickly pear to show up in the author's garden, is free-flowering and adaptable.

BOTTOM LEFT:
Opuntia 'Dark Knight' has pretty flowers as well as pads that turn a rich purple in winter.

BOTTOM RIGHT:
Opuntia 'Chinle' has become a favorite with gardeners due to its incredible flowers.

Opuntia 'Taylor's Red' has magnificently colored flowers and a dependable growth habit in the garden.

Opuntia 'Drama Queen', with bright fuchsia flowers visible from afar, and 'Dark Knight', growing together in a garden.

TOP LEFT:
Another outstanding prickly pear in the garden is *Opuntia* 'Grand Mesa Peach' with its double, peach-colored flowers and gold spines.

TOP RIGHT:
Close-up of a flower of *Opuntia* 'Dazzler'.

MIDDLE:
Uniquely colored flowers are just one reason to choose named cultivars when it comes to prickly pears for the garden. *Opuntia* 'Nambe Sunrise' boasts double, pink flowers in spring and dark pads in winter.

BOTTOM:
Opuntia 'Red Gem'—Who wouldn't be happy with this kind of show in their garden?

Barrels, Balls, Hedgehogs, and Pincushions: Jewels of the Drylands

To plant hobbyists, the barrels, the balls, the hedgehogs, and the pincushions represent some of the most collectable species in the entire plant kingdom. Sunrooms, windowsills, and greenhouses all over the world are dedicated to the cultivation of these cacti. Fortunately for those of us living in climates with severe winters, some of the most beautiful and reliable flowering of the small, ball-shaped cacti also come from such places.

A few years ago, when I first realized that I wasn't the only one interested in this type of gardening and that there is a market for cacti to grow outside, I asked a professional grower why more plants weren't marketed for gardens. He told me that not enough species can live outside to make it worth the effort to market them. This was an educated grower talking about his specialty, and that was the accepted reality at the time. Fact is, there are hundreds of cacti that can be grown outside, and we probably are still only at the tip of the proverbial iceberg.

Spider mites, mealy bugs, or various beetles can attack all of these species when plants are grown indoors, but plants grown outside are not as susceptible to these problems. It is important that temperatures at night are several degrees cooler than those during the day for many of these plants to metabolize properly. For the most part, these plants are better off if water is limited to them late in the season to force them into dormancy.

Globular cacti flowering in Steve Miles's garden.

Acanthocalycium

Acanthocalycium is a small genus of cacti from southern Argentina with unusually pretty, uniquely colored flowers. The interesting, spiny flower buds appear from a woolly growth point at the top center of the stem.

These species are only marginally cold hardy and are better able to survive if they are deeply covered in snow or mulch for the winter. They do well in an unheated greenhouse or cold frame, as long as sun does not shine directly on them while they are frozen. I have lost plants that had lived for years in the most protected part of my garden when night temperatures dropped dramatically below predictions and plants were not covered by snow or cloth. I have learned over many years that if I am to expect these plants to reliably come through winter unharmed, it is best to cover them under a couple of layers of frost cloth from late fall through early spring. The flowers that these cacti produce in spring are worth the extra effort. I would recommend these plants to collectors who are interested in keeping large numbers of species outdoors, as they are able to survive with protection. I would not recommend them to anyone looking for a sure bet.

There is a good deal of confusion as to the names of the plants in this genus. Probably there are more names than species, but all *Acanthocalycium* species are from areas that have periods of cold in winter.

Acanthocalycium spiniflorum (spiny lilac flower cactus) can become a large, upright cactus with stems that can reach a height of almost two feet (60 cm) and be over five inches (13 cm) in diameter in a heated greenhouse or outdoors where winters are warm. Even after several years they are not likely to reach that size where winters are harsh.

In my garden, they take years to get six inches (15 cm) tall. The spines are arranged neatly in rows down the stem, and the stems remain single. The showy flowers range from white to pinkish lilac and are about an inch and a half (4 cm) across. The larger these plants are when they placed in the garden, the more likely they are to survive. They are much more vigorous in the garden if they are not allowed to remain dry for long periods during the growing season. Plants respond favorably to fertilizer within reason and are much more vigorous in full sun.

Acanthocalycium violaceum (lilac flower cactus) is a bluish green cactus from the Patagonian Andes that can become several inches tall and about four inches (10 cm) wide in time but will seldom offset. The gray spines can be sparse to numerous and the flowers are a very attractive lilac-pink color. It is best to grow this cactus in a gritty, sandy loam that drains away from the base of the plant very quickly. Placing the plant in a raised position on a berm helps to keep it dry in winter. I can only grow this species in the most protected part of my garden, but it does grow and bloom year after year. This cactus needs long hours in direct sun to flower well. It can remain under heavy mulch or snow for the entire winter without harm and is much more likely to survive and grow with more vigor in spring if it does. Like most South American cacti, this one too does not benefit from being overly dry when it is actively growing.

Ariocarpus

Ariocarpus includes some of the most interesting and sought after plants in the cactus family. They grow primarily on rocky slopes in the Chihuahua desert of Mexico, but a couple of species cross over the border into Texas. These cacti grow substantial, tuberous root systems but do not have spines. Long hours of direct sun and summer heat are necessary for the long-term survival and flowering of these species. They are very slow growing plants, but are not prone to disease or insect attacks, and are able to withstand extremes of cold if kept dry in winter and given adequate water in summer. In the garden it is not advisable to cover these plants in winter, except during periods of extreme cold when snow does not cover them. Fast-draining, rocky soil is essential and they cannot be said to be reliable even then; however, in the right location in the garden they are able to survive for many years. They are easily grown in unheated greenhouses or cold frames when winter moisture is limited. I recommend these plants to collectors rather than to gardeners interested in safe choices.

Ariocarpus fissuratus (living rock cactus, star cactus) is a unique species from Mexico and near the border in Texas. It has a large natural range and does grow into areas with some winter cold. It is likely that some clones of this species are better able to adapt to colder climates than others. This cactus is spineless and grows almost level with the ground. The dark green, bulky, flat-topped, rough-textured stem can reach between five and six inches (13 and 15 cm) across. The pink flowers are over an inch and a half (4 cm) in diameter and emerge from a woolly point at the top of the stem in fall. This plant can be found in full sun, where it blends into

A handsome plant of *Acanthocalycium violaceum* (lilac flower cactus) with showy flowers in Steve Miles's garden.

its surroundings on rocky, south-facing, limestone hillsides in nature. A plant of this species in my garden went through last winter without problems, but was covered for brief periods through the worst part of the season under a double layer of frost cloth. This species survives much longer and flowers more dependably in areas where summer temperatures are hot and where downward swings in temperature are not drastic in the spring, after growth has begun.

I currently have a plant of *Ariocarpus kotschoubeyanus* var. *macdowellii* that has not been injured by the cold. It is located near a building and covered with frost cloth when temperatures are expected to stay below 10°F (-12°C) for more than a few days.

Astrophytum

Astrophytum is a genus of mostly tender but very ornamental Mexican cacti. At least two species grow at high elevations where snow sometimes occurs. One of them has proved to withstand harsh winters if plants are provided with a protected position and kept dry during winter dormancy. Several years ago, when I was visiting Mesa Garden, I learned that there was an outside chance that *A. capricorne* might be able to survive in a colder climate. I came home with a packet of seed, and in a couple of years put the theory to a test. Sure enough, all of the seedlings that were planted out survived winter but grew much more slowly than plants from the same seed packet kept in the greenhouse. After a few years, the plants in the garden even flowered.

With excellent soil drainage and a protected position in the garden, *Ariocarpus fissuratus* (living rock cactus), here growing in the author's garden, can live for several years in a cold climate.

Astrophytum capricorne (spiny star cactus) is a stunning cactus that grows in nature over much of northern Mexico, sometimes into the high mountains. Usually seven, sharp, spiraling ribs divide the stem. The plant is deep green but is covered with white flecks so it appears gray at first glance. The spines, which emerge yellow then turn gray, are long and twisted and become numerous as the plant ages. The flowers are yellow with an orange center and are about two and a half inches (6 cm) across. They emerge from a woolly point at the top of the stem. Like var. *capricorne*, var. *minor* is also resistant to cold, but several other varieties, such as var. *crassispinum*, var. *niveum*, and var. *senile*, still need to be tried. This species is much more cold tolerant than most growers give it credit for being.

I have had the same plants of this species growing in rocky soil in the most protected part of my garden for close to ten years. This area of my garden is covered with cloth if there is no snow cover and temperatures are expected to be 10°F (-12°C) or colder for an extended period. In climates that are typically wet in winter, it may be necessary to keep this cactus in a cold frame or an unheated greenhouse, but under the eave of a building might work. Larger plants are able to adapt to life in the garden with more ease than small seedlings.

Austrocactus

Plants of the genus *Austrocactus* come from southern Chile and Argentina, where they are exposed to extreme cold and wind in their

Two forms of *Astrophytum capricorne* (spiny star cactus) blooming simultaneously in Steve Miles's garden.

natural habitats. All the species make small loosely formed clusters of stems that are usually not more than a few inches tall and about two inches (5 cm) in diameter. Spider mites can be a problem for these plants if summers are too dry. In nature, some of the species are said to be fairly common plants, but they are almost non-existent in horticulture. Any species of this genus is very cold resistant. Seed from these plants does not sprout easily.

Austrocactus bertinii (prickly pickle), from the southern tip of Argentina, is exposed to more cold, wind, and wet in habitat than almost any other member of the cactus family. I struggled with this plant for a few years, until Alfred Lau, a well-known botanist and conservationist, walked through my garden and scolded me for not giving my plant enough water. Because he had studied this species in habitat and was the authority, I took his advice. A year later, my plant had more than doubled in size and bloomed prolifically for the first time.

The stems are three or four inches (7.5 to 10 cm) tall and about half that around. They resemble a gray-green pickle covered with short white and gray spines. The outstanding two- to three-inch (5- to 7.5-cm) wide flowers are a rich, glossy, golden color at the side of the stems.

Despite its reputation for being difficult, this species grew in my garden for over twenty-five years. I found it to be an easy plant to grow if it is kept cool and dry in winter and given ample moisture when it is actively growing. Many growers consider any succulent that needs more water than most to be difficult until we learn to give it more water. Because we are warned not to overwater so often, it never occurs to some of us that more water might be the solution.

Coryphantha and Escobaria

The genera *Coryphantha* and *Escobaria* include many wonderful, ornamental, and easy-to-grow cacti for gardens. All of the species have ball-shaped or elongated stems composed of tubercles, which are cone-shaped projections radiating from the center of the stem. There is a lengthwise groove in the tubercles and a cluster of spines at the tip.

Not all, but many of the following species are considered by some in science and horticulture to be in the genus *Escobaria*, instead of *Coryphantha*. In science, *Escobaria* is favored over *Coryphantha* for the disputed species, but growers and many hobbyists treat the genus names as interchangeable. Generally, the spinier species are included in *Escobaria*, but this is not a hard-and-fast rule. Plants listed in this section as *Coryphantha* are generally accepted as that. Plants listed as *Escobaria* are generally accepted as that in science. A gardener seeking these plants may find them offered by either name. Readers searching for a particular species in this volume should check under both genera.

Many of these species are miniatures, making them perfect for troughs and containers. Most of them are exceptionally resistant to cold, if they are kept dry in winter. All the species bloom in spring and early summer, usually with rings of flowers at the top of the stem. Many of them will bloom sporadically throughout the rest of the growing season, particularly after a good rain. Several species are only found growing in decomposed limestone soils in habitat, but none of them seem to object to growing in regular cactus garden topsoil as long as drainage is adequate. These are genera of very tough, adaptable plants that bloom prolifically in various settings and seldom are subject to disease or insect attacks.

The following species have been growing in my garden for at least three years, but some for over twenty years, and present no problems. All of the plants in this group remain attractive year-round and can add an immense degree of winter interest, especially when they are planted in multiples.

Coryphantha compacta (compact pincushion), like its name implies, is a small cactus. It occurs naturally at high altitudes in northern Mexico. The plants in my garden are over five years old and only about half an inch (13 mm) across, though adult plants can grow to over three inches (7.5 cm) in diameter. Had I known how slowly they increased in size, I would have kept them in the greenhouse until they were larger before planting them in the garden. The thin, straw-colored spines are sometimes hooked and leave the stems exposed. The flowers are yellow and about three-quarters of an inch (2 cm) across. Like many species in this genus, *C. compacta* could be a valuable plant for trough gardeners; it can take much heat and cold if kept dry in winter, and it would take a lifetime for it to need repotting. This little cactus is not as reliable in zone 5 (-20°F or -28°C) as most others in the genus; it needs to be covered by cloth or mulch during the harshest periods in winter if there is no snow cover. These plants need to be given water in hot, dry periods of summer.

Coryphantha difficilis (difficult pincushion) has a dull green, cylindrical stem that is flat on the top. The plant is about three inches (7.5 cm) tall and over two inches (5 cm) wide. Generally, it does not offset into clusters. The three-quarter-inch (2-cm) curved spines range from white to rust

OPPOSITE, BOTTOM:
A perfectly grown plant of *Coryphantha echinus* (sea urchin cactus) blooming in a trough in Bill Adams's garden.

Coryphantha difficilis (difficult pincushion) in the author's garden is partly hidden by an *Orostachys* species.

red, have red tips, and do not conceal the stem. When this cactus is active and growing in the summer, the crown of the plant appears to be covered in wool. The shiny, yellow flowers are over an inch and a half (4 cm) in diameter and attract attention. In nature, this species can be found in the Mexican state of Coahuila. The plant is not difficult to grow, despite the common name, but a hot, sunny location and excellent soil drainage are essential. Plants are more likely to be lost to winter moisture than to cold.

Coryphantha echinus (sea urchin cactus) is primarily a Mexican species that crosses the border in the Big Bend region of Texas. The first thing that draws attention to this cactus is the neatly interwoven gleaming, white spines. The stem is about two and a half inches (6 cm) across and can get several inches tall. This is another species that is able to take more cold than wet when it is dormant, but can be covered in mulch in winter. The glossy, yellow flower, often with a red center, is about two inches (5 cm) across, appearing in spring, and sometimes again in summer after rainy spells. An exceptionally cold tolerant cultivar of this species is sometimes available in the trade; it was originally collected by Panayoti Kelaidis in north-central Texas near Abilene. I have grown many plants of this species, and some clones are clearly much more adapted to extremes of cold than others.

Coryphantha macromeris (big needle pincushion) is native to West Texas, New Mexico, and northern Mexico. In nature, old plants can form large clusters over three feet

(90 cm) across composed of stems three to eight inches (7.5 to 20 cm) thick. The brown to white spines are thin and flexible and do not cover the fat, green tubercles. The showy flowers are pinkish purple and over two and a half inches (about 6 cm) across. This very cold tolerant species needs strong sunlight and will not tolerate moist conditions in winter. I have had plants suffer from sunburn when they were first planted in the heat of summer, but otherwise they present no problems.

Coryphantha orcuttii (syn. *Escobaria orcuttii*) (Orcutt's pincushion) from southwest New Mexico and southeast Arizona has upright stems that grow up to eight inches (20 cm) tall and more than three inches (7.5 cm) in diameter. The spines are dull white with a slight touch of pink or black at the very tip, and they densely cover and almost hide the stem. The flowers are about half an inch (13 mm) wide in varying shades of pink. Variety *koenigii* (Koenig's snowball cactus) from Luna County, New Mexico, is more densely covered with spines and has marginally larger flowers; it also is slightly more vigorous in the garden. Variety *macraxina* has slightly longer spines than the typical variety and grows at elevations above 6000 feet (1800 m) in New Mexico. I have only planted this variety recently but expect it to be as hardy as the other varieties, which grow without protection anywhere in my garden.

Coryphantha poselgeriana (needle mulee) has blue-green stems that can get as large as six and a half inches (16 cm) high and almost six inches (15 cm) across. The species grows

Another showpiece in the Barnett family's garden is this clustering *Coryphantha macromeris* (big needle pincushion) in bloom.

Coryphantha orcuttii var. *koenigii* (Koenig's snowball cactus), a popular garden cactus, growing in a trough in Bill Adams's garden.

A small plant of *Coryphantha poselgeriana* (needle mulee) in the author's garden begins to grow in spring.

Coryphantha runyonii (Runyon's pincushion) in early spring, after a long, hard winter, looking no worse for the wear.

in nature throughout a large area of northern Mexico. Plants are variable, with spines that can be white, reddish, or even black and flowers that are from light yellow to light pink. One spine in each spine cluster is erect and is sometimes up to two inches (5 cm) long. This species is marginal in my garden, but can live for many years in a protected position and can be covered by mulch or cloth for long periods while dormant in winter. This cactus is more likely to succumb to winter moisture than most, and must be kept as dry as possible during the colder months.

Coryphantha runyonii (Runyon's pincushion) comes from Texas, where it grows along the Rio Grande. Some taxonomists consider this cactus to be a smaller variety or a subspecies of *C. macromeris.* At any rate, the two plants are quite similar. The clustering, gray-green stems are about three inches (7.5 cm) tall, with long, narrow tubercles, and the showy, magenta flowers are almost two inches (5 cm) wide. This species is marginal in zone 5 (-20°F or -28°C), but can survive in a protected, sunny, south-facing position if the soil drains well. Like so many species, some individual plants prove more cold hardy than others. I tried several plants of this species before finding a few that have shown vigor in my garden.

Coryphantha scheeri (Scheer's nipple cactus) occurs naturally in a small area of southeastern Arizona, parts of southern New Mexico, and much of southwestern Texas, as well as northern Mexico, mostly in open oak-juniper wood-lands. This species has long, plump, deep green tubercles. The ball-shaped plant can be as much as six to seven inches (15 to 18 cm) across and about three inches (7.5 cm) tall, with a somewhat flat top. The spines are white or gray with pink to reddish brown tips, and are long, thin and flexible, and do not obscure the tubercles. The flowers range from a glossy, light yellow to a rich, bronze color and are about two inches (5 cm) wide. Some authors and growers lump this species into *C. robustispina* as var. *scheeri*. Although not all plants of this species are dependable, there are some remarkably cold-hardy clones in cultivation. In hot summers, this cactus is relatively fast growing.

Coryphantha sulcata (finger cactus) has showy, yellow flowers with red throats. The flowers are almost two and a half inches (6 cm) across. In nature, this species inhabits portions of northern Mexico and southern Texas. The flabby, dark green stems can be up to five inches (13 cm) tall and wide, and are made of several large tubercles that have short, white and red spines at the tip. Plants offset profusely and make large mounds with time, but are much slower growing in a cold garden than in a greenhouse. This species is marginal in zone 5 (-20°F or -28°C), but can be kept for many years in a sunny position if winter moisture is avoided. Like other *Coryphantha* species, this one has some individuals that are much more resistant to cold and wet than others.

Escobaria albicolumnaria (syn. *Coryphantha albicolumnaria*) (silver lace cactus) has an immense, natural range in West Texas. This species has narrow, upright stems that grow to about five inches (13 cm) tall and one to two inches (2.5 to 5 cm) wide and are hidden under short, stiff, silvery white spines. Old plants sometimes make clusters, but not typically. The flowers range from pink to white and are about three-quarters of an inch (2 cm) wide. This little cactus is reliable in the garden if it is given gritty soil and long periods of strong sun with dry conditions in

A flowering plant of *Coryphantha scheeri* (Scheer's nipple cactus) in the Barnett family's garden.

Coryphantha sulcata (finger cactus) shows off its huge, shiny yellow flower in the Barnett family's garden.

Escobaria albicolumnaria (silver lace cactus) with a ripe fruit in late summer.

Escobaria dasyacantha (desert pincushion) in midwinter looks better than most garden perennials at that time of year.

winter. Although it is not necessary for healthy growth, water can be given to these plants during dry periods in the growing season.

Escobaria chaffeyi (syn. *Coryphantha chaffeyi*) (Chaffey's pincushion) grows naturally in northern Mexico and within a limited area across the border in West Texas. The small plants normally consist of a single stem but sometimes branch sparingly. The stem is somewhat ball-shaped and grows to about two inches (5 cm) around. The flowers appear in spring, are pink to white, but are only half an inch (13 mm) across. The bright red fruits show through the spines at the top of the stem late in the growing season. The spines are thin and mostly white, but some have red and yellow tips and they hide the stem. This is a remarkably cold hardy species when winters are dry. It requires no extra protection.

Escobaria dasyacantha (syn. *Coryphantha dasyacantha*) (desert pincushion) is native to some of the highest terrain in the Big Bend region in Texas, where it is considered to be rare. The stem is about two to three and a half inches (5 to 9 cm) tall and an inch and a half (4 cm) in diameter, and is covered with stiff, white spines that sometimes have brown or red tips. The petals of the small, white flowers have a pink to greenish midstripe, and the flowers appear in rings around the top of the stem in spring. Bright red fruits that look like little chilies follow the flowers late in the season. This plant can be said to be a perfectly safe bet in the garden, if winters are dry and soil drains well. An occasional snowstorm is not harmful, but through most of the winter the soil should not be moist at the surface.

Escobaria duncanii (syn. *Coryphantha duncanii*) (Duncan's pincushion) from southeast New Mexico and southwest Texas is said to be a rare species in nature, but seems to have no problems adapting to life in cultivation. The stem is slightly smaller than a golf ball and about as white, with spines densely covering the entire plant. The flower is whitish, with a brown to pink vein in the petals, and is about an inch (2.5 cm) across. The plant grows a large taproot and thus thrives in the hottest and driest situations when it is established. This species can be considered dependably cold hardy if winters are dry and plants are in good sun. They grow more quickly in hot, dry summers if they are given an occasional drink.

Escobaria guadalupensis (syn. *Coryphantha guadalupensis*) (Guadalupe Mountain pincushion) can be found growing in nature at some of the highest elevations in the Guadalupe Mountains on the Texas–New Mexico border just south of Carlsbad Caverns National Park. This cactus makes clusters of three or four cylindrical stems that are four or five inches (10 to 13 cm) tall and about an inch and a half (4 cm) wide. The stems are densely covered in somewhat shaggy, white spines. The flowers are less than half an inch (13 mm) across and the petal color is from pale yellow to light pink, with a darker midstripe. This reliable and attractive cactus in the garden should be kept on the dry side in winter.

Escobaria henricksonii (syn. *Coryphantha henricksonii*) (cob cory cactus) is from a limited area in the Mexican state of Chihuahua. It makes tight clusters of upright stems, which are over six inches (15 cm) tall and about two and a half inches (6 cm) in diameter. The spines, which hide the plants, are short and thin and neatly arranged in spirals down the stem. They are mostly white, with a single dark spine in the center of each spine cluster. The flowers are pink, about three-quarters of an inch (2 cm) across, with thin, pointed petals. Unfortunately, this species is marginal in cold climates and sometimes shows some scar damage by spring, unless it is in a protected position in the garden, where it requires

TOP:
Escobaria guadalupensis (Guadalupe Mountain pincushion), with an open flower in the author's garden. This young plant has not yet started to form clusters.

BOTTOM:
Another small cactus that deserves a place wherever miniature plants are used is *Escobaria henricksonii* (cob cory cactus).

Escobaria hesteri (Hester's pincushion), seen here in the Barnett family's garden, has long been known to be tolerant of cold winters.

One of the most adaptable small cacti for gardens or containers in cold climates is *Escobaria leei* (Lee's pincushion).

dry conditions in winter. This very pretty little cactus has survived the cold in my garden for five years. Trough growers should take advantage of the size, growth habits, and esthetic qualities of this one.

Escobaria hesteri (syn. *Coryphantha hesteri*) (Hester's pincushion) is a very adaptable pincushion that grows naturally in a somewhat limited area in the Big Bend country of Texas. The green stems are not entirely hidden by the thin, normally gray or sometimes black spines. Plants can make large clusters of stems, with each stem up to two inches (5 cm) in diameter. The species is very cold tolerant if kept dry in winter. The flowers are hot purple-pink to soft pink and almost an inch (2.5 cm) across, appearing in abundance in spring and more sporadically through the summer. I have lost plants to sunburn when planting them in midsummer but find them remarkably tough otherwise.

Escobaria leei (syns. *Coryphantha leei*, *Escobaria sneedii* var. *leei*) (Lee's pincushion) has a limited natural range near Carlsbad Caverns in New Mexico. It is a tidy, well-groomed, little cactus. The spines, which hide the plant, are very short and tightly hug the stem, giving a neat, clean, white appearance. The plant forms clusters quite readily with stems that tend to vary in size. Most of the stems are so tiny that even a clump of a dozen heads may only be the size of a tennis ball. The flowers are varying shades of pink and are less than half an inch (13 mm) across. This cactus is one of the best for troughs and containers. It can be grown outside in zone 4 (-30°F or -35°C) and is known to do well in the eastern United States, but is best kept dry in winter. *Escobaria leei* is a legally protected, endangered species, but has s become readily available in cultivation. All things considered, it is highly recommended for both hardiness and ornate qualities.

Escobaria lloydii (syn. *Coryphantha lloydii*) (Lloyd's pincushion) is native to northern Mexico. In time, these plants can make large clusters of stems. This species is closely related to many of the pincushion cacti from just across the border in Texas and New Mexico. The yellow- or pink-tipped spines appear to be white at first glance. They are numerous, but thin and do not hide the stems. Stems are a couple of inches (5 cm) wide and up to five inches (13 cm) tall. The flowers are about three-quarters of an inch (2 cm) across and are mostly light pink, with a darker midstripe in the petals. This is a strong dependable species if it is given full sun and dry winters. Lloyd's pincushion should not be confused with Lloyd's hedgehog (*Echinocereus ×lloydii*).

Escobaria minima (syn. *Coryphantha minima*) (Nellie's pincushion), as the Latin name suggests, is a very small plant. It does not typically offset in nature, but plants grown in cultivation make clusters almost without exception. The twisted, short spines are corky and either cream or golden brown in color, and they uniformly cover the entire stem. The stems are not consistent in size. While most *Escobaria* species cluster primarily at the base of the stem unless they are injured, plants of this species branch anywhere on the stem. The deep to soft pink petals have a darker midstripe, and they are about three-quarters of an inch (2 cm) in diameter. Rare and protected in nature, this species has become somewhat readily available in horticulture. Its natural range is restricted to higher elevations in West Texas. In the garden this little cactus is quite reliable and blooms prolifically in spring and sporadically through the summer.

Escobaria missouriensis (syn. *Coryphantha missouriensis*) (Missouri nipple cactus) is somewhat common on the eastern plains of Colorado and has a natural range from North Dakota to Texas and from eastern Colorado to Missouri.

Another tough, little cactus from West Texas is *Escobaria minima* (Nellie's pincushion).

TOP:
One of the cacti most tolerant to cold and wet conditions is *Escobaria missouriensis* (Missouri nipple cactus).

BOTTOM LEFT:
In early spring, rings of bright red fruits appear of *Escobaria missouriensis* growing in a container in Panayoti Kelaidis's collection.

BOTTOM RIGHT:
The rare *Escobaria missouriensis* var. *navajoensis* (Navajo nipple cactus) flowering in the Barnett family's garden.

As with any species that grows over such a large area, it is variable. Mature stems vary from golf ball size to tennis ball size. The plant normally makes clusters of stems that are inconsistent in size. Plants from eastern Kansas and Missouri, where there is higher rainfall, make large clusters of many stems that grow almost level with the ground. In eastern Colorado, plants tend to be a couple of inches (5 cm) tall and have fewer stems. The flowers of this species vary from cream or yellow to very pretty, soft pink and are over an inch (2.5 cm) across, with sharply pointed petals. The fruits are bright red, and they are large enough and numerous enough to draw attention, but they do not appear until late winter or early spring of the season following flowering. There are a few recognized varieties. Variety *navajoensis* (Navajo nipple cactus), the miniature variety from western Colorado, eastern Utah, and northern Arizona, is rare. Variety *missouriensis*, the typical variety, is one of the hardiest cacti in the family, being reliable in zone 3 (-40°F or -40°C), and tolerant of wet conditions, as cacti go. Other cold-hardy varieties include var. *asperispina*, var. *caespitosa*, var. *marstonii*, and var. *similis*. Growers offering this species for sale sometimes still use the old genus name *Neobesseya* that was given to this species early in the twentieth century.

Escobaria organensis (syn. *Coryphantha organensis*) (Organ Mountain pincushion) occurs naturally only in the Organ Mountains of southwest New Mexico. It freely branches into large clusters of many heads. Stems are over an inch (2.5 cm) in diameter and four inches (10 cm) tall. The thin, quarter-inch, (6-mm) yellow spines are abundant but do not hide the stem. The flowers vary from yellow to various shades of pink, and they are about half an inch (13 mm) across, appearing abundantly in spring. This species has been growing in my garden for about fifteen years and is never stressed by even the coldest and wettest winters. It can be considered a safe bet in cold climates. Even marble-sized seedlings of this plant can be expected to adapt to the garden if they are given a little extra moisture through the first season.

Escobaria organensis (Organ Mountain pincushion) blooming in the author's garden.

Escobaria sanbergii (syn. *Coryphantha sanbergii*) (Sanberg's pincushion) is native to the higher altitudes of the San Andres Mountains in southern New Mexico. This small, upright cactus is densely covered in short, pink- or brown-tipped white spines. The stems can be up to five inches (13 cm) tall and close to two inches (5 cm) wide. The plant does not always branch, but sometimes it makes clusters of many stems. The flowers are about an inch (2.5 cm) in diameter and vary from cream to various shades of pink. The fruits are red and stand above the spines, providing color into winter. This species is reliable if grown in full sun and kept dry in winter.

Escobaria sneedii (syn. *Coryphantha sneedii*) (Sneed's pincushion) is found in nature growing in the extreme southeastern corner of Arizona through southern New Mexico, into the Big Bend region of Texas, and in adjacent areas of Mexico. The plant makes a cluster of stems that are inconsistent in size, with the largest ones usually less than an inch (2.5 cm) thick. The short, shiny white spines hide the stem when the plants are grown in full sun. Flower color ranges from white to pink, and flower size is

Certainly one of the most adaptable and reliable cacti in a variety of climates is *Escobaria sneedii* (Sneed's pincushion), here flowering in Steve Miles's garden.

about half an inch (13 mm) across. This plant is protected as an endangered species, but it is not rare in cultivation and needs no special care. It can be grown outside in zone 4 (-30°F or -35°C) with no protection. In the eastern United States, where humidity is high and rainfall is abundant, this species has been known to adapt better than most. It has thrived in my garden for more than twenty-five years and has never required any special treatment. I consider it one of the most reliable cacti in cold climates. The plant takes a few years to make large clusters and is an excellent choice for a trough or other container.

Escobaria tuberculosa (syn. *Coryphantha tuberculosa*) (cob cactus) has spines that are generally grayer than white, and that cover the stem. Like many other species in this group, this one can be found in nature from southern New Mexico into Mexico and the Big Bend area of Texas. Plants almost always branch into clusters in nature, but will not necessarily do so in cultivation. The stem is a couple of inches (5 cm) wide and about twice as tall. The flowers, in various shades of light pink, are about an inch (2.5 cm) in diameter and appear later in the season than do most *Escobaria* or *Coryphantha* flowers. Variety *varicolor* (varicolored cob cactus), a less spiny variety of this species from Texas and Mexico, has slightly fatter stems, which are sometimes somewhat cone shaped. It is also different, as the plants of this variety do not often branch in nature or in cultivation, and have shorter, thinner, gray spines with black or brown tips. This variety has suffered from sunburn during sudden autumn freezes in my garden, but is otherwise reliable.

Escobaria villardii (syn. *Coryphantha villardii*) (Villard's pincushion) has a limited natural range within the Sacramento Mountains in New Mexico. The plant makes a clump of upright, cylindrical stems that are four to five inches (10 to

The flowers of *Escobaria tuberculosa* var. *varicolor* (varicolored cob cactus) appear after rains, through the summer in the author's garden.

13 cm) tall and two and a half inches (6 cm) wide. The stems are rounded at the top and covered somewhat densely by shaggy, white spines with pink or black tips. These plants have one-inch (2.5-cm) wide, white to pink flowers, with a darker midstripe in the petals. Red fruits follow flowers in the fall. This is an attractive and vigorous species in the garden and presents no cultural challenges.

The flowers of *Escobaria villardii* (Villard's pincushion) are followed by red fruits in late summer in the Barnett family's garden.

Escobaria vivipara (syn. *Coryphantha vivipara*) (beehive cactus) has the largest natural range of any species in this genus, and is found through a large area of Mexico, and from Texas west into California, then north through Nevada, Utah, Colorado, and Kansas, all the way into Canada. It is a very common cactus, growing with grasses on the plains and in the foothills of eastern Colorado. Plants can make dense colonies of hundreds of individuals, growing in a relatively small area. Like any species with such a large natural range, this cactus can vary drastically in appearance from one area to the next. Mature stems can be over six inches (15 cm) tall or as small as an inch (2.5 cm) in height, and may be only an inch to over three and a half inches (2.5 to 9 cm) across, sometimes, but not always, with flat tops. In garden situations with extra water, stems can sometimes become even larger. The green stems may be exposed or obscured by spines, which vary dramatically in length, number, and thickness, but are generally thin, and from white to rust colored. Some plants branch freely, while others remain a single stem for life. The brightly colored flowers are over two inches (5 cm) across and range from light to dark pink, but are typically a rich, pinkish purple. In sunny situations, flowers are produced in large numbers over a long blooming period. In spring, the flowers are likely to make rings around

Clustering *Escobaria vivipara* (beehive cactus) in the author's garden.

A single-stemmed plant of *Escobaria vivipara* var. *arizonica* (Arizona beehive) in bloom in the Barnett family's garden.

the top of the stem. One unique form of this species is var. *buoflama* (Yavapai beehive) from north of Bagdad, Arizona. Plants of this variety look like large-stemmed plants of var. *vivipara*, until they bloom with flowers that are a rusty, yellowish orange color. Variety *buoflama* is hardy in zone 5 (-20°F or -28°C), but var. *vivipara*, which is among the most tolerant to cold and wet of all ball-type cacti, can be grown safely in zone 3 (-40°F or -40°C) without damage. Variety *arizonica* has a short, thick stem covered with numerous rust-colored spines.

Escobaria zilziana (syn. *Coryphantha zilziana*) (Mexican snowball cactus) is densely covered, but not concealed by thin white spines, sometimes with pink or brown tips. Plants do not normally branch into clusters. The stem is rounded, with a somewhat cone-shaped top, and is typically nearly an inch in diameter (2.5 cm) and three inches (7.5 cm) tall. The flowers are about an inch (2.5 cm) across and, like the flowers

Escobaria zilziana (Mexican snowball cactus) flowering in the author's garden.

of many other species in this group, are quite variable in color, being white to soft yellow, or maybe even green, often with a darker pink mid-stripe through the petals. This species is native to Mexico and therefore would not be expected to be tolerant of cold, but this little cactus is reliable in my garden.

Echinocactus

The genus *Echinocactus* consists of some of the most popular cacti with gardeners in warm climates. It includes *E. grusonii* (golden barrel) from Mexico, which is very cold tolerant by California standards, but is not even close to hardy where winters are severe. A few members of this genus are marginally hardy in zone 5 (-20°F or -28°C) and they are very attractive species. They are much more reliable in cold frames or unheated greenhouses, but remain in the garden year-round if care is taken to keep them from excessive winter moisture and winds. Apart from the species described here, no others are known to be even marginally hardy, and although these have been grown in zone 5 gardens, they have a reputation for living several years and growing to an impressive size, then giving up during cold, windy, wet periods of weather.

Echinocactus horizonthalonius (blue barrel, eagle's claw cactus) from the Chihuahua desert is a very attractive blue-green cactus. Dividing the stem are rounded ribs that bear clusters of a few, short, stout, grayish spines along the ridges. The flower of this heat-loving species appears at the top of the stem, and is pink and about two and a half inches (6 cm) across. In time, the plant can grow to over five inches (13 cm) wide and several inches taller, but it is very slow growing and does not offset. In nature, the species is usually found in flat, open areas, growing in loose, sandy loam in full sun. The plant is more likely to be lost to winter moisture than to cold. It is susceptible to sunburn when the temperature is below freezing and the plant is not fully dormant. This beauty can be covered heavily with mulch or frost cloth through the entire winter with no harm, but any plant covered for a long period should be uncovered during cloudy periods to avoid sunburn. I have grown this cactus in my garden for six

This flowering plant of *Echinocactus horizonthalonius* (blue barrel or eagle's claw cactus) has been growing for several years in the Dryland Mesa Garden at Denver Botanic Gardens.

years, and small plants of the species have been more reliable for me than the horse crippler, which grows in colder, wetter areas in nature. Variety *nicholii* from the Sonoran Desert is not hardy.

Echinocactus polycephalus (many headed barrel cactus) has a natural range that includes higher elevations in parts of Utah, Arizona, and Nevada, where it grows with pinyons and junipers. One reason this species is worth trying is that it can become a spectacular plant with stems that reach twelve inches (30 cm) in diameter and three feet (90 cm) in height, if the right microclimate can be found. The Latin *polycephalus* means many heads, but subspecies *xeranthemoides*, which is more cold tolerant than var. *polycephalus*, usually forms clumps of less than a dozen stems. The spines are white, yellow, and red, and strongly curve downward. The flowers are yellow and about an inch (2.5 cm) across. Extra care should be taken to protect this plant from excessive moisture at any time of the year, but particularly in winter.

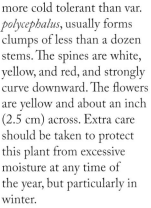

Echinocactus polycephalus subsp. *xeranthemoides* (many headed barrel cactus) is so spiny that its flowers cannot fully open.

Echinocactus texensis (horse crippler) gets its common name from its tendency to hide in tall grasses, where horses may step on it and hurt themselves. Old plants can grow close to a foot (30 cm) across and be slightly taller than that. This cactus grows in the flat grasslands and rolling plains of eastern New Mexico, parts of Oklahoma, and most of West Texas. I have had dozens of these plants live four or five years, then die suddenly during exceptionally cold periods in the spring after starting to show signs of new growth. If you are gardening where spring weather is more predictable, this species may do better for you than it does for me. I hope that in time clones of *E. texensis* will be found that prove reliable. The horse crippler is a drab green plant with many prominent ribs dividing the flat-topped stems. Plants do not branch unless they are injured. The spine clusters are spaced along the ribs, and the thick, flat, curved spines emerge red but turn gray as they age. The flowers are from almost white to light pink, with red centers, and are over two inches (5 cm) in diameter. It is important to give these plants adequate water through the first summer to allow roots to develop properly. This species is susceptible to sunburn, especially during spring and fall freezes when plants are not quite dormant, or right after they have been planted.

Echinocactus texensis (horse crippler) flowering in the Barnett family's garden.

Echinocereus

Echinocereus is, perhaps, the most valuable genus of plants available to the cold-hardy cactus and succulent garden enthusiast. It is also one of the most popular groups among people who collect

In late summer a swollen, red fruit has matured on this *Echinocactus texensis* (horse crippler) at Mesa Garden.

flowering cacti in any climate. These species range from golf-ball-sized plants that seldom cluster to large mounds composed of hundreds of tall, fat stems. The stems of all the species are divided by ribs that can expand or shrink, depending on the availability of water. The spine clusters are always on raised points along these ribs. The flower buds break through the skin of the plant along the upper edge or side of the stem, not at the top. For the most part, the flowers are exceptionally showy.

Echinos means hedgehog in Greek, and collectors around the world have known these plants as hedgehog cacti for generations. Hybridization is common between *Echinocereus* species when large numbers of these cacti are kept together and pollinating insects are present, such as in a cactus garden. Some of the hybrids produce flowers that are beautiful beyond belief, but many times they are sterile and may not set seed.

Spider mites can sometimes be a problem, but generally hedgehogs are pest-free. In nature, black longhorn cactus beetles sometimes attack the plants, but this is not a problem in a garden unless wild hedgehog populations grow in the vicinity. Many hedgehog species are among the most reliable and beautiful cacti that can be grown outdoors in cold regions. Good winter sun is helpful to insure spring flowering, and it is best not to leave these plants under cover other than snow for any length of time.

Echinocereus adustus (rufis spine hedgehog) is found in nature only at higher elevations, around the cities of Chihuahua and Durango in Mexico. The common name is derived from an older scientific name for this cactus, *E. rufispinus*. The attractive plant has a cylindrical stem about four inches (10 cm) wide and over six inches (15 cm) tall. Plants do not normally cluster. Numerous eighth-inch (3-mm) long, black,

A reliable cactus species for climates with harsh winters, *Echinocereus triglochidiatus* (claret cup hedgehog, king's crown cactus) does well in the eastern and midwestern United States and is one of the most frequently encountered cacti in northern European gardens.

brown, and white spines press tightly against the stem, almost hiding it. The bright pink flowers are spectacular and about two and a half inches (6 cm) across. Judging by where it lives in nature, this cactus should be marginal in zone 5 (-20°F or -28°C), but it has grown and flowered without problems in a sunny, south-facing exposure in my garden for five years. It would not be surprising if some clones of this species prove more cold tolerant than others. This is another species that is more likely to be lost to winter moisture than to cold.

Echinocereus albispinus (Oklahoma hedgehog) is densely covered with short, white, bristly spines that point away from the stem in all directions. These plants will make small to medium-sized clusters of cylindrical stems that are over two inches (5 cm) wide and several inches tall. This attractive hedgehog has knockout, light pink to occasionally white flowers that are over four inches (10 cm) across. Coming from Oklahoma, it can deal with wetter, more humid climates than most cacti. Without a doubt, it can be grown in zone 4 (-30°F or -35°C) with no protection. This species has grown and flowered in my garden for more than twenty-five years without ever suffering, and is known to thrive in places subject to cold winters and hot, humid summers. Botanists consider this plant a variety of *E. reichenbachii*, but it is more likely to be found as *E. albispinus* in garden centers or on the Internet.

Echinocereus baileyi (Bailey's hedgehog) is much like *E. albispinus* and is also considered by taxonomists to be a variety of *E. reichenbachii*, but plants of *E. baileyi* are much more variable. Generally, the downward-pointing spines are longer and shaggier and vary in length and color from shades of pink to black. Recently a form with cherry red spines was found. Spine color depends to some degree on the quality of light to which plants are exposed, with stronger sunlight

TOP:
A soccer-ball-sized, clustering mound of *Echinocereus albispinus* (Oklahoma hedgehog) growing in Jeff Ottersberg's garden.

BOTTOM:
Knockout, light pink flowers adorn *Echinocereus albispinus* (Oklahoma hedgehog) in Steve Miles's garden.

Few plants of any genus are as beautiful, yet as tough and adaptable as *Echinocereus baileyi* (Bailey's hedgehog).

The spectacular two-toned flower of *Echinocereus boyce-thompsonii* (Boyce Thompson's hedgehog) in the Barnett family's garden.

intensifying colors. These plants also vary much more in stem size and cluster less freely. The flowers are outstanding, being a glossy, rich pink and over four inches (10 cm) in diameter. In nature, these plants are native to Texas and Oklahoma and, recently, Jeff Thompson found plants in Kansas. This is a very tough hedgehog that can be grown outside in zone 4 (-30°F or 35°C) with no problems. Sometimes, the name *E. baileyi* var. *minor* is used for the smaller forms of this species.

Echinocereus boyce-thompsonii (Boyce Thompson's hedgehog) is native to central Arizona and can sometimes be found growing where frosts occur, but is not a high-altitude species. Benson (1982) placed this species as a variety of *E. fasciculatus*, and other taxonomists have followed that thinking, but most plant sellers consider it to be a separate species. Spines are straw-colored with dark tips, and they do not hide the stem, but do cover it evenly. Stems are an inch and a half to three inches (4 to 7.5 cm) thick and over nine inches (23 cm) tall. These plants may or may not make clusters of a few heads. The flowers are over two inches (5 cm) across and are spectacularly colored hot pink with a darker, reddish purple interior. Some botanists consider *E. bonkerae* to be a variety of this species.

Echinocereus canus (gray beard hedgehog) was found a few years ago on private land that had not yet been investigated by anyone with enough expertise in cacti to recognize it as a unique species. It was growing in a limited area on mountaintops in the Big Bend region of West Texas. These isolated areas of high terrain create islands of milder climates above the hot, dry Chihuahua desert, where unique species occur. The small, green flowers appear at the side of the stem near the bottom. The most appealing quality of this hedgehog is the long, thin, shaggy, glittering, silver spines that hide the stems. New spines emerge from the top of the plant as cardinal red and then turn a glistening, silvery white as they mature. Although it is still a rarity, this species surely will become more available soon, as it is very easy to grow and it is ornamental. This stunning cactus is hardy in zone 5 (-20°F or -28°C), but needs full sun to look its best and it does not deal well with excessive moisture, even in summer months. Stems tend to be about an inch (2.5 cm) across, several inches tall, and they do not readily offset. This cactus is considered by most taxonomists to be either a variety of *E. viridiflorus* or a very closely related species, but it has also been included as variety of *E. chloranthus* and *E. russanthus* by some.

Echinocereus
canus
(gray beard
hedgehog),
a relatively
new species,
shows much
promise. Here
it is seen
flowering for
Bill Adams.

Echinocereus chloranthus (green flower pitaya) and its taller form, var. *cylindricus* (tall green flower pitaya), grow over much of eastern New Mexico and West Texas, as well as parts of northern Mexico. The stems are about an inch and a half (4 cm) in diameter and up to eight inches (20 cm) tall. Generally, the stems will remain single but may branch into small clusters. In some plants, one longer spine at the center of the spine cluster will grow at a right angle to the stem, the rest

Looking down the barrel of a barrel cactus, *Echinocereus chloranthus* (green flower pitaya) in Steve Miles's garden.

A practical, yet stunning small garden with *Echinocereus coccineus* var. *gurneyi* (Gurney's hedgehog) as a centerpiece. This variety has taller, bulkier stems.

are short and remain pressed against the plant. The spines are yellow, silver, and red, sometimes with brown tips. The three-quarter-inch (2-cm) flowers are greenish with a red or bronze tint. This species should be considered somewhat marginal in zone 5 (-20°F or -28°C), but once these plants are established they have no problems if soil drainage is adequate and winters are dry. Like many other cacti, some clones of this species are much more cold and moisture tolerant than others.

Echinocereus coccineus (bunch ball claret cup) really does look a bit like a hedgehog from a distance as a small cluster. The species is common in much of New Mexico and West Texas. It also grows in parts of southeastern and western Colorado, as well as areas of Arizona, Nevada, and Utah, almost always on rocky hillsides, often within open areas of pinyon-juniper woodlands. This cactus starts life as a single, dull green stem about two and a half inches (6 cm) in diameter and four or five inches (10 to 13 cm) tall. In time, it may offset prolifically and become an impressive mound that is over three feet (90 cm) across with hundreds of stems. The flowers are shades of orange, about two and a half inches (6 cm) across, and unlike most cactus flowers, they remain open at night. This very spiny plant has long, needlelike spines that are close to an inch (2.5 cm) long. The spines are gray to straw colored, sometimes with black tips. The species has a large natural range, and plants are variable in stem size, spination, and ability to withstand cold. Some clones are reliably hardy to at least zone 4 (-30°F or -35°C).

This species has many recognized varieties, including var. *aggregatus*, which I can't tell from var. *coccineus*, but it is said to make mounds of more stems at maturity. Variety *arizonicus* and var. *gurneyi* have larger, bulkier stems, even as young plants. Variety *canyonensis* (synonym var. *toroweapensis*) has fiery, reddish orange spines that emerge from the crown of the stem, and is native to an area near the Grand Canyon National Park. Variety *paucispinus* (synonym var. *octacanthus*) is less spiny than most of the others. Variety *roemeri*, from further east in Texas, is reported to grow well in wetter climates. Var. *rosei* is spinier and known for uniquely colored flowers. Benson (1982) considered this species to be *E. triglochidiatus* var. *melanacanthus*, and that name is still used by some growers. It is a very adaptable species that is known to thrive in gardens in the midwestern and eastern United States.

Echinocereus dasyacanthus (Texas rainbow hedgehog) is native from eastern Arizona through southern New Mexico into West Texas, as well as northern Mexico. The show-off flowers are from three inches (7.5 cm) to over five inches (13 cm) in diameter and variable in color. Although often shades of yellow, they may be orange, pink, purple, or one of these colors blended with yellow. New spines are typically pink as they emerge but turn yellow and brown as they age, each season's growth creating a sharply defined band of color, giving the plant its common name. The spines are about half an inch (13 mm) long and are pressed tightly against the stem. This cactus can become a good-sized plant with clustering stems over a foot (30 cm) tall and close to five inches (13 cm) across in nature, but generally is much smaller in cultivation in cold climates. Clones of this hedgehog vary in tolerance to cold, but are quite tough cacti if kept dry in winter. I know

One of the few cacti that do not close their flowers at night is *Echinocereus coccineus* (bunch ball cactus). To those of us that are at work during the day that is meaningful.

Echinocereus dasyacanthus (Texas rainbow cactus) flowering in the author's garden.

of a plant of this species that was left outside in a trough through a zone 4 (-30°F or -35°C) winter and flowered the following spring.

Echinocereus davisii (syn. *E. viridiflorus* var. *davisii*) (dwarf hedgehog) is another cactus with a limited range within the higher elevations of the Big Bend region of Texas. This species is able to adapt to typical rock garden care given dry, well-draining soil. As the common name implies, this is a small plant, maybe an inch (2.5 cm) tall and three-quarters of an inch (2 cm) wide, sometimes clustering. The rusty, greenish flowers are about half an inch (13 mm) across and may appear at any point on the side of the stem. The thin, wiry, sometimes twisted spines grow at a right angle to the stem, are about three-quarters of an inch (2 cm) long, and emerge black, then turn white. This hedgehog is somewhat reliable if kept dry in winter. A legally protected species, it is listed as endangered but is not rare in cultivation. Almost all descriptions of the species in nature indicate that these plants grow with *Selaginella* (spikemoss) species, which look like mosses to most people.

Echinocereus engelmannii (Engelmann's hedgehog) has incredible purple flowers that are over three inches (7.5 cm) wide and just have to be seen. I have watched people laugh when seeing this plant bloom for the first time; because the flowers are so much larger than the stem on which they grow, the plant borders on ridiculous. The species has a large natural range, including parts of Utah, Nevada, and California, as well as most of Arizona. This results in many named varieties, two of which are very cold hardy. Variety *chrysocentrus* (Engelmann's dagger spined hedgehog), from as far north as Salt Lake City, Utah, has stems five to eight inches (13 to 20 cm) tall and about two inches (5 cm) thick covered with stiff, white and brown downward-pointing spines.

Another cactus that is rare in nature but has become somewhat common in cultivation is *Echinocereus davisii* (dwarf hedgehog).

Variety *variegatus* (Engelmann's varied hedgehog), which is more often found in eastern Utah and northeastern Arizona, typically has slightly smaller stems—three to six inches (7.5 to 15 cm) tall—and seldom makes clusters of more than four or five stems. Both varieties inhabit the Great Basin desert, a region characterized by bitter periods in winter and unbearably hot, dry summers. Cacti from the region cannot handle long periods of excessive moisture at any time of year. A third variety, known as var. *fasciculatus* (syn. *E. fasciculatus*) (Engelmann's long spine hedgehog), is perhaps as hardy, but has not been tested for as many winters or by as many gardeners. So far it has proved cold hardy in well-drained soil in a sunny position. Several other varieties are recognized, but none of them are known to be resistant to cold.

Echinocereus enneacanthus (syns. *E. dubius*, *E. stramineus* var. *enneacanthus*) (strawberry pitaya) grows naturally on rocky hillsides and dry, sandy flats throughout much of southwestern Texas and southeastern New Mexico, as well as portions of northern Mexico. In time, this hedgehog can become a large mound of many tapered stems. The flowers are a bright magenta and about four inches (10 cm) across. Stiff spines that are somewhat thin and sometimes curved cover the plants uniformly but not heavily. The spines are typically straw-colored, often with darker tips. Variety *brevispinus* has shorter spines and grows to the east of var. *enneacanthus*. This is another cactus that is more likely to be lost to moist conditions in winter rather than to cold.

Echinocereus fendleri (Fendler's hedgehog) has a large natural range that includes the area around Canon City in Fremont

One of the showiest cacti when in flower is *Echinocereus engelmannii* var. *chrysocentrus* (Engelmann's dagger spine hedgehog), seen here in Jeff Ottersberg's garden.

A small plant of *Echinocereus enneacanthus* (strawberry pitaya) blooming in the Barnett family's garden.

County, as well as Montezuma, and La Plata Counties in Colorado. It can also be found in much of northern New Mexico, and parts of Arizona where it grows primarily at higher altitudes on rolling grassy hillsides. Variety *fendleri* has somewhat cone-shaped stems that are a little over two and a half inches (6 cm) across and usually no more than five inches (13 cm) tall. The spines are variable in length and curve up and inward toward the top of the stem. Variety *kuenzleri* (Kuenzler's hedgehog) has flat, corky spines, but otherwise looks like var. *fendleri*; however, it is not as cold tolerant, and is much slower growing and shyer about flowering. Neither of these varieties normally branches, but it does sometimes happen. Variety *rectispinus* (Fendler's needle spine hedgehog) is much different in appearance, with shorter, more erect, brown and white spines, and it does cluster. The gorgeous, three-inch (7.5-cm) wide flowers are identical in all three varieties, with glossy, purple petals that dwarf the stem. A white-flowering form of the species that is always sold as 'Albiflora' looks like the typical variety in every way, except for the flower color. The white-flowering form has not been as cold tolerant, and seed from it does not always yield white-flowering offspring. This species is more likely than most to hybridize in the garden.

TOP:
Echinocereus fendleri (Fendler's hedgehog) bears gorgeous flowers in the author's garden.

BOTTOM:
Growing in troughs at Denver Botanic Gardens, these plants of *Echinocereus fendleri* (Fendler's hedgehog) have ripe fruits loaded with seed.

Echinocereus knippelianus (green peyote) is a flabby, dark green, clustering plant, with wispy spines on rounded stems that are about three inches (7.5 cm) in diameter. The entire range of this cactus in nature is in central Mexico, where it grows at high elevations that can have cold periods in winter. The plant looks best in a position that is sheltered from the midday sun in summer, and it can sunburn quite easily in autumn during sudden freezes.

For a cactus, this is a very thirsty plant in spring and early summer, and it does not flourish if it is left completely dry at that time. The flowers are over two and a half inches (6 cm) across and usually soft pink, but they can be rich pink to white. The blooming period begins early enough for flower buds to sometimes be seen sticking up through snow. In winter these cacti shrink almost flat to the ground, but healthy plants should be plump by early spring. If plants do not swell up in spring, they are too dry. This species would be a good choice for climates that are too wet for most cacti, if plants can be kept dry in winter and night temperatures are cooler than those during the day. As with any cactus, the soil must drain well. Plants grown in a heated greenhouse and those grown outside in the garden set flower buds at the same time each year.

One of the big surprises in the time I have been experimenting with succulents is how cold hardy *Echinocereus knippelianus* (green peyote) has proved itself to be.

Echinocereus knippelianus (green peyote) with fully opened flowers in the author's garden in midspring.

Echinocereus ×*lloydii* (syn. *E. ×roetteri* var. *neomexicanus*) (Lloyd's hedgehog), a naturally occurring hybrid involving *E. coccineus* and *E. dasyacanthus*, can be found scattered through southeastern New Mexico, and southwestern Texas. The plants are quite variable and may cluster or remain a single stem for life. Stem shapes and sizes are not uniform but are normally large—sometimes well over a foot (30 cm) tall and three and a half inches (9 cm) thick. It is not unusual for this hedgehog to look like one of the parent species until it produces flowers. The flowers are typically over three inches (7.5 cm) in diameter and may be solid or multi-colored with pinks, whites, reds, yellows, and oranges possible. The number of spines per plant varies tremendously, and the spines can be thin or thick and are inconsistent in length.

One plant of the highly variable *Echinocereus ×lloydii* (Lloyd's hedgehog) in Bill Adams's garden.

Another plant of *Echinocereus* ×*lloydii* (Lloyd's hedgehog) in Bill Adams's garden. The variation in flower color, as well as body shape and plant size, is remarkable.

In a protected position *Echinocereus pacificus* (little red claret cup) can grow and flower for years.

This strong, vigorous hybrid makes a good garden plant and requires no special care. In my garden it is the fastest-growing hedgehog. This cactus is highly recommended.

Echinocereus pacificus (little red claret cup) grows on some of the highest peaks in northern Baja California. This very spiny, low-growing, prolifically clustering cactus has cylindrical, green stems, which are less than an inch (2.5 cm) across. Pretty, inch-and-a-quarter (3-cm) wide, reddish orange flowers grow near the top of the stems. The spines are straw-colored and they point mostly downward, almost hiding the stems. These little cacti shrink just about flat to the ground in winter. Unfortunately, this species only survives in the most protected part of my garden and it should be considered marginal in zone 5 (-20°F or -28°C). It is a very pretty and somewhat reliable hedgehog when it is established, if it is covered for brief periods during the coldest weather, or if kept in a cold frame or unheated greenhouse. Although it is a sun-loving cactus in summer, it can sunburn easily when it is half-dormant during frigid periods in spring and fall.

Echinocereus pectinatus (comb spine hedgehog) is quite variable in appearance with some individuals densely covered by short, thin, red, pink, or silver spines, making them showy. In nature, the species is found over much of northern Mexico, and from Arizona through southern New Mexico to West Texas. Unfortunately, this hedgehog is only marginally hardy in zone 5 (-20°F or -28°C), with some individuals much more forgiving of extreme cold than others. The exceptionally showy flowers of variety *pectinatus* are lipstick pink with white interiors and are over five inches (13 cm) in diameter. The stems are several inches tall, a couple of inches (5 cm) in diameter, and do not normally cluster. Variety *wenigeri* (Weniger's hedgehog), from West Texas, branches more frequently, has cream-white spines, and more importantly is better able to cope with frigid winters; its huge flowers are yellow and white in the center with a broad band of bright pinkish purple around the outer edge. Both varieties are dependable in my garden but must be covered during harsh periods in winter. *Echinocereus pectinatus* var. *ctenoides* is classified as a variety of *E. dasyacanthus* or *E. rigidissimus* by many modern taxonomists but is sold by nurseries using any of these names.

Echinocereus polyacanthus (scarlet claret cup) is native to southern Arizona and across the border in Mexico. It is very cold hardy and survives winters in zone 4 (-30°F or -35°C) without damage. One nursery in that zone has been growing this species in open garden beds for many years. The thick, yellow- to rust-colored spines vary in length and mostly conceal the stem. The flowers are yellowish orange, to red with lighter interiors, and are over three inches (7.5 cm) in diameter. The cylindrical, cone-shaped stems are over two (5 cm) inches across and can be several inches tall. Sometimes the plant clusters prolifically, making impressive, large mounds. It is a very attractive and reliable addition to a cactus garden, particularly when it is positioned in full sun.

Echinocereus reichenbachii (lace cactus) might be the most ideal garden cactus for many climates. Its natural range is centered in Oklahoma and north-central Texas, making it more adaptable to climates with high summer rainfall and humidity. The species exists in many forms and varieties, from small, almost flat, clustering stems covered with white spines to fifteen-inch (38-cm) tall, fat stems with black spines.

Echinocereus pectinatus (comb spine hedgehog) is a very pretty plant in or out of bloom.

Marginally more cold hardy than the typical species is *Echinocereus pectinatus* var. *wenigeri* (Weniger's hedgehog).

A beautiful specimen of *Echinocereus polyacanthus* (scarlet claret cup) in Steve Miles's garden.

A cactus that deserves to be in every garden is *Echinocereus reichenbachii* (lace spine cactus), seen here in the Barnett family's garden.

The four-inch (10-cm) purple to lipstick-pink flowers dwarf the stems. This species is also known to grow well in gardens in the U.S. East and Midwest.

Echinocereus baileyi and *E. albispinus* are considered to be part of this species in science, but are generally separated in horticulture. Several varieties and subspecies of *E. reichenbachii* are known. Variety *perbellus* can be found in nature in southeastern Colorado and south and east into New Mexico and Oklahoma. Variety *caespitosus* is a low, clumping cactus from Oklahoma and parts of Texas. One of the most impressive forms is subsp. *armatus*; it has the largest flowers in the species, is found further to the south, and is not quite as cold hardy as the previously mentioned varieties, though it grows vigorously in zone 5 (-20°F or -28°C) gardens. Other varieties of this species that are as cold tolerant and decorative as var. *reichenbachii* are var. *castaneus*, var. *nigrispinus*, var. *oklahomensis*, and var. *purpureus*, which are all hardy in zone 4 (-30°F or -35°C). These vary primarily in stem size and willingness to cluster, as well as the color, number, and length of spines. Variety *fitchii* and var. *albertii*, which are the least cold hardy varieties, have survived many years in my garden near buildings. During the drought that plagued eastern Colorado for the first few years of the twenty-first century many populations of this species were lost, while other cacti species were not as affected.

Large flowers top the erect, columnar stems of *Echinocereus reichenbachii* var. *perbellus* (lace spine cactus).

Echinocereus rigidissimus (Arizona rainbow hedgehog) grows in nature throughout much of northern Mexico, south-western New Mexico, and southern Arizona. Usually the plant consists of a single, cylindrical stem over four inches (10 cm) thick and a foot (30 cm) tall. Densely covering the stem are short, neatly arranged spines that vary from red to straw colored. The flowers are at least two inches (5 cm) across, with white centers and a band of hot, pinkish purple around the outer edge. I have to keep this plant under several inches of mulch during the most frigid weather, but it is at least marginally hardy in zone 5 (-20°F or -28°C), when kept dry in winter. An outstanding form with fine, shiny, red spines, known as var. *rubrispinus*, is densely covered with bright red spines. Although I have tried growing it many times without success, it has been grown by others in the region.

Echinocereus ×roetteri (Roetter's hedgehog) is a naturally occurring hybrid involving *E. coccineus* and *E. dasyacanthus*. The resulting plants offer a surprising number of flower colors, including some almost-true reds, shades of green, yellow, orange, pink, and even creamy white. The flowers are large and showy, normally over two inches (5 cm) across. These hardy hybrids are quite variable, not only in flower color but also in length, number, and coloration of the spines, with white, pink, gray, or brown possible. Stem size is very unpredictable. Some plants produce a single stem for life, while others make clusters usually of just a few heads. In nature, this hybrid hedgehog is found sparingly from southeastern New Mexico into the Big Bend region of Texas. Plants from New Mexico are sometimes classified and sold as *E. ×roetteri* var. *neomexicanus*, but to my eye they appear to be the same. Plants of *E. ×lloydii* are sometimes sold using this same name. This exceptional garden plant is highly recommended.

The flower colors vary a great deal among plants of *Echinocereus ×roetteri* (Roetter's hedgehog), but every one that I have seen, including this plant in the Barnett family's garden, was nice.

Echinocereus russanthus (syns. *E. viridiflorus* var. *russanthus*, *E. chloranthus* var. *russanthus*) (rusty hedgehog) is another very cold hardy species from the Big Bend region of Texas. It will sometimes grow as a single, cylindrical stem over two inches (5 cm) in diameter and around nine inches (23 cm) tall, but more often it makes clumps of just a few heads. The flowers are green with a touch of rusty brown and are less than an inch (2.5 cm) in diameter. Variety *russanthus* has thin, pliable, shaggy spines that vary in length. Color also varies from rusty shades of red to yellow or silver. The spines generally point downward and conceal much of the stem. Two other varieties are just as cold hardy and also make good garden material: var. *neocapillus*, which has fine, white, hairlike spines as a seedling, and var. *cowperi*, with shorter, red-tipped, yellow spines. All three varieties are reliably hardy if conditions are not overly moist at any time of the year, and the soil does not hold moisture at the surface. If planted in full sun, they make astonishingly attractive plants year-round.

Echinocereus stramineus (strawberry hedgehog) plants can vary dramatically in their ability to endure frigid winters. I lost several of these hedgehogs before finding some cold-hardy individuals. This pretty cactus forms clumps of many stems that are almost hidden under long, stiff, white and straw-colored spines. In nature, these hedgehogs make clusters of several hundred stems, but in cold-winter gardens

TOP:
Echinocereus russanthus var. *cowperi* (Cowper's rusty hedgehog), with lighter colored spines than the typical variety, grows in the author's garden with a yellow-flowered ice plant relative, distributed as *Bergeranthus jamesii*.

BOTTOM:
The typical variety of *Echinocereus russanthus* (rusty hedgehog), here growing in the Barnett family's garden, is the one most often encountered in gardens.

this should not be expected. Those large mounds take a lifetime to become that size. The cylindrical to conical stems are about three inches (7.5 cm) in diameter and may grow to well over a foot (30 cm) tall. The flowers are a showy magenta and are up to four and a half inches (12 cm) in diameter. This species is native to rocky hillsides in southern New Mexico and parts of West Texas, as well as adjacent areas in Mexico. The plant is sometimes scarred by spring freezes after it breaks dormancy.

Cold-hardy clones of *Echinocereus stramineus* (strawberry hedgehog) can be grown perfectly, if they are not injured by frost after the growing season has started.

Echinocereus triglochidiatus (claret cup hedgehog, king's crown cactus) has one of the largest natural ranges in the cactus family in the United States. Many named forms and varieties of this species can be found growing on rocky hillsides, from central New Mexico, west through northern Arizona, into California, and north into Utah and Colorado.

One of the absolute necessities for a cold-hardy cactus garden has to be *Echinocereus triglochidiatus* (claret cup cactus, king's crown cactus), seen here in the author's garden.

In several areas within this range, the species is found at high elevations in the mountains. The flowers vary from shades of orange to almost red, are over two and a half inches (6 cm) across, and unlike most cactus flowers do not close at night. The stems vary considerably in size, from the giant, highly prized 'White Sands', with a stem up to five inches (13 cm) thick, and close to three feet (90 cm) tall, to the tiny

inch-and-a-half (4-cm) stems of plants growing high in the mountains of central Colorado.

The many named varieties and forms of this species vary primarily in body size and the number, color, length, thickness, and shape of the spines. Plants from eastern New Mexico and eastern Colorado are known as var. *gonacanthus* and have much larger stems than plants from the high desert of Utah and the western slope of Colorado known as var. *mojavensis*. The western variety has spinier stems that may get quite large, with spines that range from black to yellow when they emerge, but turn gray as they age. A rare and beautiful form of the species known as forma *inermis* (spineless hedgehog) grows naturally in western Colorado and has small, knobby stems with only a few short spines, or is spineless. This spineless hedgehog is prized by cactus collectors in general and makes mounds of small stems in time. Occasionally plants of forma *inermis* have been known to develop normal spination on new growth after being spineless for years.

Close-up of the flowers of *Echinocereus triglochidiatus* (claret cup cactus, king's crown cactus).

Echinocereus triglochidiatus forma *inermis* (spineless hedgehog) flowering in the author's garden where it is surrounded by *Delosperma cooperi* (purple ice plant).

Most varieties and forms of this species, including the spineless collector's favorite, are hardy to zone 4 (-30°F or -35°C). The plants branch freely and in time make large mounds. This is one of the showiest and most dependable cactus species that can be kept outside in climates with harsh winters.

Echinocereus viridiflorus (green pitaya) has the most northern range in the genus, growing from the Black Hills of South Dakota and eastern Wyoming, south into western Kansas and the Oklahoma panhandle. It is the common barrel-type cactus in the grasslands of eastern Colorado and it makes dense colonies from the plains to over 8000 feet (2400 m) in the mountains. The species is also common in nature throughout most of eastern New Mexico and West Texas. The flowers are smaller than those of most *Echinocereus* species, at three-quarters of an inch (2 cm) across, and are a very pretty, glossy, green to yellow-green. What they lack in size, they tend to make up for in abundance. The conical stems vary from thumb size to five or six inches (13 to 15 cm) tall. Variety *cylindricus*, from New Mexico and West Texas, gets a little taller than var. *viridiflorus* and has a bit of brown or bronze in the flowers. Often these plants offset readily and make nice clusters, but may remain unbranched for life. Stems can be level with the soil or grow several inches tall. Injury to the top of the stem will almost always result in branching. New spines are often bright red at the top of the stem but turn white as they age. Sometimes these little cacti have a long, straight, silver spine growing from the center of the spine cluster at a right angle to the stem, called a central spine, but just as often are without it. Because of its large natural range it is easy to understand why this is such an adaptable and cooperative species for the garden. It is easily cold hardy to zone 4 (-30°F or -35°C) and

Echinocereus viridiflorus (green pitaya) is among the most cold and moisture tolerant of all of the hedgehog cacti. Except for *Opuntia* spp. (prickly pears), it is the most abundant cactus on the plains of eastern Colorado.

Echinocereus viridiflorus var. *cylindricus* (green flower pitaya), growing here in the Barnett family's garden, has stems that are taller than those of var. *viridiflorus*, but like the typical variety, its flowers appear lower on the stem.

Echinocereus viridiflorus var. *correllii* (Correll's green flower pitaya) produces flowers near the top of the stem.

An exciting discovery from West Texas, *Echinocereus weedinii* (Weedin's small flower hedgehog) has already shown that it is cold hardy.

is not sensitive to moisture at any time of the year, if drainage is adequate. A very pretty form known as var. *correllii*, from the mountaintops in West Texas, has fatter, rounder stems, sometimes with golden-yellow spines, and is slightly more sensitive to moisture in winter. Many unique colonies may yet be found at the tops of the highest mountains in the Big Bend region of West Texas.

Echinocereus weedinii (Weedin's small flower hedgehog) is only known from two locations, both of which are among the highest points in the Big Bend region of Texas. This very pretty species has bristly, golden spines that almost hide the stem, and it cannot be confused with any other cactus that can be grown outside in colder climates. The flowers are copper-green and less than an inch (2.5 cm) in diameter. The stems are about an inch and a half to over two inches (4 to 5 cm) thick and from about three to eighteen inches (7.5 to 45 cm) tall, although my plants have not gotten anywhere near that size. Plants generally make clusters of only a few stems. Jim Weedin, a professor from the Denver area, is credited for this recent discovery. Because this cactus is not yet truly understood by science, it has been placed as a variety of three different species in the last few years—E. chloranthus, E. russanthus, or E. viridiflorus—but in horticulture it is generally labeled as it is here. Winter moisture is more of a problem for this cactus than winter cold and it must be grown in soil that drains well, ideally in full sun.

Echinocereus are quite likely to hybridize in gardens when a variety of species are kept together.

In some instances the resulting plants can be outstanding. Even in nature it is not unusual to find hybrids in areas where several species grow in close proximity.

This *Echinocereus* hybrid with almost true-red flowers showed up on its own in the author's garden.

When several hedgehog species are kept together and pollinators are present, hybrids will occur, like this one made by bees at Wild Things nursery.

Another *Echinocereus* hybrid from Wild Things nursery, with flower colors that might be hard to describe when the sun hits them.

Echinofossulocactus

Echinofossulocactus, as it is known in the United States, is also referred to by the shorter and more easily pronounced name *Stenocactus* in Europe. The genus consists of small Mexican grassland plants that seldom offset. The species have many subtle variations in appearance, and some of them have been named several times, causing a good deal of confusion. Except for one species, these plants have thin, wavy ribs that create exceptionally decorative patterns on their stems, making them quite interesting upon close inspection.

If you have an extra *Echinofossulocactus* plant, no matter what it is named, it is worth a try in the garden. Some plants prove to be remarkably cold tolerant. They handle cold better than moisture when they are dormant, but should be considered marginal in zone 5 (-20°F or -28°C). Both of the species named here have survived for a few years in a protected position in my garden, but must be kept dry until they show signs of growth in the spring. During the coldest periods of winter, they do best when covered with snow or frost cloth or mulch, or kept under frosted glass in a cold frame.

Echinofossulocactus plants burn easily any time of year, but particularly during sudden, deep freezes in autumn. It is advisable to provide some shade to these exceptionally ornamental cacti until they are established in the garden. Spider mites can be a problem but usually signal some other problem, such as poor soil drainage or inadequate irrigation in spring and summer. These plants resent being kept dry for long periods during the growing season. In nature, they are at home in grasslands and are more likely to thrive in topsoil that is amended with grit as opposed to rock. The plants could make great additions to troughs.

Echinofossulocactus phyllacanthus (pancake brain cactus) has stems divided by thin, wavy ribs that look like long, sharp crests. Valleys or furrows cover the entire surface of the plant. To some people, the plant looks like a green brain. The stems are almost flat on top and grow barely above the soil, but can be about three and a half inches (9 cm) wide at maturity. In my garden, plants do better with some shade in the hottest part of the day. When stressed by too much sun, the blue-green stems turn pink. They also turn pink or yellow in autumn and are more likely to do better if they are covered until spring. This very pretty cactus has a woolly point at the top of the stem where flowers and new growth appear. The spines are short, flat, and mostly red or pink as they emerge, and flowers are yellow and less than an inch (2.5 cm) across.

Echinofossulocactus zacatecasensis (Zacateca brain cactus) has the same wavy margins covering the surface of its stem as *E. phyllacanthus*. The plants of this species are about two inches (5 cm) tall and over three and a half inches (9 cm) wide, with straw-colored, one-inch (2.5-cm) long, flat spines that curve inward. The one-inch (2.5 cm) wide, white flowers feature a violet midstripe in each petal. Unless this cactus is planted in the right position where it can be viewed at close range, such as near the top of a tall berm, it is hard to see its detailed, ornate qualities. The delicate ribs that cover the entire plant cannot be fully appreciated at a distance. None of the species in this group are sure-fire survivors in climates with long, cold winters, but it is surprising to see how capable many individuals are of long-term survival in the right microclimate.

Few plants can rival the interesting qualities of *Echinofossulocactus* species, such as this *E. phyllacanthus* (pancake brain cactus), when it is closely examined.

Echinomastus

Echinomastus is a valuable genus of plants to the cactus and succulent enthusiast, the rock gardener, and the trough devotee because it includes several very pretty, small cacti with exceptionally ornate spination and eye-catching flowers. One of the nicest things about these plants is their early flowering season, as most of them will bloom while night temperatures still dip below freezing. Their attractive flowers appear as rings around the upper edge of the stem. All the plants in this genus are likely to produce a single stem for life. They are tough cacti that are better off with limited winter moisture and a south-facing position in full sun.

Gardeners who want to succeed with this genus should follow the example of Don Barnett and his son, Donnie, who have been growing all of the *Echinomastus* species for many years. All the soil in their garden has been amended to drain freely, and is virtually without organic matter. The Barnetts also take great care to provide perfect growing conditions with carefully placed rocks and berms providing a variety of microclimates.

Echinomastus dasyacanthus (Chihuahua pineapple cactus), here flowering in the Barnett family's garden, has proved reliable if kept dry in winter.

Echinomastus dasyacanthus (syn. *E. intertextus* var. *dasyacanthus*) (Chihuahua pineapple cactus) grows naturally along the Mexican border, from southeastern Arizona through southern New Mexico into the Franklin Mountains of Texas. The stems of these cacti are densely covered with shaggy, gray spines that have somewhat of a pinkish cast. Most plants form small, upright stems to about five inches (13 cm) tall and two to three inches (5 to 7.5 cm) in diameter. The flowers appear early in the season, often when snow is still on the ground, and are white, sometimes with a touch of pink, and about an inch (2.5 cm) in diameter. This cactus is very reliable in cold climates if kept dry through winter. Note that *Echinocereus dasyacanthus*, *Escobaria dasyacantha*, and *Echinomastus dasyacanthus* are not the same species. They share a specific epithet, which means thickly spined, but are otherwise separate species.

Echinomastus intertextus (woven spine pineapple cactus) is a common cactus in the higher elevations of West Texas and southeastern New Mexico. It is frequently encountered in Big Bend National Park. The species is very closely related to *E. dasyacanthus*, which is sometimes reduced to a variety of *E. intertextus*. The average gardener can recognize the difference instantly by the neater appearance of the spine arrangement of *E. intertextus*, which really does give the impression of being neatly woven like a basket. The stem size and shape, the flowers, and the early blooming season are much the same as *E. dasyacanthus*. This species is reliable in the garden and requires no protection other than from excessive moisture in winter.

Echinomastus johnsonii (Johnson's pineapple cactus) is a ferocious-looking, cylindrical cactus that grows over eight inches (20 cm) tall and up to three and a half inches (9 cm) in diameter. Its shaggy, reddish, daggerlike spines are stout, over an inch (2.5 cm) long, and evenly cover the stem but do not conceal it. In nature, this species can be found in parts of eastern California, through southern Nevada, into northwestern Arizona, sometimes growing with *Yucca brevifolia* (Joshua tree), always in areas of limited rainfall. The plant is sensitive to prolonged periods of moisture at any time of year. Flower color varies from pinkish or magenta to greenish yellow, and the flowers are about two and a half inches (6 cm) across. I have had the best results with this cactus when the plants are growing in sandy soil, with long hours of full sun.

Echinomastus intertextus (woven spine pineapple cactus), like so many smaller cacti that might become lost in the landscape, is displayed to advantage in this container in Bill Adams's garden.

Echinomastus johnsonii (Johnson's pineapple cactus) is one more blooming treasure in the Barnett family's garden.

Echinomastus mariposensis (Mariposa cactus) grows along the border of Mexico and Texas in the Big Bend region. The stems are sometimes over three inches (7.5 cm) tall, two inches (5 cm) wide, and are hidden by spines. At first glance, these cacti appear to have pure white spines, but a closer look will show that older spines turn dark brown or black and make an interesting contrast. Even for an *Echinomastus*, this is an early bloomer, with frilly flowers that are white or very light pink and a little over an inch (2.5 cm) across. The species was once considered rare, but field studies have revealed it to have a larger natural range than was once believed.

Echinomastus warnockii (Warnock's cactus) is a common cactus in Big Bend National Park and the surrounding area on both sides of the Rio Grande. Plants have ball-shaped stems that are about three and a half to six inches (9 to 15 cm) across and are almost hidden by stiff, tan-colored spines with dark tips. The flowers are white but may have a pink or green tint and are slightly more than an inch (2.5 cm) in diameter. In my garden, this species is among the first cacti to bloom each year. I have had plants live and flower for several years in a row and then be killed by hard freezes in the spring after they have started to show signs of growth.

One of the first cacti to bloom each year is *Echinomastus warnockii* (Warnock's pineapple cactus), here growing in the Barnett family's garden.

Epithelantha

The genus *Epithelantha* consists of some of the smallest members of the cactus family. The plants are covered in tiny, neatly arranged spines that hide the stem completely. In nature, these cacti are scattered throughout northern Mexico, parts of Arizona, much of southern New Mexico, and West Texas.

Epithelantha micromeris (button cactus) occurs in nature from eastern Arizona across southern New Mexico and northern Mexico into West Texas. Mature stems can be over two inches (5 cm) tall, but plants that are offered for sale or found in nature are usually well less than half that size. The clean, white spines grow tightly against the stem, and the plants feel smooth to the touch. The flowers are light pink and less than half an inch (13 mm) across, followed by fruits in the fall that look like tiny, red chilies at the top of the stem. Although I have had the best luck with this tidy, little cactus in rocky soil, I consider it marginal; I can only keep it alive in the most protected part of my garden, where it has lived for about ten years. Some plants of this species are more adaptable to frigid winters than others. Generally, this cactus is more likely to withstand cold periods when it is dry. Plants grown from seed collected near Albuquerque, New Mexico, are the most reliable in my experience. While this species is more likely to survive winter in a cold frame or unheated greenhouse than in an open garden, it is well suited for troughs or containers.

Epithelantha micromeris (button cactus), seen here with ripe fruits in the author's garden, is another miniature that adds little to the garden if it is not placed in a position where it can be easily viewed.

Ferocactus

Ferocactus is a genus of primarily large barrel cactus. Some of the species assigned to it are the largest cacti of the American Southwest deserts, other than the treelike *Carnegiea gigantea* (saguaro). A few *Ferocactus* species grow into higher terrain, where winters can be severe for at least brief periods, but most species are among the least cold hardy cacti discussed in this book. These species are able to withstand more cold than moisture in winter and are much more dependable in cold frames or unheated greenhouses. Larger plants are considered more cold tolerant to a point. Small seedlings are not reliable, but the same could be said for plants that are over a couple of feet (60 cm) tall.

Ferocactus hamatacanthus (Turk's head cactus) is the most cold-tolerant species in the genus. It can become an impressively large plant that reaches two feet (60 cm) tall and one foot (30 cm) wide. The reddish, fishhook shaped spines are close to three inches (7.5 cm) long, and are numerous, but do not hide the stem. The flowers are over two and a half inches (6 cm) across and are yellow, sometimes with red throats. This species is native to northern Mexico and West Texas, where it does encounter some periods of bitter cold in midwinter. In general, medium-sized plants are easier to establish in the garden than large or small ones. This cactus benefits from a protected position as it is marginal in zone 5 (-20°F or -28°C). I have been somewhat successful with it in colder parts of zone 5 (-20° to -15°F or -28° to -26°C), but I know of plants that have grown with more vigor and have survived a succession of winters in the warmer parts of that zone (-15° to -10°F or -26° to -23°C).

Ferocactus hamatacanthus (Turk's head cactus) is generally considered to be the most cold-hardy plant in this genus. This plant has gone through a couple of winters in the author's garden.

Ferocactus wislizeni (candy barrel cactus) is a huge barrel cactus with a natural range that straddles the Mexican border from southern Arizona through New Mexico into Big Bend country in Texas. In favorable situations, mature plants from Arizona can be close to ten feet (3 m) tall and two and a half feet (75 cm) in diameter. Plants from Texas are closer to three feet (90 cm) tall. The flowers are yellow to orange and appear at the top of the stem in rings around the outer edge. The flat, hooked spines on the stem are reddish, yellow, or gray and are over three inches (7.5 cm) long. In my garden, grapefruit-sized plants lived through two winters but died during a very, wet period in the third winter. With enough protection from both cold and wet, this species could be kept out in zone 5 (-20°F or -28°C), but it should not be considered truly hardy there. This species is known to survive and grow for several seasons in cold climates, but when it reaches a fairly large size, it suddenly dies. Wild plants come from a wide range of climates, indicating that cold hardiness varies greatly in the species.

it is hard to believe how nicely this huge *Ferocactus wislizeni* (candy barrel) is doing in the Barnett family's garden.

Glandulicactus

Plants in the genus *Glandulicactus* come from New Mexico, West Texas, and Mexico. Like so many genera in the family Cactaceae, this genus causes disagreements among taxonomists. Some growers currently use the genus name *Sclerocactus* for these species. Over time, taxonomists have placed these species in several genera, including *Ancistrocactus*, *Hamatocactus*, and *Ferocactus*. More work needs to be done before the issues can be resolved. Whatever their name, these typically cylindrical cacti seldom branch into clusters, and they have long, fishhook-shaped spines. Wet weather in winter is more likely to cause trouble for these cacti than cold.

Glandulicactus tobuschii (syn. *Ancistrocactus tobuschii*) (Tobusch fish hook cactus) is a large-stemmed, yellow-flowering species with hooked spines from South Texas. I still have not tried growing it but other gardeners in my area are successfully growing it outside in loam soils that have no organic matter. It is best if these plants are kept on the dry side year-round.

Glandulicactus wrightii (syn. *G. uncinatus* var. *wrightii*) (eagle claw cactus) is found throughout southwestern Texas, where it grows at elevations up to 5000 feet (1500 m). The plant is a pretty, gray-green to blue-green color, with rows of long, hooked spines that point upward on the upper portion of the stem. The inch (2.5-cm) wide flowers are a unique, coppery orange color and appear at the top center of the plant. The stems are three to six inches (7.5 to 15 cm) tall and two to three inches (5 to 7.5 cm) wide, and seldom branch. Some cactus growers and sellers confuse this species with *Sclerocactus wrightiae* from Utah, but they are not the same species. Gritty soil without any organic material and dry conditions in winter are said to be the secret with this species.

A young plant of *Glandulicactus wrightii* (eagle claw cactus) in the author's garden in early spring.

Gymnocactus

Gymnocactus is a small genus of cacti from Mexico that grow primarily in the higher mountains. The genus is closely allied to and sometimes submerged into *Turbinicarpus*, but the name used here is still more often encountered in horticulture, especially in places like California where these have been popular cacti in collections for years.

Gymnocactus beguinii (glass-spined cactus) is an alpine species from the state of Coahuila, Mexico. The plant grows in rocky, fast-draining soil if given additional water during hot, dry periods and kept reasonably dry in winter. In my garden this incredibly ornate cactus starts showing signs of growth early in the spring when night temperatures are still freezing. The shiny, silver spines have dark brown to ebony tips and almost entirely hide the bluish green stem. In nature, this small plant seldom becomes more than six inches (15 cm) tall and three inches (7.5 cm) wide, but greenhouse-grown plants get much larger. The top of the stem is white and slightly woolly when the plant is actively growing and flowering in spring and summer. The reddish pink flowers are about an inch and a half (4 cm) across and appear at the top center of the stem. Some growers suggest acid plant food for this species when flower buds first appear in the spring. I have grown this species in my

What a pretty cactus! *Gymnocactus beguinii* (glass spine cactus) flowering in the author's garden in early spring.

garden for about ten years and have never covered it in winter. Because it sets flower buds so early in the year, it should not be deprived of sun in late winter or early spring. I do not believe that anyone in a cold climate has tried to grow the form known as var. *senilis*, with soft, hairlike growth between the spines, but it may very likely be just as hardy, if not more so.

Gymnocalycium

The large genus *Gymnocalycium* is widely distributed through much of South America. Many of the species are tropical, but a handful of cold-hardy species exists in southern Argentina. Plants included in this genus have been popular with collectors in Europe for many years because of their ease of culture and their prolific, large, flashy flowers. As cacti go, these are shade lovers and they do much better with protection from midday sun. They are not drought tolerant and thus need supplemental water during dry periods in the growing season. This quality makes them a good choice for climates that get a fair amount of moisture. The common name chin cactus is used for these cacti, referring to a dimplelike projection below the spine cluster.

Currently, many *Gymnocalycium* species are being tested and some will be found to be dependably cold tolerant. Clones of all the species discussed here vary considerably in their ability to deal with extreme cold, but some are quite impressive and have been unharmed by temperatures as low as -20°F (-28°C) and weeks of temperatures that remain below freezing. Even some of the subtropical members of this genus will thrive in an unheated greenhouse. Like most South American cacti from colder regions, these plants are much more dependable if they are covered through the heart of winter.

The following species have been growing in my garden for at least three years, and unless otherwise noted, they have survived without cover. In winter, many of these plants shrink below the soil surface.

Gymnocalycium baldianum (spider spine chin cactus) is native to the Andes in Argentina. Its flat-topped, dark gray-green stem is divided by rounded ribs. The spine clusters are at raised points on the ribs and the thin, stiff, white spines are slightly twisted and leave the stem almost entirely exposed. The flowers are about two inches (5 cm) wide and in most cases range from red or reddish purple to white.

Some plants produce flowers that are among the most indescribable, eye-catching colors in nature. Stems do not typically branch and are about three and a half inches (9 cm) tall and two and a half inches (6 cm) in diameter.

This cactus is certainly among the best choices for troughs or containers. It can sunburn more easily than most cacti on sunny, frigid days in spring and fall if it is not covered by snow or mulch. In my garden, plants grow in an area where leaves from deciduous trees tend to collect and are left until late winter. Leaving the plants covered until later than that may inhibit flowering, as flower buds begin to appear in early spring. When in flower, these plants are worth any effort involved in giving them extra protection.

The amazing color variation in the flowers of *Gymnocalycium baldianum* (spider spine chin cactus) can be seen in these plants in the author's garden.

Gymnocalycium bruchii (Bruch's chin cactus) flowers in the author's garden in early spring while nights are still freezing.

Gymnocalycium bruchii (Bruch's chin cactus) has many variable traits. The whisker-thick spines are arranged differently from plant to plant and are mostly white, but can be shades of brown, and some spines are slightly twisted. The blue-green stem typically branches into clusters, but stem size varies greatly from plant to plant and at maturity can be a quarter inch (6 mm) up to about two and a half inches (6 cm) in diameter. For the most part, the top of the stem hardly rises above the soil level, but offsets grow at any point on the stem, including the top. The flowers range from almost white to deep pink, sometimes with midstripes in the petals, and they are about two inches (5 cm) across. The blooming period is early and buds often appear while night temperatures are still falling below freezing. Even the shape, length, and number of flower petals are inconsistent; sometimes petal tips are pointed and sometimes rounded.

According to one theory, floral variation is a result of the wide elevational range in which these ornate, little cacti grow. Since plants growing at lower altitudes bloom earlier than those at higher ones, these plants have to attract a wider variety of pollinators than most plants to ensure that seed is produced to start the next generation. This species is one of the most reliable South American cacti in cold climates, but like other species, some of its clones are more capable of dealing with frigid temperatures than others. In my garden, I occasionally find volunteer seedlings that thrive for years without winter cover.

Gymnocalycium calochlorum (clustering chin cactus) from southern Argentina makes low, flat-topped clusters of many stems that grow level to soil. The spines are wispy and mostly pinkish brown. The light pink flowers are trumpet-shaped and do not open as widely as most chin cactus flowers, but are over two inches (5 cm) across at the widest point. The blue-green stems are about an inch and a half (4 cm) tall and over two inches (5 cm) in diameter. Variety *proliferum* is as cold tolerant as var. *calochlorum*. Many California nurseries sell both varieties as *G. proliferum*. This species has seeded itself around in my garden, where it has been living and flowering for more than ten years. It is not necessary to cover these plants in winter, but doing so is not harmful if the cover is removed by early spring. Flower buds form early in the season and plants that are covered in midspring may not bloom.

Gymnocalycium chubutense (Chubut chin cactus) is a dwarf cactus from southern Argentina that makes clusters of purplish green stems with short, stiff, gray spines. The stems remain level with the soil. The plant is very slow growing and could be kept in a trough or container for many years without outgrowing its home. The trumpet-shaped, white flowers are quite large when compared to the size of the stem, which is typically less than an inch (2.5 cm) in diameter. The flowers do not fully open, but are frilly and ornate. In my garden, these plants survive winters without being covered, but by spring they may be scarred.

Gymnocalycium gibbosum (fat chin cactus) lives in nature over much of southern Argentina and is very adaptable. In time, plants can grow to more than five inches (13 cm) across and four inches (10 cm) tall, but are not likely to branch. The two-inch (5-cm) wide flowers appearing at the top of the stem in spring are usually white, but may also be red.

An old plant of *Gymnocalycium calochlorum* var. *proliferum* flowers in the author's garden.

Like many cacti with a large natural range, this species has many varieties, forms, and subspecies. Subspecies *ferox* (fierce chin cactus) has stout spines that cover the stems more densely than any other form of this species, but unfortunately is not as cold tolerant.

The following varieties are very cold hardy and are among the most dependable South American cacti for me in the garden. Variety *nigrum* (black chin cactus) has almost-black stems and short, stiff spines that leave the stem exposed. This unique variety is considered the most reliable in this area. Variety *fenellii*, var. *gerardii*, var. *leonense*, var. *leucanthum*, and var. *nobile* differ primarily in the number and length of spines, as well as the size and color of the stem. I have grown all these varieties in my garden for at least five years and in some cases for over ten. They are very slow growing and need light shade and extra water in the heat of summer. In winter these plants will shrink into the ground and then swell up with amazing speed in early spring. Sunburn can be a problem for these plants, especially during sudden frigid periods in autumn, so care should be taken when choosing a position for them in the garden. These cacti are much better able to cope if they are covered for the coldest months.

TOP:
Two varieties of *Gymnocalycium gibbosum* (fat chin cactus) flowering side by side in the author's garden: var. *gibbosum* (left) and var. *nigrum* (right).

BOTTOM:
This plant of *Gymnocalycium gibbosum* var. *leonense* (fat chin cactus) has been growing in the author's garden since it was a small seedling.

Gymnocalycium guanchinense (red chin cactus) is a very slow growing species from the Andes in Argentina, but the plants are hardy and even large seedlings will normally adapt to the garden. These plants will be much more reliable if they are covered in winter. The rounded, reddish green stem is lightly covered with short, stiff, slightly curved spines. The ornate, white flowers are about an inch (2.5 cm) across and appear at the top of the stem in spring. Mature stems are about three and a half inches (9 cm) tall and five and a half inches (14 cm) wide. In my garden this is one of the slowest growing chin cactus species and it does not flower reliably.

Gymnocalycium guanchinense (red chin cactus) with flower buds in early spring in the author's garden.

Gymnocalycium quehlianum (Haage's chin cactus) is a fairly good-sized cactus with rounded, reddish green stems over five and a half inches (14 cm) in diameter and about an inch and a half (4 cm) tall. The stems seldom branch and are divided by a number of narrow ribs with short, thin spines spaced evenly along them. The flowers are white with red centers and are over two inches (5 cm) across. The natural range of this species is limited to southern Argentina. I have been growing this species in my garden for several years now, but it is shy about flowering. It needs to be covered through the coldest months of winter or it will likely be scarred by springtime. Although it is a cactus, this species is not drought tolerant and it needs some light shade in summer.

Gymnocalycium weissianum (Weiss' chin cactus) is a low-growing cactus with rounded stems. Native to Argentina, it has long, thick, white spines that do not hide the dark, drab green stems. The plants, which are shaped like sea urchins, are over three inches (7.5 cm) tall at maturity and can be over five inches (13 cm) across but do not normally branch.

Some shade is recommended in the heat of summer as plants can sunburn at any time of year. In my garden some additional irrigation is required for these plants to grow with any vitality. The pink, funnel-shaped flowers are about an inch (2.5 cm) wide. Plants are much more vigorous in spring if they are covered through the coldest periods in winter.

Lobivia

The large genus *Lobivia* has a natural range that includes many semiarid areas in South America, mostly at higher elevations. These plants do not mind being covered with snow or protective mulch for long periods when they are dormant in winter. In fact, like most South American cacti they are more likely to thrive if they are. Most species make small to medium-sized clusters. These plants have always been popular in European and Japanese cactus collections because of their showy, colorful flowers and adaptable nature.

Unfortunately, the group is confusing to science. Many plants have been assigned multiple names, but it is worth wading into the confusion to seek out some of these exceptional cacti. At present, many species are lumped into *Echinopsis* or *Trichocereus* by some botanists and growers. Some of the species that are most appealing to gardeners are placed in *Rebutia* and offered by plant sellers under that name. Because it is easier to find those plants in nurseries or on the Internet using that name, the disputed species are included in this work under *Rebutia*. Another source of confusion is that many of the plants that have been accepted as varieties for years are now sold using the variety name as the species epithet. For instance, *Lobivia haematantha* var. *rebutioides* may be offered by that name or as *L. rebutioides*, and the plants in question are exactly the same.

This *Gymnocalycium weissianum* (Weiss' chin cactus) was just uncovered after a long hard winter.

Lobivia is an anagram of Bolivia, where some of the first plants placed into the genus grow in nature. Almost all of these species can be kept in unheated greenhouses or cold frames if sun does not shine directly on them through clear glass. These plants do better outside where winter nights fall below freezing than they do in a heated greenhouse. I grew many species in a greenhouse that was kept above 50°F (10°C) for several years and the plants bloomed well. When I built a second greenhouse where night temperatures were allowed to drop below freezing, all of the lobivias that were moved to that structure flowered more vigorously.

Lobivia aurea (golden Easter lily cactus) is an incredibly variable species native to some of the coldest regions in Argentina. This cactus has an uncountable number of varieties, and some have been proved cold hardy and prolific flower producers in zone 5 (-20°F or -28°C). Variety *aurea* has rich yellow flowers up to three inches (7.5 cm) across. The thick, stiff spines vary drastically in length and may be from white to black. The plants can reach about three inches (7.5 cm) tall and two inches (5 cm) across. Variety *dobeana* has deep, waxy green, rounded stems. The short, stout, sometimes-reddish spines that alternate with long, white ones do not hide the stems. The knockout, fire-engine-red flowers are slightly less than three inches (7.5 cm) across. Variety *leucomalla* has glossy, yellow flowers and short, bristly spines that are the color of bleached straw, and hide the columnar stems. After several years of growing many varieties of this species outside, I have come to the conclusion

Lobivia aurea (golden Easter lily cactus) var. *leucomalla* looks nothing like the other varieties of *L. aurea*.

Lobivia aurea (golden Easter lily cactus) var. *dobeana* has been growing in the author's garden for several years, but is covered with frost cloth in the winter.

Lobivia haematantha var. *rebutioides* (Easter lily cob cactus) starting to show signs of growth in the author's garden in early spring.

that this one is the most reliable. Also quite reliable when covered for the winter is var. *riograndensis*, with spines that emerge looking waxy and pumpkin color and then turn white the second season. The stems may get as large as three and a half inches (9 cm) across and three inches (7.5 cm) tall. With a little extra water in the growing season, these plants increase in size rather quickly. In spring, they produce a succession of unbelievably showy, three-inch (7.5-cm) wide, yellow flowers that can be quite impressive. None of these varieties are drought tolerant and are more likely to survive if they are covered in winter.

Lobivia haematantha (Easter lily cob cactus) is as confusing as its relative *L. aurea* when it comes to the number of named varieties that don't look anything alike. The flowers of all varieties are about an inch and a half (4 cm) across. Variety *densispina* is a low-growing, round plant to about three inches (7.5 cm) across and a couple of inches (5 cm) tall. Flowers vary from yellow to orange and the spines are flexible and do not hide the deep green stem. Variety *elongata* has stems two inches (5 cm) wide and four inches (10 cm) tall, covered with short, dark, hooked spines; it produces yellow flowers. Variety *kuenrichii* is a shorter and fatter plant with long, dark brown, hooked spines and orange to yellow flowers. The most reliable variety and the one that has grown most energetically in my garden for the longest time is var. *rebutioides*. This very pretty plant is densely covered with short, soft, bristly, white spines that grow close to the stem or slightly away from it. The dark gray-green stem is about two inches (5 cm) wide and three inches (7.5 cm) tall. Flower color is orange to yellow. All varieties of this species are from high altitudes in the Andes of Argentina and are buried under snow in winter. Like so many other South American cacti, these plants are more likely to survive if they are covered through the colder months.

Lobivia thionantha (gray stem Easter lily cactus) is the toughest and most reliable species in the genus, and in my experience is the most dependable South American cactus in cold climates. The plant reaches about four and a half inches (12 cm) tall and three and a half inches (9 cm) in diameter. The stems are a very attractive, powdery blue-gray and typically do not branch. The short, thick, black spines are gray at the base and about half an inch (13 mm) in length, leaving the stem entirely exposed. Native to southern Argentina, this species has beautiful, deeply colored flowers that are about an inch and a half (4 cm) across and may be white, red, or bright yellow. The intensity of the flower color is astonishing and has to be seen to be believed. This exceptionally pretty cactus is capable of withstanding extreme cold, and though it does better when covered by snow or cloth during winter, such protection is not necessary for survival.

Lobivia thionantha (gray stem Easter lily cactus) displays its intensely colored flowers. This plant has been in the author's garden for many years.

Mammillaria

Without a doubt, the most popular genus of cacti with collectors around the world is *Mammillaria*. These species are primarily native to Mexico, but several of them can be found in the U.S. Southwest, and a few inhabit areas as far south as northern South America. The genus is one of the larger genera in the cactus family, with conservative taxonomists recognizing more than one hundred and seventy species. This huge group of plants includes some of the most adaptable members of the cactus family. Most growers and collectors would also agree that it includes some of the most ornately spined cacti. It has been said that there are more mammillarias living in collections in Europe than any other kind of

cactus, simply because they refuse die. If you pay attention to the assortment of cacti found in grocery store plant departments, you will find that plants of this genus dominate them.

It is common for these plants to make rings of flowers around the top of the stem in winter and early spring. Many species will remain a single stem for life, but some will become large clusters. The stems of these plants are composed of tubercles, much like plants in the genus *Coryphantha*, but the tubercles are not grooved. The spines vary a great deal from species to species and may be straight or hooked. Several species are native to the higher terrain of northern Mexico and need to be tried in gardens where winters are harsh. For now, the following species are the ones I have found to be most cold tolerant.

Mammillaria grahamii (Graham's fishhook cactus) grows in nature on dry hillsides from California to Texas, scattered along both sides of the Mexican border. Marginally hardy plants from south-central New Mexico will grow and flower in a protected site in zone 5 (-20°F or -28°C) gardens. It is important for the survival of these plants that winter moisture be limited or avoided. The stems of this cactus may grow to over six inches (15 cm) tall and up to four inches (10 cm) wide, but they seldom branch. The longest spines are hooked and range from white to reddish black. The flowers are about an inch (2.5 cm) in diameter and are very showy, being hot pink, with a narrow, white edge on the petals. If these plants are covered in winter, it should be only for a few days at a time, when temperatures are the coldest. If cloth is used as the covering, keep in mind that hooked spines will cling to it, causing damage to the plant if removal is not done carefully. *Mammillaria* species with hooked spines are often referred to as Velcro plants by hobbyists and growers alike, as they readily attach to anything.

A nearly perfect ring of flowers encircles hooked spines atop a stem of *Mammillaria grahamii* (Graham's fishhook cactus) in the Barnett family's garden.

Mammillaria heyderi (Heyder's pincushion) is an almost flat, disc-shaped cactus to over five inches (13 cm) across but is usually not much more than an inch (2.5 cm) tall. The spines are thin and pliable and do not obscure the green stem. The three-quarter-inch (2-cm) flowers are white, sometimes with a pink blush, and the petals have a greenish brown midstripe. Variety *heyderi* occurs naturally in most of West Texas, except for the panhandle, and it is also found in southeastern New Mexico and adjacent areas in Mexico. Variety *bullingtoniana* (Heyder's western pincushion) is from southwestern New Mexico and southeastern Arizona. It differs in having slightly larger stems and thicker, stouter spines. Both varieties grow impressively large, tuberous root systems. I have grown both varieties in my garden for over ten years. They have never had any detectable problems and have always flowered reliably.

A small plant of *Mammillaria heyderi* (Heyder's pincushion) in the author's garden.

This plant of *Mammillaria heyderi* var. *bullingtoniana* (Heyder's western pincushion) in the author's garden has been there for more than ten years.

Mammillaria meiacantha (pancake cactus) has the most northern natural range in the genus and is found growing in great numbers in the rolling grasslands of eastern New Mexico, not too far south of the Colorado border. Its distribution is scattered through eastern New Mexico into the Big Bend region of Texas. This cactus is so low growing that the crown of the stem shrinks below the soil level in winter or during dry periods in summer. The species is similar in appearance

Mammillaria meiacantha (pancake cactus) growing in the author's garden from seed collected in northern New Mexico near the Colorado border.

to *M. heyderi*, but with fewer, shorter, and stiffer spines. In late spring, rings of white to light pink, three-quarter-inch (2-cm) flowers appear. The flowers have petals with a darker midstripe. Showy, red fruits follow the flowers in late summer. I have grown this species in the garden for at least fifteen years and it has never suffered, even in the hardest winters. It is by far the most reliable species in this genus in cold climates.

Mammillaria meridiorosei (Peloncillo Mountain fishhook cactus) from southwestern New Mexico grows at an altitude of about 6000 feet (1800 m) in the Peloncillo Mountains.

Mammillaria meridiorosei (Peloncillo Mountain fishhook cactus) thrives in hot, dry, sunny situations where soil drains well.

The species also grows further south into Mexico. The ball-shaped stem has hooked spines that vary in color from black to white. Clusters of spines grow at the tips of long, cone-shaped tubercles, creating stems that are about three inches (7.5 cm) tall and wide. In early summer, the top of these plants is covered with two-inch (5-cm), reddish pink to reddish purple flowers. This is another cactus that is more likely to be lost to moisture than to cold in winter. If soil drains well and plants are in good sunlight, this species can grow quickly during periods of summer moisture. Some taxonomists consider this plant to be a southern form or variety of *M. wrightii* (Wright's fishhook cactus). To the eye of the average gardener there is little difference in appearance between the two, but this one is less thirsty in summer and prefers dry, rocky soil.

Close-up of the flowers of Mammillaria meridiorosei.

Mammillaria viridiflora (green flowered fishhook cactus) occurs in parts of western New Mexico and eastern Arizona in nature, growing mostly on rocky hillsides. The three-inch (7.5-cm), ball-shaped stems are almost hidden by dark, hooked spines. The plants may make small clusters, but not always. The nice flowers, sometimes yellow-green, are about an inch (2.5 cm) in diameter. The plant is marginal in zone 5 (-20°F or -28°C), but it lives and flowers without winter cover in the right microclimate. When grown in soil that dries quickly, these plants can live for years in a protected, south-facing position close to a heated building. It is recommended that plants are kept dry in winter.

Mammillaria viridiflora (green flowered fishhook cactus) flowers are not always yellow-green, as this plant in the Barnett family's garden proves.

Mammillaria wrightii (Wright's fishhook cactus) grows in nature from Santa Fe, New Mexico, south into Mexico, west into Arizona, and southeast into Texas. Plants are often found growing among pinyons and junipers, where the soil contains more humus than surrounding soils. This cactus does better in the garden with a little organic material worked into the soil where it is planted. The somewhat flat-topped stem seldom clusters and is about three inches (7.5 cm) tall and wide. As the common name implies, the dark-colored spines are shaped like fish-hooks; they do not hide the deep green stem. The especially pretty, bright pinkish purple flowers are close to two inches (5 cm) across. Unfortunately, many gardeners in zone 5 (-20°F or -28°C) report having this cactus either grow rapidly and flourish or rot just as quickly. Slightly acidic soils are said to produce much stronger plants. This very cold hardy species is not likely to be lost to frigid winter temperatures.

Notocactus

Notocactus is a genus of mostly tropical and subtropical cacti native to Brazil, Argentina, Paraguay, and Uruguay. Oddly enough, the plants that have been able to adapt to colder climates are from northern Argentina and Uruguay, where winters are not nearly as severe. These species are at home in grasslands. The plants grow best in humus-rich soil, and they should not be left dry for long periods during the growing season. In the summer months it is best to give them some shade during the hottest part of the day. Most of the plants in this group do not make clusters unless they have been injured. The flowers emerge from a woolly growth at the top of the stem, but unfortunately, these plants are shy about flowering when they are subjected to harsh winter temperatures. All the species are easily sunburned during frigid spells in fall and need a protected position in zone 5 (-20°F or -28°C).

While they are dormant, notocacti are more likely to grow vigorously when they are covered by cloth or mulch, if snow does not cover them. The flowers make any extra effort worth the trouble. The plants are easily grown in cold frames or unheated greenhouses, and many species have been popular houseplants for generations. All of the species would make excellent additions to troughs or other containers.

In his book *The Cactus Family*, Edward Anderson moves all of the notocacti to the genus *Parodia*. It is unlikely that all cactus nurseries will follow this lead, as the genus name *Notocactus* has been recognized and used by growers and cactus hobbyists for generations. According to the rules of taxonomy, however, *Parodia* is the older name and thus has priority over *Notocactus*.

Another species from northern New Mexico that is cold hardy is *Mammillaria wrightii* (Wright's fishhook cactus).

Notocactus agnetae (syn. *Parodia concinna* subsp. *agnetae*) (golden suncup) is a dull green, four-inch (10-cm) wide, five-inch (13-cm) tall cactus with whisker-thick, curved, bristly, yellow spines that grow against the stem but do not cover it. The glossy, yellow flowers are over three inches (7.5 cm) in diameter and emerge from white wool at the top of the stem. This cactus, which turns orange as winter approaches, shrinks drastically in the fall and then swells up almost overnight as the weather gets warmer in spring. In my garden it is the most reliable species in the genus, but the plants are still better off under cover through the winter. They can survive without being covered but are likely to be scarred. The natural range of this species is limited to areas around Lavalleja and Maldonado in southeastern Uruguay.

Notocactus agnetae (golden suncup) has grown in the author's garden for several years, but it is shy about flowering.

Notocactus mammulosus (syn. *Parodia mammulosa*) (Tom Thumb cactus) can grow up to two and a half inches (6 cm) tall and wide in rich soil amended with humus. I killed more than a couple of these cacti before realizing that they are not able to withstand midday sun in the summer at the altitude of my garden, which is 6000 feet (1800 m). Plants are especially susceptible to sunburn when they have been allowed to remain dry for any length of time. The flowers are pink around the outer edges, fading to yellow in the interior, and are about two inches (5 cm) across. The short, bristly, yellow spines are arranged in rows that run from the top to the bottom of the stems. The stems are about three inches (7.5 cm) tall and five inches (13 cm) wide. This species is native to parts of southern Brazil, Uruguay, and northeastern Argentina. I have never had these plants survive for many years, unless they were covered for most of the winter and kept well watered.

Notocactus sellowii (syn. *Wigginsia sellowii*) (Wiggins' suncup) is a low, flat-topped cactus divided by several sharp ridges, radiating like spokes on a wheel from the woolly center of the stem. The waxy, green stems can be over five inches (13 cm) across, and in strong sunlight they have a reddish cast. The few, short, thin, but stiff spines do not conceal the stems. The flowers are a glossy, bright yellow and about an inch and a half (4 cm) across. In nature, this species is found in parts of southern Brazil, Argentina, and Uruguay. These cacti need a cover through the winter and protection from midday sun during the growing season, as they can sunburn quite easily. Because they come from a humid, subtropical climate, they also require a little more moisture in dry climates than rain alone.

If covered through the winter, *Notocactus sellowii* (Wiggins' suncup) can survive outdoors for many years.

Notocactus submammulosus (syn. *Parodia mammulosa* subsp. *submammulosa*) (bristly suncup) forms a three-inch (7.5-cm), flat-topped, ball-shaped stem with rows of short, stiff, straw-colored spines. This very pretty cactus has canary yellow flowers over two inches (5 cm) across. Variety *pampeanus* resembles var. *submammulosus*, except for having a few more spines and a more polished-looking, green stem. The natural range of this species is Uruguay and Argentina. Both varieties are capable of growing and flowering in cold climates, but must be covered in winter and given irrigation to be reliable.

Parodia

Parodia includes a few species adaptable to gardens in zone 5 (-20°F or -28°C). Many of them grow at high elevations in the Andes. Most of the plants form spiny, ball-shaped stems that do not normally cluster.

Among taxonomists, there is a trend toward making this a super genus that would include about a half dozen long-recognized, South American genera, including *Notocactus*. Several of these genera have been popular with hobbyists for many generations, and it will take years for cactus nurseries to rename their offerings.

Any species with short, hooked spines is likely to do well in an unheated greenhouse, and can be grown outside if it is covered in winter. I have tried several parodias with straight spines and not as many of them survived. In South America, cold weather is likely to be accompanied by moisture, and a blanket of snow will insulate the plants while temperatures are bitter. In cultivation, it is not harmful to most South American cacti to keep dormant plants in the dark.

Parodia maasii (flame flower cactus) is a variable species, and some clones survive in cold climates even in an unprotected position. Most do much better if they are covered through winter and kept close to a heated building. This cactus becomes quite large in warmer climates, but is likely to be no more than three inches (7.5 cm) tall and wide in cold climates. Prominent ribs divide the stems into rows, with short, sharply curved or hooked spines along the ridge. The flowers are reddish orange to yellow,

This *Parodia* species with straight spines and bright orange-red flowers has proved cold hardy in Steve Miles's garden.

about an inch (2.5 cm) across, and they appear at the top center of the stem. This species is native to northern Argentina and southern Bolivia, where it grows at high altitudes in the Andes.

In my garden, the plants that did best had eighth-inch (3-mm), hooked, yellow spines and reddish orange flowers. These individuals were planted while they were still small seedlings; they grew near a heated building and were covered each year from early autumn through late winter. After four years, when they were flowering-size plants about a couple of inches (5 cm) tall, I decided that they must be tough enough to survive without a winter blanket. None did.

Pediocactus

The genus *Pediocactus* consists of cacti from the U.S. Southwest that have proved challenging for many growers. Nonetheless, some of the species are among the most cold tolerant in the cactus family. Except for *P. simpsonii*, all the species are rare and legally protected by the U.S. Endangered Species Act.

The first named species in this genus was discovered in the high mountains of central Colorado, when Colorado was still part of Kansas Territory, and thus the plant was recorded as being from extreme western Kansas. Later, when botanists who were unaware of that fact created a new genus for these species, they picked the name *Pediocactus*, from the Greek *pedion*, meaning plains. Of course, this was a reference to western Kansas as it is today. As a result, the mountain ball cactus has a botanical name that translates to the plains cactus.

All the species grow at high altitudes or in climates with low humidity, where nighttime temperatures drop significantly.

If you are gardening where the humidity is high, these may not be the easiest plants for you to grow outside. The plants are touchy about water when they are not actively growing. Also, they are easier to grow in troughs or in the ground than in small, plastic containers.

In my garden, I have had better luck with plants if they are not covered in winter, except for brief periods of extreme cold when snow is not present. All the species except for *Pediocactus simpsonii* and *P. knowltonii* need a dry, resting period in summer. In nature, many of these cacti are found only in special soils and will not thrive in typical garden soil. For that reason, growers sometimes offer grafted plants for sale. If you are purchasing such plants, it would be wise to know if they are grafted to plants that are cold hardy.

This genus is one of the most studied genera in the entire plant kingdom, but it seems that more confusion than understanding comes from these studies. Taxonomists sometimes include *Pediocactus* species in either *Sclerocactus* or *Turbinicarpus*, but growers or cactus collectors never label plants in that way.

The seed from most of these cacti does not germinate readily for most people, and the seedlings are finicky about too much or too little moisture. They are also resentful of being repotted. Because most of these species are federally protected, the seed cannot be freely collected from wild plants, which means they will always be rare in collections.

I must admit that I am quite jealous of this trough full of perfectly grown *Pediocactus despainii* (San Rafael Swell cactus).

The rare *Pediocactus bradyi* (Marble Canyon cactus) blooming in the Barnett family's garden.

Pediocactus bradyi (Marble Canyon cactus) comes from northern Arizona and grows only in a limited area near the Marble Canyon of the Colorado River. The soil in this area is composed primarily of Kaibab limestone chips. This species is somewhat plentiful within its range, but the plants blend into their surroundings and are hard to find. The plant is typically less than two and a half inches (6 cm) tall and wide, and will sometimes make clusters, but it should not be expected. The stem shrinks into the ground during summer's heat and winter's cold, and is sometimes covered by wind-blown sand in nature. This fascinating, little cactus has somewhat rounded stems that are covered evenly, but not hidden by, short, thin, cream-colored spines. In early spring, the golf-ball-sized plant produces two-inch (5-cm) wide flowers that may be peach, pink, or light yellow.

Pediocactus despainii (San Rafael Swell cactus) can only be found in nature in the San Rafael Swell in Emory County, Utah, where it grows on south-facing slopes at the edge of pinyon-juniper forests. Soils in this area are made primarily of decomposing limestone. This small cactus measures about two inches (5 cm) tall and three inches (7.5 cm) wide after spring snow melts and late summer rains. During hot, dry periods

Another rare cactus, *Pediocactus despainii* (San Rafael Swell cactus), blooming in the Barnett family's garden.

of summer and through the severe cold of winter, the plants shrink into the ground. The pale yellow to salmon-pink flowers are about an inch (2.5 cm) in diameter and appear in early spring. The thin, straight spines are white and tend to elongate as the plants age, until they reach about two inches (5 cm). If these plants are growing in strong sunlight, the spines will almost entirely hide the stem. Plants will sometimes cluster but that is not typical.

Pediocactus knowltonii (Knowlton's cactus) has a limited natural habitat along the Los Pinos River in northwestern New Mexico and southwestern Colorado at altitudes mostly above 6500 feet (1900 m) elevation. The soil in which it grows is a mixture of river rock and humus. In nature, this plant is usually less than an inch (2.5 cm) tall and wide, with clusters of minute, white spines at the tips of tubercles, but in cultivation plants are frequently much larger. These tiny cacti have pink flowers about an inch (2.5 cm) in diameter. It is common for the flower buds to form in the fall, persist through the winter, and open in early spring. This species is more likely to branch into clusters than other species in the genus. It also is one of the easiest *Pediocactus* species to grow successfully, and professional growers have less trouble coaxing these plants along from seed. Although it is one of rarest cacti native to the United States, it is becoming easier to find plants for sale in cultivation. The stem does not shrink into the ground in summer and winter.

Pediocactus knowltonii (Knowlton's cactus) begins to form flower buds in late fall that do not fully develop until the following spring.

Pediocactus knowltonii (Knowlton's cactus) with fully developed flowers in the Barnett family's garden.

One more rare cactus in the Barnett's garden is this perfectly grown plant of *Pediocactus paradinei* (Houserock Valley cactus).

Pediocactus peeblesianus var. *fickeiseniae* (Fickeisen's Navajo cactus) is another prize plant in the Barnett family's garden.

Pediocactus paradinei (House Rock Valley cactus) has light pink to yellow flowers that are about an inch (2.5 cm) wide and appear at the top of stems. The plant, which is about two inches (5 cm) tall and an inch and a half (4 cm) in diameter, sometimes forms clusters. In nature, the species grows only within the area around House Rock Valley to the upper Kaibab Plateau of northern Arizona, in limestone soils, with grama grass, among scattered pinyon-juniper communities, and with sagebrush at altitudes up to about 7000 feet (2100 m). Like other specialized members of this genus, this plant shrinks into the ground in summer and winter and becomes impossible to find at that time. Spine length increases as plants age, and mature plants are covered, but not hidden, by one-inch (2.5-cm) long, whisker-thick, silver spines.

Pediocactus peeblesianus (Peebles' Navajo cactus) is an easily recognizable species from Arizona with short, twisted, corky, white spines. The stem, which is about two inches (5 cm) wide and slightly taller than that, seldom forms clusters. The lemon-colored flowers are about half an inch (13 mm) in diameter. Variety *peeblesianus* has a limited range near Holbrook, Arizona, in Navajo County. Although var. *fickeiseniae* (Fickeisen' Navajo cactus) has a larger natural range, it is small enough to be contained within the boundaries of the Grand Canyon National Park; this variety is a bit fatter, with a slightly spinier appearance. In their native habitats both varieties grow primarily in very rocky, alkaline soils. Most hobbyists that have success with this species are growing grafted plants, which are not nearly as demanding. On its own roots, this cactus is very difficult to keep alive for any length of time. The plants shrink into the soil, except during moist periods in early spring and after summer monsoon rains begin.

Pediocactus sileri (gypsum cactus) grows naturally only in the area of Pipe Springs National Monument in northern Arizona. The plant is mostly solitary but may branch and can be up to ten inches (25 cm) tall and nearly four inches (10 cm) in diameter, making it one of the larger plants in the genus. The spines are about three-quarters of an inch (2 cm) long and are mostly silver, but the thickest and most noticeable spines are brown to black. Although numerous, the spines only hide about half of the blue-green stem. As the common name implies, this specialized species grows only in gypsum soil. The greenish yellow flowers are about an inch (2.5 cm) across, and the spines do not allow them to fully open. This plant does not shrink significantly in summer or winter as so many other plants in this group do.

Pediocactus simpsonii (mountain ball cactus) has by far the largest natural range in the genus *Pediocactus*. It can be found in New Mexico, Colorado, Utah, Nevada, Wyoming, Idaho, Montana, Washington, and Oregon, growing at elevations mostly above 7000 feet (2100 m). It is the only species in the genus that does not enjoy legal protection throughout its range. It also is the one most likely to be encountered in horticulture and is the easiest to grow. As might be expected of any cactus with such an expansive range, the plants vary

The numerous spines of *Pediocactus sileri* (gypsum cactus) prevent the flowers from opening completely. Note the thinner white spines and the thicker dark-colored spines. This plant is growing in the Barnett family's garden.

Another form of *Pediocactus simpsonii* (mountain ball cactus) in Panayoti Kelaidis's collection. This white-flowered form was grown from seed collected in Nevada.

Pediocactus simpsonii (mountain ball cactus), Snowball Form, flowering in Panayoti Kelaidis's collection.

in the color and length of spines as well as stem size and flower color.

Typically, plants of this species are one to five and a half inches (2.5 to 14 cm) tall and from an inch and a quarter to five and a half inches (3 to 14 cm) across. The spines range from reddish brown or black to white, and from about a quarter inch to an inch (6 mm to 2.5 cm) long. In some but not all cases the spines hide the stem. Most plants produce flowers in soft shades of pink, but others produce white, red, or even purple flowers.

All the varieties of *Pediocactus simpsonii* can cluster but it is not typical. Variety *minor* is isolated to higher altitudes and has been documented growing above 11,000 feet (3,300 m). Its small stem has a rounded top and is usually not more than a couple of inches (5 cm) above the soil level, but can sometimes be larger. This variety is among the most cold-tolerant members of the cactus family. Variety *nigrispinus*, named for its dark spines, is generally considered to be a form of var. *robustior*, but it is almost always sold as a separate variety. From the perspective of a gardener, it should be treated separately due to its unique appearance, with a dense covering of black spines. Variety *robustior* grows naturally in eastern Washington and Oregon and has the largest stems and the shaggiest appearance. Normally var. *robustior* has stout, reddish brown spines and is more likely to branch into clusters than other varieties. It is also the variety most able to cope with dry situations.

No variety of this species has special soil requirements and they can be grown in the same garden soil that is used for other cacti. For the most part, these are alpine plants that need more water than most cacti.

Pediocactus winkleri
(Winkler's cactus) is known
to grow naturally only in
alkaline soils within a limited
area in Wayne County, Utah.
Temperatures in this area can
reach 105°F (40°C) in midsummer and -30°F (-35°C)
in winter. Because this cactus
is dormant for much of the
year and shrinks into the soil,
making it hard to find, the

Another
very rare
cactus that
the Barnetts
have been
successful
with is this
flowering
plant of
*Pediocactus
winkleri*
(Winkler's
cactus).

species was only discovered and named in 1979. Typically, the
plant is about two and a half inches (6 cm) tall and an inch
and a half to two inches (4 to 5 cm) in diameter. The flowers
range from salmon to pink and are about half an inch (13
mm) across. The clusters of small, white spines do not obscure
the stem. Grafted plants of this species are sometimes offered
for sale and are much easier to grow.

Rebutia

The genus *Rebutia* is a group of exceptionally ornamental
and free-flowering cacti from Bolivia and Argentina.
Many of these plants are native to high altitudes in the
Andes, so it is not hard to understand how they can adapt
to climates with frigid winters. These cacti bloom more
prolifically when they are exposed to cold temperatures in
winter, and all are worth trying in an unheated greenhouse
or cold frame. In the garden the plants can be covered with
snow or mulch for long periods in winter without harm.
Like so many South American cacti, they actually benefit
greatly from being buried under cloth or snow.

At one time, *Rebutia* consisted of only a handful of species. Today it encompasses those original species plus a host of species from other smaller genera. The genus name *Mediolobivia*, for example, is not as commonly used by growers as it once was, and the species that were assigned to it are now considered *Lobivia* species by many botanists, but in horticulture, *Rebutia* is the preferred name due to the size and overall appearance of the plants. Many of the former *Mediolobivia* species are likely to adapt to gardens with cold winters. Mesa Garden sells these plants as lobivias, but it is the exception; most nurseries offer these charming cacti as rebutias. No matter what genus name is used, they are exceptionally nice, little cacti. The genus name *Digitorebutia* is also acceptable and might be used for some of these species.

Most rebutias have thin, pliable spines that do not project from the stem and are not painful to touch. In all my years of experimenting with South American cacti in the garden, I have found this group to include some of the most reliable species. It really is a sin that they are not familiar to trough gardeners, as they are perfect plants for that use. All of the following species are well known to the general cactus collector and are easily found to purchase from many mail-order cactus nurseries. Many more species in this genus should prove valuable to gardeners in cold climates, but so far these are the most adaptable species.

Rebutia atrovirens (syn. *Lobivia atrovirens*) (red flower crown cactus) is an incredibly attractive miniature cactus with inch (2.5-cm) wide, blood red flowers that grow at the side of the stem in spring. Rounded, reddish green to purplish green stems are about an inch and a half (4 cm) tall and wide. The soft, bristly spines cling to, but do not cover, the stem. In time, the plant makes a small cluster of closely crowded stems and grows large, tuberous roots.

Even without flowers *Rebutia atrovirens* (red flower crown cactus) is a very attractive little cactus that could be a star in a container.

All varieties of this species are likely to be cold hardy. Although I have not grown all of them for a succession of winters, I would be terribly surprised if any of them failed. Other than var. *atrovirens*, the typical variety, three other varieties are known: var. *haefneriana*, var. *ritteri*, and var. *yuncharasensis*. The varieties vary primarily in stem size, but they all have flowers that are rich shades of red. I have grown plants of this species that were covered through winter and others that were not, and all survived without scarring. Nevertheless, it is advisable to cover plants as those that are covered through the cold months grow faster and bloom more prolifically.

Rebutia "densipectinata" (syn. *Lobivia densipectinata*) (thimble crown cactus) is one of the choicest miniature plants. Thumb-sized, it is densely covered with short, hair-thick, silver and brown spines. The spines grow tightly against the stem but do not conceal it. Over time these cacti will make small clusters of stems. The reddish orange flowers appear at the base of the stem and are close to an inch (2.5 cm) across, which is much larger than the half-inch (13-mm) thick stem. The only potential problem with this plant in the garden is its size: it is so small that it may not be seen when it is not flowering. The placement of such small plants must be carefully considered to enjoy them. In my garden this species has been growing for about six years and has never shown any signs of winter damage. The name "*densipetinata*" is illegal per the *International Code of Botanical Nomenclature* as it was published without a description. This has not stopped growers and hobbyists from using it.

Rebutia "densipectinata" (thimble crown cactus) flowering in the author's garden. Note the size of the stem in relation to the flower.

Rebutia haagei (Haage's crown cactus) in the author's garden with a flower bud starting to form near the base of the stem.

Rebutia haagei (syn. *Lobivia haagei*) (Haage's crown cactus) is very similar to the two previous species in general appearance, but it has pink flowers and fewer spines. There are many named varieties of this species, all of which grow in nature at high altitudes in the Andes. The flowers of all the varieties are various shades of pink and the rounded, thumb-size stems make clusters. Variety *canacruzensis* has striped flower petals. Variety *eos* has exceptionally small stems. Variety *mudanensis*, var. *orurensis*, var. *pelzliana*, and var. *violascens* vary in stem size, in the shade of pink in the flowers, and in spination.

Rebutia pygmaea (syn. *Lobivia pygmaea*) (pygmy crown cactus) has an immense natural range and through the years has collected an unbelievable number of synonyms and named varieties. These plants have dark green to purplish, rounded stems that are about an inch and a half (4 cm) tall and wide. They are covered evenly, but not densely, with light-colored, hair-thick spines that grow tightly against the stem.

Rebutia pygmaea (pygmy crown cactus) with a flower in early summer.

The inch (2.5-cm) wide flowers in varying shades of orange appear near the base of the stem. The plant makes low, flat clusters of tiny, bullet-shaped stems from a single, large, tuberous root. Named varieties in cultivation include, but are not limited to, the following: var. *colorea*, var. *diersiana*, var. *iscayachensis*, var. *rauhii*, and var. *tafnaensis*. These varieties vary in the color and size of the stem, as well as the shade of orange in the flowers. Any variety name may be used as a species name by growers who are selling these plants.

Sclerocactus

The genus *Sclerocactus* is native to the U.S. Southwest, with Utah being the hot spot. These cacti are very cold tolerant, but many of them are touchy about prolonged wet conditions, particularly in winter and midsummer when they tend to be dormant. I have had the best luck with them under the eave of a building, where they are shielded from rainfall just a few feet away. To grow them in this manner I have to give them a little extra water in early spring. The entire natural range of this genus is in areas of low rainfall. This is not to say that these plants thrive on constant dry conditions; in late winter and early spring when snow melts they will swell up and need good moisture. In nature, they begin to grow again when the monsoons come in late summer. In midsummer these plants are best left dry, but they will not be hurt by an occasional rainstorm if the soil drains well.

Taxonomically, this genus is confusing to cactus growers and botanists alike. Even though botanists have studied it as much or more than most plant groups, no two of them agree about relationships within this genus. The U.S. Endangered Species Act protects all *Sclerocactus* species, and many of them will always be rare in collections. Although these are sun-loving cacti, they can be sunburned when they are planted in midsummer without some kind of temporary shade being provided. None of the plants in this genus tend to branch, except when they have been injured at the crown.

Generally, *Sclerocactus* species are hard to find in the market place, and they are a little more expensive than most other cacti. This is partly because seed does not sprout freely, and young plants are finicky in small nursery pots. Once these cacti are established they seem to be reasonable to grow, but

A perfect plant of *Sclerocactus cloverae* (Clover's fishhook cactus) flowering in the Barnett family's garden.

Sclerocactus glaucus (Uinta Basin hookless barrel) with flowers in the Barnett family's garden.

my experience is that not every plant that is put in the garden will survive. Most cacti will transplant quite easily, but plants of this genus are an exception. If you try any of these species, pick a spot for them where they will not be disturbed.

Sclerocactus cloverae (Clover's fishhook cactus) has spiraling ribs on a blue-green stem. The stem can be over five inches (13 cm) wide and nine inches (23 cm) tall, but is usually much smaller. The plants are partially obscured by the red to white, inch-and-a-half (4-cm) long, hooked spines. The flowers range from pink to purple, and are over two inches (5 cm) across, appearing at the top of the stem in spring. This species grows naturally in fine sandy soil in the Four Corners region, where New Mexico, Colorado, Utah, and Arizona meet. A recognized subspecies, subsp. *brackii*, is named for Steven Brack, the owner of Mesa Garden in Belen, New Mexico. Edward Anderson considers this species to be the same as *S. parviflorus* in his book *The Cactus Family*.

Sclerocactus glaucus (Uinta Basin hookless barrel) is a small cactus with rounded stems up to four and a half inches (12 cm) tall and almost three and a half inches (9 cm) thick. The stems are a very pretty blue-green color and are divided by rows of fat, round tubercles. These plants are not hidden by the inch (2.5-cm) long spines, which may be from brown to white, and can be slightly curved, to sometimes hooked. The flowers are shades from pink to purple and about two inches (5 cm) in diameter. This species is rare, but can be found on rocky, dry, south-facing slopes from around Grand Junction, Colorado, south into New Mexico, and west into Utah, growing at altitudes up to about 6000 feet (1800 m). This species is one of the easier *Sclerocactus* species to establish in the garden.

Sclerocactus mesae-verdae (Mesa Verde cactus) was discovered shortly before World War Two in Mesa Verde National Park in the southwest corner of Colorado. Charles Bois-sevain, the senior author of *Colorado Cacti*, is credited with finding it and introducing it to science. At that time, a new genus was proposed for the species and it was to be called *Coloradoa*. The idea of creating a new genus for this plant was really never accepted by taxonomists and it has been known as a *Sclerocactus* since the 1940s. In nature, these plants will only be found growing in fine, sandy loam. In the garden the same type of soil is recommended, but nothing ensures success with this species. The dimpled, gray-green stems grow to around four inches (10 cm) tall and three inches (7.5 cm) wide. The short, curved, gray spines that hug the tubercles do not hide the stems. The greenish yellow flowers are close to an inch (2.5 cm) across.

Sclerocactus mesae-verdae (Mesa Verde cactus) blooming in the Barnett family's garden.

Sclerocactus nyensis (Nye County fishhook cactus) is native to the mountainous terrain of southern Nevada. The stem is about four inches (10 cm) tall and two inches (5 cm) in diameter with reddish spines that may or may not be hooked. The rose-colored flowers are about an inch (2.5 cm) across. I have not tried this one myself, but it is being grown successfully by some gardeners in the region.

Sclerocactus parviflorus (devil's claw cactus) has one of the largest natural ranges in the genus *Sclerocactus*: plants are scattered through most of northern Arizona, eastern Utah, and northwestern New Mexico, as well as the western edge of Colorado. These cacti can become quite good sized, with stems that are up to ten inches (25 cm) tall and five inches (13 cm) thick, but are usually much smaller. The hooked

Close-up of the flowers of *Sclerocactus parviflorus* subsp. *intermedius* (devil's claw).

LEFT:
Sclerocactus parviflorus (devil's claw cactus) in full bloom is another outstanding plant in the Barnett family's garden.

RIGHT:
Sclerocactus parviflorus subsp. *terrae-canyonae* (San Juan County devil's claw) blooming in the Barnett family's garden.

spines are slightly flattened and are arranged in spirals from the bottom of the stem to the top. The spines are white to reddish, and if the plants are in full sun the stems will be concealed. The flowers are over two inches (5 cm) across and can be white, yellow, pink, or purple, depending on the subspecies. Subspecies *parviflorus* has pink or purple flowers and the largest natural range in the species. It is considered the most reliable plant in the genus for most gardeners. Subspecies *havasupaiensis* has almost white flowers and thinner spines. Subspecies *intermedius*, which has purple flowers and a touch of pink in the spines, occupies a natural range that reaches 7000 feet (2100 m). Subspecies *terrae-canyonae* grows with pinyons and junipers at high altitudes, and has yellow flowers. The authors of *Colorado Cacti* (Boissevain and Davidson 1940) confused this species with *S. whipplei* from Arizona.

Sclerocactus polyancistrus (Mojave devil's claw) is one of the least cold-tolerant species in this group, but it will take frigid temperatures if kept dry in winter. This ferocious-looking, spiny cactus has a stem up to fifteen inches (38 cm) tall and over three inches (7.5 cm) in diameter. The stem is hidden under a dense layer of hooked, red to yellow spines. The rose- to magenta-colored flowers are about two inches (5 cm) across. In nature, the species is at home in the Mojave Desert, growing on both sides of the Nevada–California border. Some plants are known to grow at altitudes up to 7000 feet (2100 m), but most are usually found at lower elevations. It is the high-altitude plants that will be most successful in cold climates. Before purchasing plants, it is important to know where the seed was collected.

Sclerocactus pubispinus (syn. *S. sileri*) (Great Basin fishhook cactus) grows along the Utah–Nevada border on rocky hillsides. It can be found with sagebrush, junipers, and pinyons, mostly at elevations above 6000 feet (1800 m). The ball-shaped plant gets to about five and a half inches (14 cm) tall and wide. The dull green stems are partially hidden by red to yellow or white spines that are somewhat flat and are strongly curved or hooked. The flowers are an inch and a half (4 cm) across and may be yellow, green, pink, purple, or peach with deeper coloration through the center of the petal. This species is not as challenging as some of the others in the garden.

Sclerocactus spinosior (desert valley fishhook cactus) is not reliably hardy in zone 5 (-20°F or -28°C) but can be grown in protected microclimates, such as near the south side of a heated building. The stem of a mature plant is approximately three and a half inches (9 cm) wide and five and a half inches (14 cm) tall. This well-armed cactus is densely covered with cream to black, sharply hooked spines. The flowers are reddish purple to lavender and close to an inch and a half (4 cm) across. In nature, this species grows in southern Nevada and southwestern Utah at elevations between 5000 and 6000 feet (1500 and 1800 m). Subspecies *blainei* has longer spines.

Sclerocactus spinosior (desert valley fishhook cactus) in flower in the Barnett family's garden.

Sclerocactus wetlandicus (Uinta Basin barrel) flowers prolifically in the Barnett family's garden.

Sclerocactus wetlandicus (Uinta Basin barrel) is very similar in size and general appearance to *S. glaucus*, and may be identical to it, or not. Experts do not seem to agree, but time will tell. At any rate, they are closely related species but grow at some distance from each other. *Sclerocactus wetlandicus* is worthy of inclusion in a dry garden by any name. The plant

Sclerocactus whipplei (Whipple's devil's claw) in full bloom in the Barnett family's garden.

can be found in nature in a limited area of eastern Utah, growing on dry, rocky slopes. This species was recently named but it has found its way into cultivation rather quickly. Most gardeners agree that larger plants are more easily established.

Sclerocactus whipplei (Whipple's devil's claw) grows primarily on gravel hillsides in northeastern Arizona, but is said to enter into southeastern Utah. This species is generally found at elevations between 5000 and 6000 feet (1500 and 1800 m). The blue-green stems are divided by prominent ribs and grow to about five inches (13 cm) tall and four inches (10 cm) in diameter. The flat, hooked spines are somewhat purple or pink and appear to be arranged in rows that spiral down the sides of the stem. The flowers are yellow and quite pretty but only are allowed to open about three-quarters of an inch (2 cm) because the spines block them.

Sclerocactus wrightiae (Wright's fishhook barrel) from south-central Utah has soft green, ball-shaped stems about three inches (7.5 cm) tall and wide. The stems are densely covered with but not hidden by inch-and-a-half (4-cm) long, white, curved or hooked spines. The whitish to pink flowers are about an inch (2.5 cm) across. Benson (1982) referred to

Flowering *Sclerocactus wrightiae* (Wright's fishhook cactus) in the Barnett family's garden.

this species as the transitional link between *S. mesae-verdae* and *S. whipplei* in *The Cacti of the United States and Canada*. I tried this species and the plants grew for several years. They were killed almost immediately when I disrupted roots, close to the surface of the soil, by pulling weeds near where the plants were growing.

Toumeya

Toumeya is a genus of only one species and its relationship to the rest of the cactus family is not clearly understood. Recent DNA studies lean toward this species finding a permanent home some day in the genus *Sclerocactus*. The U.S. Endangered Species Act protects this little cactus. Though it is somewhat rare in nature, the species is occasionally offered by a number of reputable nurseries.

Toumeya papyracantha (grama grass cactus, paper-spined cactus) is placed in a new genus on a fairly regular basis, but is always returned to this one. This miniature cactus comes from parts of Arizona but mostly from New Mexico where it can be found with *Bouteloua* species (grama grasses). It has flat, flexible, straw- to gray-colored spines that camouflage the little plants as they hide in dead, dry blades of grass. The club-shaped stem is only one or two inches (2.5 to 5 cm) tall and three-quarters of an inch (2 cm) in diameter. The flowers are white and about an inch (2.5 cm) across. This is an exceptionally choice cactus for troughs or other containers, but it has a tendency to heave from the ground in spring, as soil freezes and thaws. Add grit to the soil if this is a problem.

Toumeya papyracantha (grama grass cactus, paper-spined cactus) with a flower open in the Barnett family's garden.

Turbinicarpus

The genus *Turbinicarpus* is composed entirely of small but quite ornamental cacti from northern Mexico. Many of these plants have limited natural ranges and all of them are considered rare. In the future, more plants will probably prove their tolerance of cold conditions, but for now, the following is the only one that I feel safe to recommend even though it is marginal. Mexican law protects all cacti, and species of this genus are considered endangered in the wild. In horticulture, these plants are common in Arizona or California cactus nurseries.

Turbinicarpus valdezianus (felt spine cactus) is a flat-topped, ball-shaped plant about an inch (2.5 cm) wide and an inch and a half (4 cm) tall. The stem is covered by clusters of soft, white spines. The flowers are white to magenta and close to an inch (2.5 cm) across. I have only had luck with this species when it is buried under frost cloth during the coldest periods in winter. Even then it does not bloom as well for me in the garden as it does in the greenhouse.

A ten-year-old plant of *Turbinicarpus valdezianus* (felt spine cactus) in the author's garden is only about the size of a grape.

Lovable Oddballs: Unusual Members of the Cactus Family

The oddballs are both North and South American natives, and like oddballs of all kinds, include some real charmers among them. I certainly do not use this term in a negative manner. Rather, these cacti simply do not fit neatly into one of the other three basic categories described in this chapter. At least from the gardener's perspective, these plants have unique qualities. Among this group are some of the most southerly members of the cactus family in nature. Many botanists consider several of the unusual species to be members of the genus *Opuntia*, meaning they are closely related to chollas and prickly pears. Most of these plants have club- or egg-shaped stems and do not match the description of either group. Other members of this artificial grouping are only distantly related to the chollas and prickly pears. Still other members are crested cacti from any genera. Some of these oddball plants are showy and interesting species that deserve a place in any cold-climate cactus garden.

Oddball plants, such as this beautiful, old, crested *Pediocactus simpsonii* (mountain ball cactus) at Chelsea Nursery, can be interesting and valuable plants.

Grusonia

Grusonia species are closely related to the upright chollas (*Cylindropuntia*) and the prickly pears (*Opuntia*) and at one time comprised Section *Cornyopuntia* of genus *Opuntia*. These unique, low-growing plants with club-shaped stems have since been separated into the new genus *Grusonia*, a position supported by DNA studies. In this oddball group I also include *G. pulchella*, a distinctive cactus with many synonyms. None of these plants are prone to insect or disease problems, but they may be sensitive to excessive moisture or poor drainage.

Grusonia bulbispina (tiny mound cholla) is another miniature that deserves a place in troughs or other containers.

Grusonia bulbispina (syn. *Opuntia bulbispina*) (tiny mound cholla) is native to cool, high mountain valleys in northern Mexico. This cactus is not one you will ever have to worry about taking over your garden. I have been growing plants of this species for a few years and they still take less space than my fist. My plants have not flowered, but the flowers are said to be reddish. Each egg-shaped joint is about a quarter to a half inch (6 to 13 mm) long and decorated with short, light-colored spines. The species is perfect for trough and container gardens, and that might be the best place for it. The plants in my garden have done best in gritty loam without rock under the root system. Unfortunately, this species is marginal in my garden and plants do best if they are covered during periods of extreme cold. These tiny cacti need a protected position to survive winter, as well as a little extra water in the heat of summer. I have tried fertilizing them to encourage faster growth and have not seen it be that effective.

Grusonia clavata (syn. *Opuntia clavata*) (club cholla) is another species that is closely related to both the chollas and the prickly pears, but the general shape of the plants does not fit into either group. It does fit nicely into dry gardens. The Latin *clavata* means club-shaped and that is not a bad description if one thinks of a very fat, almost egg-shaped club. These plants are adorned with attractive, broad, flat, shiny, white spines that cover the top half of each inch- to inch-and-a-half (2.5- to 4-cm) long joint. The flowers are a medium shade of yellow and a little over an

The broad, flat, white spines make *Grusonia clavata* (club cholla) an attractive plant for any cactus garden.

inch (2.5 cm) across. Common throughout most of central New Mexico, where it grows in sandy soils, this low-growing plant crawls along the ground, making a somewhat flat, very clean-looking, white mat. Variety *major* resembles var. *clavata* in every way, except it has much larger stems. This species has been very dependable in my garden for over twenty-five years without any damage, even in the worst winters. Although it was included in *Colorado Cacti* (Boissevain and Davidson 1940), it has never been found growing naturally within the state borders since that time.

Grusonia pulchella (syns. *Opuntia pulchella*, *Cylindropuntia pulchella*, *Micropuntia pulchella*) (sand cholla) is from central Nevada, where it grows huge, thick taproots in flat, dry, sandy loam. The plant appears to be a small cactus above the soil, with pencil-like green stems that barely stick above ground. The common name cholla is generally used for these cacti, but they are not like the shrubby plants that we typically think of when we use that term. The flowers are showy, being a bright pinkish purple, and are about an inch (2.5 cm) across, which is amazingly large coming from such tiny stems. Plants are able to withstand extremes of heat, wind, and cold. They can be hard to establish in the garden as they are sensitive to excessive moisture, especially in the coldest months and in the heat of summer. Also, they are sensitive to sudden drops in temperature after they have broken dormancy in spring. This cactus is probably a good choice for container culture, so water can be more carefully monitored, but it can be grown in the right soil in the garden. In places where summers are hot and dry, these plants thrive in gritty soil.

Grusonia pulchella (sand cholla) flowering in the Barnett family's garden.

Grusonia schottii (dog cholla) with a flower in the Barnett family's garden.

Grusonia schottii (syn. *Opuntia schottii*) (dog cholla), from the Big Bend region of Texas and northern Mexico, looks like a larger, taller version of *G. clavata*. The stems of this species are more upright and grow a few inches off the ground, and the plants make fiercer-looking mats. The flat spines vary from grayish white or straw-colored to almost red. This cactus is perhaps slightly less cold tolerant than *G. clavata*, but is still able to withstand temperatures several degrees below 0°F (-18C) in the open garden without showing any signs of stress. The flowers are bright yellow and about an inch (2.5 cm) across. Closely related to this species and broadly fitting the same description are *G. grahamii* and *G. stanlyi* (syn. *G. emoryi*). These species are mostly from West Texas and have about the same ability to withstand cold. All of these plants have survived a succession of winters in gardens and are tolerant of any soil that drains well.

Maihuenia

Maihuenia species are among the most southern-dwelling members of the cactus family in nature, being primarily from Patagonia and the southern Andes. Many species have been named in the past, but today only two species are recognized. Both are resistant to cold and available commercially, but *M. poeppigii* is more commonly seen for sale than *M. patagonica*. For cacti, these are unique species that cannot be mistaken for any other plants in the family. They have short, cylindrical, deep green leaves that remain year-round. Either species is a valuable addition to a pot or trough, as well as a rock garden, and both will be their best if grown in full sun. These plants can be buried in snow for the entire winter without harm and probably prefer such a situation, though it is not necessary.

Maihuenia patagonica (syns. *M. albolanata*, *M. andicola*, *M. brachydelphys*, *M. cumulata*, *M. latispina*, *M. tehuelches*) (spiny green blanket) has white flowers that are over two inches (5 cm) across at the top of short, upright, club-shaped stems. As the specific epithet implies, this species is native to Patagonia; it also can be found high into the Andes. The small stems are covered with evergreen leaves, making the plant unique among cacti. In winter, the plant looks no different than it does in the growing season. The plant slowly makes a dense mat of stems, closely crowded together. Eventually, the mat becomes a low mound up to several feet across and over a foot (30 cm) tall. This slow-growing cactus takes ages to do this, and the mat is only an inch (2.5 cm) or so above the soil for many years. Without a doubt, this is the one of the most wind- and cold-tolerant members of the cactus family, if not of all plants. The long, thin spines are brown to white and are plentiful, with the sharply pointed tips reaching through the foliage like needles. These plants do not require regular irrigation or fertilizer, except during dry spells, but in the heat of summer they respond favorably if this is done. I recommend a gritty soil more than a rocky situation for these plants.

Maihuenia poeppigii (syns. *M. caespitosa*, *M. philippi*) (green mat cactus) has stems that are hidden by shiny, green, cylindrical leaves. The two-inch (5-cm) wide flowers are light yellow and grow at the tops of stems, but these plants may take several years to bloom. This species is native to southwestern Argentina and southern Chile and is very resistant to cold. It can grow in an open garden bed in zone 4 (-30°F or -35°C) for many years. It can also take the heat if it is adequately hydrated, as it also grows well where summer

Many people might not recognize *Maihuenia poeppigii* (green mat cactus) as a member of the cactus family due to its bright green leaves.

temperatures are often over 100°F (38°C). I never realized how vigorous this plant could be until I tried it in gritty, humus-rich loam and gave it more moisture than I recommend for most cacti.

Maihueniopsis

Maihueniopsis is a genus of South American cacti that were once thought to be part of the genus *Opuntia*, but are now considered a unique group. All of the species are ground huggers with segmented stems and impressively large, tuberous root systems. In nature, the species are limited to climates with severely cold winters, including high altitudes in the Andes. These are charming plants in the garden or in troughs, but can also be kept in a cold frame or an unheated greenhouse. Many species have not been tested in northern gardens for their ability to withstand cold, winter conditions. It would be surprising if more of them were not found to be good garden plants in time. As a group, these cacti have deep, tuberous root systems and require deep containers or troughs. None of the species tolerate dry conditions in the heat of summer, and the plants turn yellow when left too long without water. The following species have been in my garden for ten years and have had very few problems with cold winters.

Maihueniopsis darwinii (Darwin's cactus) resembles some forms of *O. fragilis* in the shape and size of the joints or stems. It also has the ability to spread itself when loosely attached joints break away from the main plant and root wherever they land. It is interesting that *O. fragilis* has one of the most northern ranges in the cactus family, while *M. darwinii* has one of the most southern, being from Patagonia at the southern end of South America. This cactus forms a large root system, with taproots up to more than a foot (30 cm)

Maihueniopsis darwinii (Darwin's cactus) blooming in the demonstration garden at Mesa County Fairgrounds.

long on plants that appear to be quite small above ground. This very decorative species has yellowish orange flowers about an inch (2.5 cm) wide. The broad, flat spines are more numerous on the upper half of the inch to inch-and-a-half (2.5 to 4 cm), egg-shaped stems. Variety *hickenii* is more striking than var. *darwinii*, with a greater number of spines that are longer, broader, and showier, but it is much slower growing. Both varieties make low, thick mats or mounds over time and are most vigorous in deep, loamy soils with some supplemental water during hot, dry spells. These odd, little cacti do not mind being buried under a thick layer of mulch, cloth, or snow for the entire winter, but it is not necessary.

Two varieties of *Maihueniopsis darwinii* (Darwin's cactus) growing together: the spinier variety *hickenii* (left) and the typical variety *darwinii* (right).

Maihueniopsis glomerata (copana cactus) is a smaller and sometimes less spiny version of *M. darwinii*, with oval to elongated, egg-shaped stems. It, too, deserves to be drawn to the attention of trough enthusiasts, as it is a unique and attractive miniature that could remain in the same container for life. The plant is very slow growing besides being small. The spines are about as thick as coarse hair and cling to the stem in some forms, so that the plants are not painful to touch. Other forms are much spinier. In a rock garden, this tiny plant needs to be placed where it can be seen. It has a carrot-sized taproot and does best in garden loam that is gritty, but not rocky. Like most alpine plants, it should not be kept excessively dry in summer. In its high mountain habitats this charming, little cactus is often buried under snow for long periods of winter. It does not require such a covering, but the plant is better able to survive without cold damage when a layer of mulch protects it if there is not snow cover during the harshest months.

Maihueniopsis glomerata (copana cactus), seen here in the author's garden, is a miniature plant that must be placed in a position where it can be seen. It is a perfect choice for a container.

Pterocactus

Pterocactus is a South American genus distantly related to *Opuntia*. Adult plants of *Pterocactus* are distinctive and would be hard to confuse with any other genus. Because the plants produce huge, tuberous roots, it is not recommended to move them once they are established in the garden. The species are susceptible to sunburn until they settle in and need soil that drains well; otherwise, they tend to have few cultural problems. There are other species in this genus that will be proved just as hardy as time goes by. In harsh winters, if these plants are not covered, they will sometimes lose their stems and grow new ones in the spring. Plants that have large roots when they are planted are more reliable in the garden.

Pterocactus decipiens (Medusa cactus) has proved tolerant of frigid winters in the garden; however, it does not produce as many flowers if left outside as it does in the green-house. The flowers are copper-yellow and about an inch (2.5 cm) across. The plant is quite interesting, with floppy, long, brownish, pencil-thick stems sprawling along the ground in all directions and looking something like skinny, brown snakes or worms. Cacti of this type grow swollen, tuberous roots that make up, by far, the largest portion of the plant's body. The spines are almost hairlike and cling tightly to the stems and are not noticeable without close examination, but they grow from light-colored, woolly points that are visible and attractive. In a raised position, where stems can drape over rocks, this cactus can draw attention. It prefers deep, sandy loam, with some additional water in the growing season.

With enough imagination, one could see the stems of *Pterocactus decipiens* (Medusa cactus) as little snakes emerging in the author's garden.

Pterocactus megliolii (winged seed cactus) is very much like *P. decipiens* but has shorter stems that have a more erect growth habit. The flowers are about an inch (2.5 cm) across, copper-yellow, and very pretty, but last only a day. This unique and interesting cactus is definitely worth including in any cactus garden, even in warm climates. Because the massive, tuberous root that it develops does not take to being moved, it is better if a permanent spot is found for these plants at the time of planting. This would also be a good species for a container, especially at the edge of the pot, where the stems can dangle over the rim. The plant grows larger and blooms more frequently if it is covered in winter and given extra water when it is actively growing.

Another South American native that has found a home in cold-climate cactus gardens is *Pterocactus megliolii* (winged seed cactus).

Crested Cacti

When the growing point or crown of any type of cactus plant is injured, it sometimes causes the growth to elongate, or become deformed, in a strange and fascinating manner. This growth is referred to as monstrose growth, fasciation, or cresting. Some species are more likely to crest than others, but many species have this ability. The unique plants that result from cresting can become quite valuable to collectors and instantly get attention in the garden. Crested plants are, in many cases, not as hardy as plants of the same species that have not been injured, but often they are strong enough to live for many years in the garden, and large plants can become showstoppers. These plants are also much slower growing than would be normal for the species, but sometimes they grow to a much larger size.

A handsome crested plant of the normally barrel-shaped *Echinocereus canus* (gray beard hedgehog) in Jeff Thompson's collection. See the photo on page 128 for comparison.

Opuntia polyacantha 'Wavy Gravy' is the most frequently offered crested cactus that is truly cold hardy and not costly. Notice that even the flowers are misshapen.

A small plant of *Echinocereus viridiflorus* (green pitaya) begins to show signs of being crested. The odd growth is the result of an injury suffered when a horse stepped on the plant.

6

COLD-HARDY
SUCCULENTS

Exceedingly
few plants
provide
year-round
interest
in a dry
garden
as well as
agaves
and yuccas,
seen here
in the Conrad
family's
garden.

lthough cacti are by far the most iconic New World succulents, they are not only ones. Woody lilies, a large group of plants in the agave family, or Agavaceae, are almost as well represented in cactus gardens throughout the world as are cacti. (Botanists belonging to the school of thought that there are fewer and more diverse family groups prefer to place yuccas and agaves in the lily family, or Liliaceae.) It would be hard to imagine a dryland garden of any size without the sculptural qualities that these plants contribute. Yuccas and agaves, the best-known woody lilies, add an exotic, subtropical quality to a cold-hardy cactus planting that simply makes them indispensable. Hesperaloes, relatives of the agaves and yuccas, are used in all kinds of dry gardens to add color through the season. Some of the smaller plants in this group are incredibly ornate and useful.

Unfortunately, an abundance of misinformation has been published by people with good intentions about the cold tolerance of many cold-hardy succulents. Agaves, yuccas, and their relatives are all rosette-forming plants with massive, succulent root systems when they are established. Most of the Agavaceae are native to Mexico, but some species are present in parts of South America. What is important to those of us with an interest in cold-hardy succulents is that a few of these plants can be found in the United States, growing at high elevations. That means they have adapted to extremes of cold in habitat. Another fortunate trait is that many of these species are able to cope with harsher winters in cultivation than what they have to endure in nature.

Dozens of succulent wildflowers also add charm to a dry garden. The purslane family, or Portulacaceae, includes several valuable gems. For example, the neat, attractive rosettes, as well as showy the flowers of *Lewisia* species, have made them favorites with rock gardeners everywhere. The prolific flowering habit of *Talinum* (syn. *Phemeranthus*) species adds color and variety in the heat of summer after most dryland garden plants have finished blooming. Though the flowers are small, they make up for it by opening in large numbers.

When compared to Europe or Asia, colder regions of the New World have fewer members of the crassula family, or Crassulaceae, but some of them are very pretty. New World crassulas include many small, ornate plants that add interest as well as detail to a cactus garden.

In nature succulent plants are often found growing with cacti. This alone makes them obvious companions for cacti in gardens. The texture, color, and form of these species, as well as the contrast in shape to cacti, make for a more interesting and appealing garden in the end.

Agaves: Stars of the Dry Garden

Agave is a genus of leathery leaved plants that grow in nature from the Southwest United States to Central America, with most species native to Mexico. Most agaves, also called century plants, have a basic shape similar to an artichoke. The plants can create the illusion of being in a subtropical, desert garden. Few other plants can add as much to a dry garden or could be used as effectively as a unique and interesting focal point. Century plants have always been standard, cactus garden plants in places like Texas, California, and Arizona, as well as in southern Europe. More recently, U.S. gardeners in regions as diverse as the Southeast and Pacific Northwest have had success in growing a number of species. These plants are favorites in the Mediterranean gardens of France, Spain, and Italy.

Century plants are grown in most warm climates worldwide, often as a source of industrial fiber. The plants are also used in the production of tequila, which is not only economically important to Mexico, but is also a great conversation starter in the garden. In the Southwest United States, century plants were an important source of food and fiber for Native Americans, who are responsible for increasing the ranges of many species, by moving agaves near their villages to farm.

Agave rosettes die after flowering, but are replaced with a large number of offsets at that time, if not before. I can say from experience that having a century plant bloom leaves the gardener with mixed emotions: losing an old, mature specimen, but having an exciting event in the garden. The flower-spike is always exceptionally tall when compared to the size of the rosette it rises from, and it shoots up quite quickly. In most, but not all species, the tube-shaped flowers are yellow and can be quite showy when viewed closely. Many species are self-fertile, meaning that viable seed can usually be obtained from a single blooming plant, if pollination occurs.

In cold climates century plants do best in the sunniest exposure possible, preferably a raised position with excellent drainage. In cold climates, plants located where they can be protected from excess moisture and wind in winter are more likely to thrive. In spring and summer all agaves will grow more rapidly if they are fertilized and given additional water during hot, dry weather, but it is not necessary. The common name, century plant, came about because of the enormous amount of energy that these plants obviously put into flowering. Travelers passing through the desert years ago assumed that it would take a hundred years to store that much vitality. I have at times lost small cacti and succulents growing near century plants, when offsets or suckers emerged and displaced them.

All agaves have leaves with hard, sharp, pointed tips that can penetrate skin with ease, and many have teeth at the edge of the leaf that can tear clothing or skin. It would be wise to take these dangers into account when placing any of these plants in the garden. It does not harm the plant to dull or remove these leaf tips for safety's sake. The plants of some species vary greatly in their ability to withstand cold. It would be a great assistance to gardeners if commercial growers of *Agave* would isolate and name hardier cultivars. To some degree, this is already starting to happen.

Agave deserti (desert century plant) has long, stiff, upward-curving, gray-green leaves.

Century plants can be an important element in xeric gardens, but they can cause problems when they are placed close to slow-growing plants such as this small cactus. The agave pup will quickly dominate the site, obscuring the cactus.

When mature, the plant forms a rosette twelve to eighteen inches (30 to 45 cm) tall and about two feet (60 cm) across. Sharp teeth edge the leaf, which ends in a spiny tip. New leaves have an attractive imprint of the edge of a leaf on the upper surface. This species does not cluster as freely as some of the others in this genus, but it will occasionally make pups. The number of pups, or offsets, produced varies from clone to clone. Although this species does not experience extended periods of cold in nature, it is able to withstand temperatures well below 0°F (-13°C) without damage. It is a slow-growing century plant from northern Mexico, as well as parts of Arizona, and California at elevations up to about 5000 feet (1500 m). Like most medium-sized agaves, this one blooms in about twenty years, with a flower-spike that may be more than twelve feet (3.6 m) in height and have a few, small, lateral branches near the top.

Agave deserti (desert century plant) in the Dryland Mesa Garden at Denver Botanic Gardens.

Agave gracilipes (slim foot century plant) is among the more cold tolerant *Agave* species. Many botanists consider this plant to be a naturally occurring hybrid involving *A. lechuguilla*, which also grows in the area. In nature, *A. gracilipes* is found from southeastern New Mexico into West Texas and in adjacent areas in Mexico, mostly growing on rocky hillsides. It is a small plant for the genus, with stiff, narrow leaves edged with prominent teeth. The leaves are normally less than a foot (30 cm) long and form rosettes about that wide. The flower-stalks are about eight feet (2.4 m) tall, with short, lateral branches extending from them. Some plants of this species have been known to create an abundance of offsets over a period of time.

Agave gracilipes (slim foot century plant) growing in the Barnett family's garden.

Pups in the author's garden left by an *Agave havardiana* (Havard's century plant) that bloomed after twenty years in the author's garden.

Agave havardiana (Havard's century plant) has been an important element in my garden for over thirty years and has seen temperatures as low as -20°F (-28°C) with little or no harm. This good-sized plant makes an impressive focal point in a raised position. The two-foot (60-cm) tall and thirty-inch (75-cm) wide, symmetrical rosettes are broad and open. The slightly concave, blue-green leaves are about half as wide as they are long. The base of the rosette ascends, but the tips of the leaves curve outward. The leaves of these attractive plants have strong teeth along the margins and imprint patterns. In my garden the original plants of this species came from the Davis Mountains and bloomed after growing for more than twenty years. Flowering plants develop massive, laterally branched spikes that are about sixteen feet (4.8 m) tall. In nature, these agaves can be found on rocky, limestone hillsides in the Big Bend region of West Texas and in adjacent areas in Mexico. Plants of this species make offsets, but not as prolifically as some of the other agaves. The specific epithet is sometimes misspelled "harvardiana" and then mistakenly referred to as "Harvard's century plant."

Agave lechuguilla (Chihuahua desert shin dagger) makes impenetrable colonies on rocky hillsides in parts of West Texas, and southeastern New Mexico, as well as in the state of Chihuahua in Mexico. This species has a sizeable natural range, and plants from some areas are more adaptable to cold and wet than others. The stiff, olive-green leaves of this century plant are thicker and narrower than those of most century plants, with regularly spaced teeth along the

An old plant of *Agave lechuguilla* (Chihuahua desert shin dagger) in the author's garden.

edge, and spiny tips. This plant makes a unique silhouette, forming open, upright rosettes, which are about eighteen inches (45 cm) tall and two feet (60 cm) wide. Care should be taken in the selection of a position for this plant in the garden as it suckers prolifically, an effect which can be nice between large boulders or disastrous in a bed filled with miniatures. The flowers are quite attractive, being yellow and reddish, on an unbranched spike that normally is about fifteen feet (4.5 m) tall. Sometimes this species blooms when it is younger, but typically it takes about twenty years. A plant growing in my garden for over twenty-five years has never shown any signs of cold damage, even at -20°F (-28°C).

Agave mckelveyana (McKelvey's century plant) has long, narrow, gray-green leaves that are edged with small, evenly spaced, sharp teeth. The leaves create a balanced rosette a little over a foot (30 cm) tall and wide. Often the plant makes numerous offsets but not always. This species is native to northwestern Arizona, where it grows on rocky hillsides with junipers and desert shrubs to an elevation of about 6000 feet (1800 m). In my garden this plant flowered after twenty years, producing a narrow, ten-foot (3-m) tall spike. Winter moisture is more likely to be harmful to the plant than cold. Although it is not the most dependable species and it is often scarred in winter, it does have the ability to live a long life and flower in cold climates.

Agave neomexicana (syn. *A. parryi* var. *neomexicana*) (New Mexico mescal) is the most reliable century plant in climates where winters are harsh. The full, powdery gray to blue-green rosette is perfectly symmetrical, a little over a foot (30 cm) tall and about two feet (60 cm) wide. The broad, sharply pointed leaves have dark, daggerlike tips that curve

The attractive flowers of *Agave lechuguilla* (Chihuahua desert shin dagger) on tall stalks can add interest to a garden.

This plant of *Agave neomexicana* (New Mexico mescal) has been growing in the author's garden for twenty years.

slightly inward. They are edged with small, evenly spaced teeth. The natural distribution of this species is throughout the mountains of southeastern New Mexico and south-western Texas, as well as across the border into Mexico. The flower-stalk is generally about ten feet (3 m) tall, with short, lateral branches. Some individuals of this species produce numerous pups, or offsets, from the time they are young, and some make only a few at flowering time.

Agave parryi (Parry's century plant) has an immense natural range that includes much of Arizona and south-western New Mexico, as well as northern Mexico. Varieties from the southern habitats, such as var. *huachucensis* and var. *truncata*, become larger and are popular in gardens in Phoenix and Tucson; these varieties are said not to adapt well to colder climates in some literature, but several old plants of var. *huachucensis* are growing in zone 5 (-20°F or -28°C) gardens. In contrast, plants from north-central Arizona growing at altitudes over 8000 feet (2400 m) are among the most cold-tolerant agaves.

This attractive species has that classic, artichoke shape, but with pale blue-gray, evenly toothed leaves. The rosettes vary in size, but generally are about two and a half feet (75 cm) wide and about one and a half feet (45 cm) tall. It is not unusual for an older plant to send up a branching, twenty-foot (6-m) tall flower-spike after about twenty years. Some clones pup pro-lifically from the time they are young, while others create few offsets in a lifetime.

Agave parryi (Parry's century plant), Flagstaff form, with a flower-stalk in Kelly Grummons's garden.

A somewhat miniature, prolifically clustering variety of this species from west-central Arizona, known as var. *couesii*, is cold hardy. Compared to the typical variety, this variety has thinner, shorter leaves, a shorter flower-spike, and slightly smaller flowers. Two named cultivars are known to be reliably cold tolerant. These are the Camp Verde form, which has been proved hardy in zone 5 (-20°F or -28°C), and the Flagstaff form, which is marketed as cold hardy to zone 4 (-30°F or -35°C).

Agave parryi var. *couesii* (Parry's century plant) in Lola Nafziger's garden.

Agave polianthiflora (red flower century plant) is a charming little century plant that looks more like a miniature *Yucca* than a typical *Agave*. The narrow, blue-green leaves end in pointed tips and have long, white bands on the upper surface. Numerous, white, curly, fibrous filaments edge the leaves. Mature rosettes are close to six inches (15 cm) tall, well less than a foot (30 cm) across, and are crowded with many leaves. These plants grow for about ten years and then produce a six-foot (1.8-m) tall flower-spike that is reddish pink, as are the flowers. This species is not likely to offset vigorously, but it does send out a few pups, particularly at flowering time. I have grown this species in the garden for over ten years and have only seen it suffer slight damage when temperatures remained colder than

These small pups are all that's left of *Agave polianthiflora* (red flower century plant) in the author's garden after the mature plant bloomed.

Close-up of the flowers of *Agave polianthiflora* (red flower century plant).

Agave scabra (rough leaf century plant) is an impressive focal point at Kendrick Lake Park in Lakewood, Colorado.

-10°F (-23°C) for an extended period. This species is native to the high mountains in Mexico and could be considered an alpine, meaning that it should not be left dry for long periods in the growing season. *Agave polianthiflora* should not be considered bullet proof, but in the right microclimate it will live for many years.

Agave scabra (rough leaf century plant) can make an impressive focal point in any cold-hardy cactus garden if the right clone is used. This species forms the largest century plant that can be grown successfully in colder climates, but it cannot be said to be dependable. There is much variation within plants of this species when it comes to adapting to temperature extremes. Also, these plants are known to live for several years and then die suddenly, during cold or wet spells in winter. In nature, *A. scabra* can be found scattered through the Chihuahua desert, at elevations ranging from 5000 to 6500 feet (1500 to 1900 m) as far south as San Louis Potosí state, Mexico. It goes without saying that plants from seed collected at higher altitudes is more capable of withstanding frigid weather than seed collected at lower elevations. The rosettes can reach three feet (90 cm) tall and over six feet (1.8 m) wide. They are composed of heavily toothed, three-and-a-half-foot (1-m) long, six-inch (15-cm) wide, gray-green leaves. The leaves curve strongly outward, creating an interesting, balanced, architectural form. Some clones offset freely. Excessive moisture, particularly in winter, can be fatal to this century plant. It is of utmost importance that soil drainage is excellent, and it is preferable to grow plants in raised beds. The flowers are yellow and appear after about twenty-five years, on twenty-foot (6-m) tall, laterally branched spikes.

Agave toumeyana (Toumey's century plant) from east-central Arizona survives temperatures well below 0°F (-18°C) without harm if it is kept mostly dry in the coldest months. This very pretty species makes crowded rosettes of many, thick, deep green leaves. The leaves have white imprints on the upper surface, and the leaf margins are heavily covered with hairlike filaments instead of teeth. The rosettes are typically about a foot (30 cm) tall and wide, and sometimes offset profusely, making thick stands that crowd out anything nearby. This propensity should be taken into consideration when planning a place for it in the garden. The decorative subsp. *bella* has more filaments on each leaf and more leaves per rosette. The leaves are about half as long as in var. *toumeyana* and have brown edges. The flower-stalks do not branch, but may be up to eight feet (2.4 m) tall with greenish yellow blossoms. Finally, subsp. *bella* offsets exceptionally vigorously.

Agave toumeyana subsp. *bella* (Toumey's century plant) in the author's garden.

Agave utahensis (Grand Canyon century plant) is generally considered one of the most cold-tolerant century plants because it grows farther north than the rest of the species in the genus, in northern Arizona and southern Utah. In my experience, although it is cold tolerant, it is one of the touchier species when it comes to winter moisture. The rosettes, which are about a foot (30 cm) tall and slightly wider, are made of many, narrow leaves with teeth along the margins.

Agave utahensis var. *eborispina* (ivory tooth century plant) in the Barnett family's garden.

Agave utahensis subsp. *kaibabensis* (Grand Canyon century plant) growing in Bob Pennington's garden at Agua Fria Nursery.

It is not unusual for this century plant to offset prolifically, creating dense mats of pointed leaves, a factor that must be considered when deciding placement of these agaves in the garden. The species has three recognized varieties. Variety *utahensis* has yellow or gray-green leaves and medium-sized teeth. Variety *nevadensis* is marginally smaller and bluer. The most prized of the bunch is the exceedingly ornamental var. *eborispina* (ivory tooth century plant), with thick, ivory-like teeth on the edge and the tip of the leaves. Subspecies *kaibabensis*, which is much like var. *utahensis* but grows much larger in the garden, is also greener and offsets less frequently. The flower-spikes of all varieties and the subspecies are over ten feet (3 m) tall and are not branched.

Agave utahensis (Grand Canyon century plant) in the demonstration garden at Mesa County Fairgrounds is cold tolerant but very sensitive to winter moisture.

Yuccas: Lilies of the Drylands

Some of the most impressive and certainly some of the largest succulent plants for a cold-hardy cactus and succulent garden are members of the genus *Yucca*. Some of these species are treelike, creating a focal point that cannot be equaled by anything else in northern climates. When mature, these plants remind many people of palm trees. Other species form very charming, small plants that always attract attention in the proper garden setting.

Yucca species are native to almost all areas of North America, and since the 1600s they have been used in gardens throughout Europe. Their widespread use has made them easily recognized plants to most gardeners. Almost all yuccas make neat, balanced rosettes, mostly with long, narrow leaves and sometimes with trunks. Most of the cold-tolerant species lack stems.

To the delight of most gardeners, many yuccas are able to withstand much colder winters in cultivation than they are forced to withstand in their natural habitats. Regular watering in spring and summer increases the plants' growth rate, as long as the soils drain well. Extra irrigation is not necessary for most species once the plants are established nor is fertilizer necessary for yuccas, although the plants do respond well to fertilizer if it is not overdone.

To establish yuccas in the garden, it is necessary to give additional moisture for at least the first season, including spraying the foliage. Until the tree-type yuccas are established, it is advised to water them whenever they are dry. Antidesiccant sprays are sometimes used to establish these plants, particularly before the onset of winter and during that season.

Yuccas are touchy about having their roots disturbed and do not like being transplanted. When planting them, pick a garden site where they will be able to remain. It is a good

A spectacular grouping of *Yucca* trees stands at the entrance to Denver Botanic Gardens, one of the first gardens in the United States to emphasize native and xeric plants.

practice to disturb the root system as little as possible when moving these plants from containers. Yuccas have a reputation for losing all growth above the soil, then sending up new rosettes next to where they were originally planted. Spider mites can be a problem, especially when yuccas are grown in containers, but also until they have become established in the garden. In containers, these plants will sometimes also attract scale insects or mealy bug.

All *Yucca* species are night blooming and are pollinated by specific moths that lay eggs in the flowers. The larvae then feed on a portion of the yucca seed. In the species that become trees the oldest leaves die and then fold downward, clinging to the trunk. One theory suggests that removing the old, dead leaves exposes the trunk and makes the plant less able to withstand cold. This theory has not held up in my experience, as I know of several plants with leaves that have been removed on the trunk and they are thriving. The flower-spike always develops in the center of the rosette in late spring or early summer, but yuccas do not bloom every year. Taxonomists disagree greatly about this genus, and there are many more species names than species. By now that should not surprise anyone reading this book. The fibers from *Yucca* plants are strong and were often used by Native Americans to weave baskets.

Yucca aloifolia (Spanish dagger) is an ornamental species composed of stiff, flat, deep green leaves, with painfully sharp tips. Some clones turn red in winter. In nature, this yucca is found from Virginia to Louisiana and Florida, making it much more adaptable to wet climates. That does not mean that good soil drainage is not important for successful cultivation. This species is very desirable and has been grown in European gardens since the 1600s. In cultivation, the plant requires additional soil moisture through the growing season just to survive. A position that is protected from winter winds is helpful, but the plant is capable of thriving with very low humidity. The flowers are white, with a hint of purple and green, and grow on stalks that reach a few inches above the foliage. The plant forms an upright trunk, or elongated stem, over time, sometimes multiple trunks, and can reach ten feet (3 m) in height. In some situations, the stem lies down and spreads out along the ground. The leaves are about eighteen inches (45 cm) long and over an inch (2.5 cm) wide. There are a few fantastically attractive, variegated cultivars of this species, but all of them are a little tender for gardens in zone 5 (-20°F or -28°C).

Yucca baccata (banana yucca) has a sizeable natural range that includes western Colorado, parts of Utah, Nevada, and Arizona, as well as New Mexico, Texas, California, and Mexico. As with any species with such a large territory, it has a variable growth habit. The number of leaves per rosette varies, as does the length of the leaves and the number of offsets produced. Plants also have dramatically different appearances when they are grown in dissimilar light exposures. Rosettes that are crowded together create a less-attractive silhouette, so to discourage prolific offsetting, this species is best kept on the dry side once it is established. Extra offsets that are removed at soil level can be rooted during warm weather, if desired. The interior of the blossom is white but the buds are reddish on the outside. The flower-spike is not as tall as the rosette. The concave, blue-green leaves, which can be up to thirty inches (75 cm) long and over two inches (5 cm) wide, have coarse, thick, curled

Yucca baccata (banana yucca) with a flower-stalk beginning to form.

fibers along the edge and stiff, pointed tips. Old plants sometimes have short trunks generally less than a foot (30 cm) tall. The fleshy seedpods were an important food source for Native American tribes in the U.S. Southwest. Variety *vespertina* is as cold hardy as variety *baccata*, but has bluer leaves that form more upright rosettes and a touch of a maroon in the flower bud. Young plants of both varieties growing in small nursery containers almost always have oddly twisted leaves. Soon after they are in the ground, the leaves begin to straighten and be more like adult plants.

An old plant of *Yucca baileyi* (alpine soapweed) in the rock garden at Denver Botanic Gardens in late fall.

Yucca baileyi (syn. *Y. navajoa*) (alpine soapweed) naturally occurs in the Four Corners region, where Colorado, Utah, Arizona, and New Mexico meet, and from there it grows north into Wyoming. This exceptionally pretty plant has full rosettes that sometimes develop a short trunk, but not quickly. It is very dependable and cold hardy, with many, thin, straight leaves that vary in length, but are generally less than two feet (60 cm). The leaves are edged with curling, hairlike filaments. The plant sometimes makes an abundance of crowded offsets. The white flowers grow on short stalks that reach slightly above the foliage. Subspecies *intermedia* has fewer filaments and is widespread through New Mexico.

This perfect *Yucca brevifolia* (Joshua tree) growing in the demonstration garden at Mesa County Fairgrounds was started from seed by Don Campbell.

Yucca brevifolia (Joshua tree) has a large altitudinal range, and plants from the upper elevations are hardy to at least 0°F (-18°C) if they are kept dry in winter. Some taxonomists separate these high-altitude plants into var. *jaegeriana*. The leaves are only about four inches (10 cm) long, and trunks are less than twenty feet (6 m) tall—about half the size of the Joshua trees that dominate the Mojave Desert at lower altitudes and are known as var. *brevifolia*. The shorter variety is considered by others a horticultural recognition rather than an actual scientific designation. A perfect specimen of the shorter Joshua tree grows in an open planting in the demonstration garden at Mesa County Fairgrounds in Grand Junction (see photo on page 221). The plant is about four feet (1.2 m) tall, and the flower-spikes, which stand about eighteen inches (45 cm) above the rosette, are so loaded with cream to greenish white flowers that the weight sometimes keeps the stalks from standing up straight. In nature, this species is at home through much of the Mojave Desert in parts of Utah, Nevada, California, and Arizona.

Yucca elata (soap tree) can become a magnificent specimen plant in a dry garden, forming thick, tall trunks that may be over fifteen feet (4.5 m) in height. Unfortunately, they are slow growing and only gain about six inches (15 cm) a year at most. It is also unfortunate that specimen-sized plants of this species do not always survive transplanting, and they are relatively expensive. The flower-stalk is impressive—about fifteen feet (4.5 m) tall, laterally branched, and loaded with large, waxy, white blossoms. After flowering, the stems often divide to make branched trunks. The dark green leaves are edged with curly, hairlike filaments near the center of the rosette. The leaves vary from one to three feet (30 to 90 cm) long, but are only a quarter inch (6 mm) wide and have dartlike tips. The natural range of this species includes southern Arizona, southern New Mexico, and southwestern Texas, as well as northern Mexico. The species has been growing in my garden for more than thirty years and has been exposed to temperatures of -20°F (-28°C) without ever being damaged.

Yucca elata (soap tree) in the Dryland Mesa Garden at Denver Botanic Gardens.

Close-up of *Yucca elata* (soap tree) flowers.

Yucca faxoniana (palma yucca) is one of the most remarkable plants that can be grown in a cold climate.

Yucca faxoniana (palma yucca) is found in nature through a good portion of northeastern Mexico, but it also is native to parts of West Texas. The massive plant bears stiff, thick, yellow-green leaves to about four feet (1.2 m) long. Old plants form rosettes up to eight feet (2.4 m) across. The rosettes sit on top of thick trunks that may be up to twenty feet (6 m) tall. These plants have been known to be exceptionally cold hardy for many years. Many old, well-established specimens grow in places in zone 6 (-10°F or -18°C), such as Santa Fe (New Mexico) and Amarillo (Texas), and a number of huge plants have survived in Pueblo (Colorado) in zone 5 (-20°F or -28°C) for some time. Most of the larger plants offered for sale in cultivation are field collected and have little or no root systems, but they can be established with regular watering for a couple of growing seasons. Unfortunately, these plants grow painfully slowly, and large plants, which are typically sold by the foot, are quite expensive; however, smaller seed-grown plants are available in the nursery trade and adapt to garden life with ease. The flower-spike is between three and four feet (90 and 120 cm) tall, with numerous, short side branches. The stalks are loaded with white or greenish white flowers. A few years ago I bought a few small seedlings of this species, and though they show no signs of growing trunks, they quickly settled in the garden. This is a reliable species when it has become established.

Yucca filamentosa (Adam's needle) has thin, one-inch (2.5-cm) wide, flexible, green, to blue-green leaves that are about eighteen inches (45 cm) long and edged with many, hairlike filaments. It is the prominent filaments, of course, that give the plant its botanical name. The rosettes are often over four feet (1.2 cm) across and can offset abundantly, but these plants do not make trunks. This species is native to the east coast of the United States, from New Jersey, and Pennsylvania, south to northern Florida. This has been the most popular yucca in both American and northern European gardens since the 1700s. These plants are not drought tolerant and are happier with nutrient-rich garden soil, and the culture that most garden perennials want. There are many named cultivars of this species. These include some very ornamental, variegated forms such as 'Color Guard', with cream streaks running lengthwise through the center of the leaf. Another is 'Bright Edge', with bright yellow margins. Cultivars such as 'Ivory Tower' can be quite striking, with flower-stalks that may be fifteen feet (4.5 m) tall and carry a large numbers, of three-inch (7.5-cm) wide blossoms. Another quite desirable cultivar is known as 'Rosenglocke', which is grown for pinkish white flowers. There are two sub-species besides *filamentosa* that are sometimes available from nurseries. The one that I have seen offered for sale most often is known as subsp. *smalliana*, which is a slightly smaller plant with flowers that have a green vein in the petals. Sometimes, subsp. *concava* can be found for sale, this is also smaller than the typical species and does not offset as readily. These two subspecies are sometimes offered as hardy to zone 5 (-20°F or -28°C) in chain store garden departments, but neither of them survived for me. I might not have been generous enough with water for them to become established.

Yucca filamentosa (Adam's needle) with a flower-stalk developing in a streetside planting.

Yucca filamentosa (Adam's needle) 'Color Guard' at Paul and Lola Nafziger's Last Go Round Ranch.

Yucca flaccida (flaccid leaf yucca) in the Conrad family's garden.

Yucca flaccida (flaccid leaf yucca) is native to the Appalachian Mountains. Like its close relative *Y. filamentosa*, it requires more typical perennial garden conditions than yuccas from the drier western United States. That makes it a good choice for gardens in climates that receive more than fifteen inches (38 cm) of rainfall in summer. The normally stemless plant produces an abundance of offsets. The rosettes are up to five feet (1.5 m) across and about three feet (90 cm) tall. The thin, flexible leaves have pointed tips, are over an inch (2.5 cm) wide and two and a half feet (75 cm) long, and are edged with long, straight, hairlike fibers. The cream-colored flowers appear on spikes that are normally over six feet (1.8 m) tall. There is an unusually handsome, variegated cultivar named 'Golden Sword', as well as several named varieties that vary mostly in the shade of blue-green in the leaf. In the right garden this plant could be a valuable focal point.

Yucca glauca (common soapweed) is by far the most cold-tolerant *Yucca* species, but it is equally adaptable to extreme heat. It grows abundantly on the plains of eastern

A flowering plant of *Yucca glauca* (common soapweed).

Colorado and can be found high into the mountains. Its range also includes areas of Oklahoma, Texas, and New Mexico. From there it grows north into Alberta and Saskatchewan in Canada. Even plants growing in proximity can show tremendous variation in leaf length—from a little over six inches (15 cm) to three feet (90 cm) long. The ultimate size of most plants is dependent on soil type and available moisture. The glaucous-green leaves, generally about a quarter inch (6mm) wide, have sharp tips, and white edges, sometimes with filaments. The plants are usually stemless and sometimes cluster but may remain a single rosette. The mostly white flowers are about three inches (7.5 cm) across and grow on a stalk that is a little taller than the rosette. Besides subsp. *glauca*, there are several recognized varieties and subspecies, including subsp. *albertana* from Alberta, Canada, and subsp. *stricta* (syn. *Y. gurneyi*), a miniature from Oklahoma, New Mexico, and Colorado.

   Yucca harrimaniae (Harriman's yucca) grows in western Colorado, parts of Utah, northern Arizona, and northwestern New Mexico, mostly at altitudes above 7500 feet (2250 m) elevation. This exceptionally variable species has several named varieties and forms, most of which make choice garden material. The plants sometimes have short trunks, but not always. The leaves range in length from about four to eighteen inches (10 to 45 cm) and in width from half an inch (6 mm) to an inch and a half (4 cm). The yellow-green to blue-green leaves have needle-sharp tips and are edged with a thin, brown stripe and numerous, thin, white, hairlike filaments. This species needs quick-draining rocky or gritty soil and as much sun as possible to look its best, but it will out-perform most plants in the hottest, coldest, and windiest sights. The waxy, greenish white flowers appear on stalks between one and three feet (30 and 90 cm) tall. A recognized form that might be encountered is subsp. *gilbertiana*, which grows in the area around Salt Lake City, Utah, and has greenish yellow flowers.

Yucca harrimaniae (Harriman's yucca) in full bloom with a nice variety of wild flowers.

Yucca nana (syn. *Y. harrimaniae* var. *nana*) (dwarf yucca) is a real attention getter, especially when given the right placement in the garden. As the common name suggests, it is one of the smallest yuccas and thus is perfect for situations where space is limited, such as container culture. Because it is such an attractive plant, it has become popular with gardeners in relatively little time. It was found near Glenn Canyon in southern Utah in 1985 by Rod Haenni, a talented and knowledgeable gardener from the Denver area, and was described as a new species in 1998. The showy rosettes are composed of densely packed leaves edged with many, curly, white, hairlike filaments. At maturity, the plant has deep green leaves about eight inches (20 cm) long. The flower-stalks are about three feet (90 cm) tall and have bell-shaped, greenish white blossoms. In time, new rosettes spring up around established plants. Many taxonomists and some plant sellers consider this species to be a uniformly small variety of *Y. harrimaniae*, but it is definitely unique from the gardener's point of view.

A handsome specimen of *Yucca nana* (dwarf yucca) in the Conrad family's garden.

Yucca neomexicana (New Mexico soapweed) is native to parts of southeastern Colorado, northeastern New Mexico, the Texas panhandle, and western Oklahoma, where it grows in flat, sandy grasslands. The flat leaves are light blue-green, about a quarter inch (6 mm) wide, and over two feet (60 cm) long, with thin, white margins and an abundance of hairlike filaments, especially near the center of the rosette.

Yucca neomexicana (New Mexico soapweed) with a flower-stalk starting to show.

The flower-spike is three to four feet (90 to 120 cm) tall and the flowers are white. Some taxonomists consider this yucca a subspecies or variety of *Y. glauca* or *Y. harrimaniae*, but to the eyes of a gardener it is not the same. Plants in my garden have remained single, but some clones are known to send out large numbers of offsets. The rosettes formed by these yuccas are generally about two feet (60 cm) across and are a little taller than that.

Yucca neomexicana (New Mexico soapweed) flowering in the author's garden.

Yucca pallida (pale leaf yucca) is an ornate species native to central Texas. This unique, interesting plant has twisted, rippled, pale blue-green leaves edged with white to yellow bands. The leaves are about an inch (2.5 cm) wide and a foot (30 cm) long. The plant does better with typical garden conditions and regular irrigation than it does in dry, gritty soil. In some situations, this stemless yucca offsets prolifically, making countless twenty-inch (50-cm) tall, thirty-inch (75-cm) wide rosettes, but some clones remain single. The flower-spikes range from three to over seven feet (90 to 210 cm) tall and are densely covered with pure white flowers. Plants of this species have been through temperatures as cold as -15°F (-26°C) in my garden without being damaged. I do have to admit that I killed the first plant of this species that I tried to grow by not giving it enough water. This is a great choice for climates that have rainy summers, if it is provided with full sun and soil that drains well.

A young plant of *Yucca pallida* (pale leaf yucca) growing in a rock garden in midwinter.

Yucca recurvifolia (Roman candle yucca) grows naturally in the southeastern United States, where rainfall and humidity are high. This could make it a practical choice for wetter climates where other yuccas may not thrive. Soil that drains well is advised no matter what climate these plants are grown in. This decorative species is widely cultivated and is occasionally found in chain store garden departments. Sometimes it is found under the name *Y. pendula* or mislabeled as a variety of *Y. gloriosa*. The deep blue-green leaves, which have almost flat surfaces and are thin enough to be floppy, are about two inches (5 cm) wide and up to three feet (90 cm) long, with no filaments on the edges and they bend in the center so that the tips point downward. Some beautiful, variegated cultivars of this species are available, but they are not as cold hardy. The flower-stalks stand about two feet (60 cm) above the foliage, and the three-inch (7.5-cm) wide flowers are clear white. Plants form trunks up to ten feet (3 m) tall, sometimes branching from the base. The rosettes are three to four feet (90 to 120 cm) wide. In my garden this yucca is a much prettier plant when grown in part shade and given regular irrigation.

Yucca recurvifolia (Roman candle yucca) is an outstanding addition in almost any garden.

Yucca rostrata (beaked yucca) is one of the tallest and most impressive, trunk-forming *Yucca* species that can be grown in colder climates. It makes a valuable addition to any kind of dry garden. Normally, the fat, treelike trunks, which can reach fifteen feet (4.5 m) tall, are single, but after flowering they sometimes branch. The half-inch (13-mm) wide leaves are a pale blue-green, quite pliable, and may be one to two feet (30 to 60 cm) long, with yellow margins, and needle-like tips. The three-inch (7.5-cm) wide, white flowers grow on stalks about two feet (60 cm) tall. This species is native to the Big Bend area of Texas and northern Mexico, but plants growing in cooler climates have repeatedly withstood temperatures below -15°F (-26°C) without harm. In summer these yuccas grow more quickly when given routine watering during hot, dry weather. They also are very drought tolerant and can survive permanently without additional moisture once they have been established. Mainstream plant wholesalers are now growing this species and offering it as hardy to zone 5 (-20°F or -28°C). Mary and Gary Irish consider this species a variant of *Y. thompsoniana* in *Agaves, Yuccas, and Related Plants*. There is probably good reason for this combination from a scientific approach, but from a gardener's perspective both plants are easily distinguishable.

Yucca rupicola (twisted leaf yucca) makes an interesting garden plant with showy, curving, twisted, ribbonlike leaves. The two-foot (60-cm) long, two-inch (5-cm) wide, thin, olive-green leaves have slight yellow and red margins. The plant is without a stem or a trunk, although it is attractive. Sometimes it makes several rosettes over two feet (60 cm) high and three feet (90 cm) wide. The greenish white flowers are about three inches (7.5 cm) across and grow on stalks up to five feet (1.5 m) tall. This species is native to the Edwards Plateau of Texas, near Austin, but it is hardy to warmer areas

Yucca rostrata (beaked yucca) can become a large tree in time, but even when small it can be an impressive focal point.

This is a young plant of *Yucca rupicola* (twisted leaf yucca) two years after being planted from a six-inch (15-cm) container.

in zone 5 (-20°F or -28°C). The plant grows more quickly with a regular water schedule, but is drought tolerant when established, and it is able to grow better in light shade than most yuccas. I have had plants of this species living in my garden for more than five years and have never seen damage by winter temperatures, even around -15°F (-26°C).

Yucca ×*schottii* (mountain yucca), believed to be a hybrid between *Y. elata* and *Y. baccata*, lives naturally in foothills and in the mountainous areas of southeastern Arizona and southwestern New Mexico, as well as northern Mexico. In habitat, it often is found in forest openings; thus in warmer climates it is often recommended for use in shadier situations. Where winters are harsh, plants that are in full sun always appear to have more vitality. This yucca can become a large specimen, with concave, blue-green leaves close to three feet (90 cm) long and a little over an inch (2.5 cm) wide. In time, the plant forms a large rosette at the top of a thick trunk, which can be over six feet (1.8 m) tall, and is likely to offset at the base. In a larger garden, this striking species definitely makes an attractive focal point. The flowers are white and develop on stalks that are usually over thirty inches (75 cm) tall. Plants benefit from supplemental water during hot, dry seasons, but it is not necessary when they are established. This is another species that suffers from late frosts.

This small *Yucca* ×*schottii* (mountain yucca) can become a huge plant given time.

Yucca sterilis (syns. *Y. harimaniae* subsp./var. *sterilis*) (sterile yucca) grows naturally in parts of eastern Utah. It is a nice garden yucca, but it does make suckers and therefore gardeners should provide space for extra rosettes around the base of the plant. Sometimes suckers surface a surprising distance from the original plant. When small, the suckering rosettes can easily be moved to containers or other spots in the garden. As the common name suggests, this is a sterile species; though it regularly produces flowers, it does not set seed. Flower-spikes are generally less than eighteen inches (45 cm) tall. The bluish green leaves, which are broad, thin, and not stiff, may vary in length but are generally about a foot (30 cm) long with a few filaments. *Yucca sterilis* is a reliable species in cold climates and adapts to any well-drained soil.

Yucca sterilis (sterile yucca) in full bloom.

Yucca thompsoniana (Thompson's yucca) can be found in nature from southeastern New Mexico into West Texas and in much of northern Mexico, sometimes at high altitudes. The foot (30-cm) long, half-inch (13-mm) wide, blue-green leaves are stiff, with sharply pointed tips. The plant forms a tight rosette on a trunk that may be up to ten feet (3 m) tall. Sometimes the stem branches after flowering, creating an appearance somewhat like that of a Joshua tree (*Yucca brevifolia*), but it may remain as a single trunk for life. This species is very drought tolerant once it has been established, but it grows much more quickly if it is offered water during hot, dry periods. The white flowers are densely packed on three- to five-foot (90- to 150-cm) tall, branching spikes. Some taxonomists combine this species with *Y. rostrata* as an extreme form, but from the perspective of a gardener they are not the same.

Yucca thompsoniana (Thompson's yucca) flowering at Denver Botanic Gardens.

More Cold-Hardy Woody Lilies: Valuable Drylanders

Although agaves and yuccas are essential features in traditional cactus gardens, they are not the only members of the family that will add interest to a planting. The closely related dasylirions can be a very effective focal point. Manfredas with fat succulent leaves, nolinas with grasslike foliage, and hesperaloes that add color are well suited to xeric gardens. All of these plants grow with cacti in the natural world and are often used by gardeners in milder climates due to their ease of culture.

Dasylirion

The genus *Dasylirion* is primarily composed of plants that resemble yuccas, often with saw-tooth edges, on long, flat, thin, straplike leaves. Most dasylirions are from warm climates, and in Texas, Arizona, or Southern California are valuable garden plants that can become quite large. Two species are at least marginally hardy in zone 5 (-20°F or -28°C). In slightly milder climates or in an unheated greenhouse that is large enough, they should do fine, if excessive winter moisture can be avoided. Both species have survived a succession of winters in my garden in an open spot, but they lose a little vigor each season until they give up, due to late freezes after they have broken dormancy. The longer that these plants are established, the more winter hardy they become where hard freezes are not normal after mild spells in spring. Dasylirions do best in a sunny location, growing in soil that is low in organic material, preferably in a raised position where moisture drains away from the base of the rosette. Denver Botanic Gardens has an established plant of a third species, *D. leiophyllum* (green sotol), which makes a large and beautiful plant.

Dasylirion texanum
(sotol) has a natural range from central and West Texas into parts of Mexico. It is the most cold tolerant of the two species, and in a carefully chosen spot, where winter moisture can be limited, it can make a nice addition to a dry garden. In time, the dark green rosettes can become as large as five feet (1.5 m) tall and wide. The spear-shaped flower-spike is densely covered with white blossoms and may be up to eight feet (2.4 m) tall.

Dasylirion texanum (sotol) in the Barnett family's garden in early spring.

LEFT:
A towering flower-stalk of *Dasylirion texanum* (sotol).

Dasylirion wheeleri
(desert spoon) is native to the high-altitude grasslands of Arizona and Mexico, and is much like the sotol in its general appearance and flowering habit. The most obvious differences are that the desert spoon has bluer leaves and, given enough time, can develop a fat trunk. The plant makes a large rosette composed of three-foot (90-cm) long leaves. The flower-stalks are unbranched and can be over eighteen feet (5.4 m) tall. Unfortunately, this species is only marginally cold hardy, and generally it is scarred more often than the sotol in bad winters. This plant is one more choice for the adventurous gardener, not for anyone looking for a sure thing; however, some plants of this species have been doing quite well for several years in cold-climate gardens.

Dasylirion wheeleri (desert spoon) in the Dryland Mesa Garden at Denver Botanic Gardens.

Hesperaloe

Plants of the genus *Hesperaloe* can be found throughout the southwestern United States, growing in exposed, baking-hot situations. In cities like Albuquerque (New Mexico) and Phoenix or Tucson (both Arizona), these plants are relied on to flower in roadside plantings, where little other than cacti will survive, let alone thrive. Some hesperaloes have shown that they are not only adaptable to dry, sun-baked situations, but they are also able to withstand extremes of cold.

All the hesperaloes perform best in well-drained soils, with long periods of full sun exposure. The only likely cultural problems are too much winter moisture, too little direct sun, and possibly spider mites. The presence of spider mites probably indicates some other problem, like poor soil drainage. Antidesiccant sprays that are sometimes used on evergreens can be helpful in limiting winter damage to some of the more tender members of this group. In *Agaves, Yuccas, and Related Plants*, Mary and Gary Irish report that hesperaloes hybridize easily. Such behavior could result in some interesting garden material becoming available.

Hesperaloe funifera (giant red yucca) has been growing near the entrance to Denver Botanic Gardens for several years.

Hesperaloe funifera (giant red yucca) is native to northeastern Mexico, where it doesn't have to face extremes of cold. This very attractive species is large enough to be the centerpiece in a small garden. The four- to six-foot (1.2- to 1.8-m) long, two-and-a-half-inch (6-cm) wide, concave, leathery, yellow-green leaves are edged with long, thick, curled fibers. The plant forms an upright rosette that is similar to the rosette of some *Yucca* species. The inch (2.5-cm) wide flowers are creamy white on the interior and a rich shade of red on the exterior. The flowers are crowded on stalks that typically are over twelve feet (3.6 m) tall. This species needs to be kept as dry as possible in winter, but it does not object to additional moisture in the growing season, especially during dry spells. It is not the most reliable species in cold climates, but in the right microclimate it does quite well and can be a valuable addition to a dry garden.

Hesperaloe parviflora (red flower yucca) is by far the most well-known and reliable species in the genus, especially in cold climates. Even where winters are mild, this is a popular garden plant and it is certainly worthy of space in any dry garden. Plants grown in full sun bloom more prolifically. Some irrigation is necessary for profuse flowering, but not the plant's survival. Without a doubt, this is the most cold-tolerant *Hesperaloe* species, as it is easily able to withstand temperatures in zone 5 (-20°F or -28°C). The somewhat cylindrical leaves are stiff, with hairlike filaments along the edge, and they curve inward. Branching flower-stalks keep growing through the summer and may become several feet tall. Fresh flowers continue to open through the growing season at the end of the stalks. Typically, the tubular blossoms, which attract hummingbirds, are pinkish red, but cultivars with yellow flowers are commonly available. The rosettes are mostly upright, but have a lopsided appearance, as some leaves are longer than others. Despite the common name, this species looks less like a typical yucca than the other members of the genus. Over time the plant becomes a mass of tightly crowded leaves, with many, tall, branching flower-spikes. In nature, this species occurs throughout most of West Texas and parts of northeastern Mexico.

Close-up of the flower of *Hesperaloe funifera* (giant red yucca).

Hesperaloe parviflora (red flower yucca) in bloom at Kendrick Lake Park in Lakewood, Colorado.

Manfreda

A couple of unique and interesting species in the genus *Manfreda* are well worth including in a cold-climate cactus and succulent garden. These plants form huge tuberous roots and low, open rosettes that are generally evergreen but can die back if winters are harsh enough. In that case, new growth emerges from the center of the rosette when temperatures warm in spring. Plants that are covered through the coldest periods of winter have much less leaf damage in my garden. Both species have leaves that are semisucculent or fleshy and could be confused for an *Aloe* species. Also both species need some additional water through the growing season to be their best.

Manfreda maculosa (spice lily) has half-inch (13-mm) wide, foot (30-cm) long, flabby, green leaves that are randomly blotched with rusty, red spots. The stronger the sun exposure, and to some degree the drier the situation, the deeper the shade of the red markings will be. Individual plants vary in the number, size, and shade of reddish spots, even among those grown from a single seedpod. The plant is about a foot (30 cm) across and half that tall and clusters freely to make many rosettes. The fragrant, new flowers are cream colored, with a little pink, but in a few days they turn brownish rose. New and aged blossoms are present at the same time on stalks that keep growing from late spring until hard frost. This species is native to areas from south-central Texas to the

Manfreda maculosa (spice lily) with a flower-stalk forming in the spring in Jeff Ottersberg's garden.

Gulf of Mexico. There is no apparent reason that these plants should be able to withstand the degree of cold that they have proved they can. However, if soil drains well and plants are in a sunny position, they are dependably hardy in zone 5 (-20°F or -28°C) if they are planted early in the growing season after all chances of frost.

Manfreda virginica (false century plant) grows in nature from West Virginia to Missouri and as far south as Florida. This species can be found in a variety of habitats, making it adaptable to many garden situations. It is very cold resistant and can adapt to wetter winter conditions more easily than most succulents. The leaves are over a foot (30 cm) long with fine teeth at the edge. The rosettes are about eighteen inches (45 cm) tall and almost two feet (60 cm) across. This species is perhaps less ornamental than *M. maculosa*, but it is more cold tolerant. The spice-scented flowers are greenish yellow, and new blossoms open toward the top of the spike, which grows taller through the summer and may reach close to six feet (1.8 m) in height. Plants appreciate deep watering during dry periods in the growing season.

Nolina

The genus *Nolina* includes species that are exceptionally carefree, attractive, and useful in the garden. For the most part, they are tropical and subtropical plants that are often used in gardens in Southern California. They are closely related to the well-known ponytail palm (*Beaucarnea recurvata*), which has always been a popular houseplant and a garden tree in frost-free climates. The species that are suitable for gardens in climates with cold winters are slow growing, but very tough and are capable of withstanding temperatures well below 0°F (-18°C) without injury. In cold climates, it would be advisable to keep these plants as dry as possible through the winter months.

The general appearance of nolinas is something like that of pampas grass when it is not in bloom. In winter, nolinas remain green and as attractive as they are in summer. In spring and summer, plants respond to fertilization and regular watering by growing more vigorously. Once nolinas are established, they can survive extremely dry conditions.

The following species would make great substitutes for some of the ornamental grasses that have become a presence in gardens over the last few years. These plants require even less maintenance than the tall grasses. They don't even need a yearly shearing and never have to be watered when they are established. Like most xeric plants, they need water the first season until they are well established. Some taxonomists place this genus in the family Nolinaceae.

Nolina lindheimeriana (devil's shoestring) in the Conrad family's garden.

Nolina lindheimeriana (devil's shoe-string), from the Edwards Plateau in Texas, has flat, stiff, green, pampas-grasslike leaves. The leaves have frayed tips and minute, but sharp teeth along the margins. The plant becomes a clump two to three feet (60 to 90 cm) tall and wide, with leaves that arch gracefully. Although it is drought tolerant, in soil that drains well the plant will take advantage of a regular water schedule during the growing season. It is suitable for either sun or part shade. The white flowers are crowded on stalks that stand well above the foliage. This species is not common in the plant industry, but it can be found for sale from time to time.

Nolina microcarpa (common bear grass) is a tall, clumping species to five feet (1.5 m) in height and becomes a massive clump seven feet (2.1 m) wide. In nature, it is at home in parts of southern Texas, New Mexico, and Arizona, as well as north-central Mexico. This reliably cold-hardy species needs no special protection in cold climates. The flat, slender, arching, grasslike leaves are olive green, or yellow-green, edged with small, but very sharp teeth. Often, the ends of the leaves are frayed, which creates an interesting visual element in a breeze. The light green, almost white flowers are numerous and are crowded together on three-foot (90-cm) tall spikes that have many, thin, and wiry lateral branches. The plant requires deep irrigation the first season to become established, but then can be left to natural rainfall.

A five-year-old plant of *Nolina microcarpa* (common bear grass) in the author's garden.

Nolina texana (Texas bear grass) can be found in nature growing in scattered colonies from central Texas into eastern and southern New Mexico. It is present in parts of Arizona and northern Mexico. A single colony of this species is known to occupy a limited area in southeastern Colorado. The plant forms a clump about three feet (90 cm) tall and wide, with smooth, narrow, leathery, green leaves. The flower-spike does not grow above the foliage, but is full of small, white blossoms. This extremely resilient species can be grown in strong sun that would cook many traditional, garden perennials. It can also cope with a fairly shady position, but its growth rate will be quite slow, so it is advisable to start with the largest available plants. This ornate bear grass is a logical choice for climates that receive reasonably regular rainfall. Plants are reliably cold hardy in zone 5 (-20°F or -28°C).

Crassulaceae is the family of succulents with the most plants that are familiar to gardeners in cold climates. It includes the genera *Sedum* and *Sempervivum*, which are by far the best-known and most widely grown garden succulents throughout the world. This family also includes familiar houseplants, such as *Crassula argentea* (jade plant). The Crassulaceae are spread primarily through Asia, Europe, Africa, and the Americas. They grow in amazingly varied situations from moist, high mountains to hot, dry deserts. Fewer members of this family are native to colder regions in the New World when compared to the number of species from northern Europe and Asia. As may be expected with such a large group of succulent plants, most of the species are from warm tropical and subtropical climates, and are not cold tolerant.

Dudleya

Dudleya cymosa subsp. *pumila* (mountain live forever) blooming in the author's garden.

Dudleya species grow primarily along the Pacific coast, from Oregon south through the Baja Peninsula in Mexico. Most of the plants in this group are active and growing through the winter. Dudleyas make star-shaped rosettes of just a few triangular leaves, which are only slightly fleshy, but are succulent. In nature, dudleyas are typically found in rocky soils or fissures, often on almost vertical slopes.

Dudleya cymosa (mountain live forever) grows in the coastal mountains of California, and has waxy leaves that are gray-green with a touch of magenta. The plant forms a balanced rosette a little more than two inches (5 cm) wide and about half that tall. In spring, reddish orange flowers appear on six-inch (15-cm) candelabra-like stalks. Subspecies *pumila* is similar to subsp. *cymosa*, but is found at higher altitudes and is capable of surviving in zone 5 (-20°F or -28°C).

To many gardeners this is a confusing group of plants that tend to grow in the cool months and go dormant in the heat of summer. Plants do not benefit from being allowed to remain dry for long periods at any time of the year, but should have excellent drainage. They are thirsty in the early spring and in the fall, after it is wise to restrict water to most of the other plants in a cactus garden. To me it is worth the extra effort of hand watering dudleyas, but this should be a consideration if they are to be included in a dry garden. In my garden the plants only live for a few years, then begin to lose vigor, but are very attractive when spring weather cooperates and are worth replacing from time to time. Think of this as a plant that is likely to be enjoyed by the adventurous gardener but will require some special attention. I would not recommend it to anyone looking for a sure thing, but given the right microclimate it should live for at least a few years.

Sedum

Some of the best-known and most widely used succulent plants are members of the genus *Sedum*. The common name stonecrop is often used for these plants, due to the rocky terrain that they frequently inhabit in nature. This genus has species growing on almost every continent and surviving incredibly varied environmental conditions. In the colder climates in Europe and Asia, these are common succulent plants with many species being represented. Relatively few species of the genus are native to North America, and none in horticulture are from cold climates in South America. Most of the North American sedums are not commonly encountered in cultivation, but many would make excellent subjects for use in troughs or other containers, as well as with miniatures in a rock garden.

Sedum borschii (Montana stonecrop) is a slow-growing, miniature species from Montana, Idaho, and parts of Canada. The plant makes a tiny rosette of waxy, reddish foliage and has bright yellow flowers on short stems. In nature, this species can be found in rocky soils at altitudes up to 7000 feet (2100 m) and is very cold hardy. It is not commonly grown in horticulture, but it is sometimes available from rock garden specialists that deal in rarities. The compact clumps of plants are slow to spread. All of the tiny alpine species need water during warm, dry periods, but sharp drainage is equally important.

Sedum debile (Great Basin stonecrop) grows on rocky slopes, in the high mountains of Nevada, Utah, Idaho, and eastern Oregon where the plants are buried under snow for months. This is a small, clustering species with fat, shiny leaves making spirals at the top of short stems. If not covered with snow through the winter months, it is best if these plants are kept as dry as possible. Plants of this species are slow growing and it will take years for them to become a few inches across. The flowers are bright yellow, and quite large when compared to the size of the tiny rosette of leaves.

Sedum lanceolatum (lance leaf stonecrop) has become more commonly available in cultivation than it once was. The species has a large, natural range that includes most of the high mountains of Colorado, but also rocky terrain through much of the western United States and parts of Canada. The gray-green leaves are cylindrical and somewhat curved, narrowing to a point at the tip. The plant can vary drastically in appearance, depending on light and soil conditions. The flowers are vivid yellow and appear in multiples on short stalks. In nature, this species is often found in open areas in pine forests.

Close-up of the flower of *Sedum lanceolatum* (lance leaf stonecrop).

Sedum oreganum (Oregon stonecrop) has fat, succulent leaves and looks like it should adapt well to harsh, dry situations, but the truth is, it is native to the moist, coastal mountains of Oregon and it needs adequate water to thrive in summer months. This attractive species is well-known and somewhat readily available in cultivation. It is the same as, or is very similar to, a plant often sold as *S. obtusatum*. The leaves are a waxy, shiny green with red edges, when they are growing in full sun. The small, star-shaped flowers are yellow. I have had the best results with this plant in my garden when it is covered with snow or with leaves from deciduous trees through the coldest months. In milder climates the plant requires no protection. It slowly makes low, dense mats, if it is growing in deep, rich soil.

Sedum oregonense (Cascade stone crop) is not readily available in horticulture, but is worth searching for. It makes a great trough or container plant and can be used with miniatures in the garden, as it grows relatively slowly. This exceptionally pretty *Sedum* has fat, spoon-shaped, blue-green leaves edged with a little pink if they are growing in strong sun. The flowers are cream-colored in summer, but not plentiful. In the garden this plant likes rocky, fast-draining soils, but it does not want to be constantly dry during warm weather. It might make a good choice for climates with rainy summers. In nature, plants of this species are deeply covered with snow for long periods in winter. I grow this plant as I do South American cacti.

A three-year-old plant of *Sedum oregonense* (Cascade stonecrop) in the author's garden, after a late winter dusting of snow.

Sedum spathulifolium (Pacific stone crop) makes a very attractive mat in the garden, with crowded, spiraling rosettes of disc-shaped, silver leaves. In nature, this species occurs in the coastal mountains from northern California to Washington. It is currently the most common New World *Sedum* species in garden centers. At lower altitudes the plant may be able to thrive in full sun. At higher elevations, such as in my garden, plants are weakened by the intense radiation, so light shade is necessary. The flowers are yellow and appear in summer. A popular and desirable cultivar from Cape Blanco, Oregon, is known as 'Cape Blanco'. The form has powdery, white foliage and is commonly available in the nursery trade. These are thirsty plants in summer that do best in a protected, semishady position in the garden. Although not the slowest-growing species in its genus, it generally spreads slowly enough to be controllable in a container. In my garden this *Sedum* is only a long-lived plant when it is covered through the winter.

Sedum spathulifolium (Pacific stonecrop) tumbling over a rock in Edie Gibson's garden.

In addition to the New World species, a large number of *Sedum* species from the Old World are right at home in a cactus garden. Most garden centers carry a good assortment of these plants, which for our purposes can be divided into two basic groups: the low, spreading groundcovers and the tightly clumping, upright growers.

Among the groundcovering types is *Sedum spurium*, cultivated for generations, and known from its many cultivars such as "Dragon's Blood" ('Schorbuser Blut'), 'John Creech', 'Tri-color', and 'Voodoo'. These plants can spread aggressively through a garden and their placement should be considered. *Sedum album*, *S. acre*, *S. kamtschaticum*, and *S. reflexum* are found easily wherever plants are sold and will make lush mats. One of the best of groundcovers is *S. rupestre*, with blue-green foliage that turns reddish in winter, and its cultivar 'Angelina', with yellow-green foliage in summer that becomes rich shades of orange in the colder months.

Many of the upright, clumping types have long been popular in gardens, and almost no gardener is unaware of *Sedum* 'Autumn Joy'. Two of the best clumping species are *S. cauticola* and *S. sieboldii*, both somewhat dwarf. *Sedum* 'Matrona', *S. sieboldii* 'Mediovariegatum', and *S. telephium* (Atropurpureum Group) 'Möhrchen' are among the readily available hybrids and cultivars that make attractive, somewhat drought-tolerant

Sedum rupestre 'Angelina' growing with Echinocereus fendleri (Fendler's hedgehog) in the author's garden.

garden plants. Variable in size, as well as in flower and in leaf color, these and many others are suitable companions for cacti in the garden. The fine-leaf species *S. hispanicum* is tough as nails, but looks delicate.

Sempervivum

Sempervivum species and hybrids produce plump, succulent rosettes that are well known as hens and chicks and have been used in gardens forever. In cold climates few succulents make better companions to cacti than these members of the crassula family, and they are found wherever plants are sold. There is no advantage to growing true species over hybrids, except to the purist. The rosettes may be from bright green to deep red in color. Species such as *S. arachnoideum* are covered in cobweblike fuzz. Plant color changes dramatically, depending on temperature and intensity of light. Sempervivums are among the best plants at slowing erosion on berms when they are positioned correctly, and in time make dense mats, or mounds, of rosettes. Many *Sempervivum* species are native to Europe, and some have been used in gardens for so long that their natural origin is not known.

The Purslane Family in the Americas: Choice Small Succulents

The purslane family, or Portulacaceae, does not offer an abundance of species for the cold winter garden, but it does include some very popular and attractive plants. Most gardeners know the moss rose, or purslane (*Portulaca oleracea*), which has been a standard garden annual for many years. The showy bitterroot (*Lewisia cotyledon*), which is the state flower of Montana, is also part of this group. Not all members of this family are succulent, but in North America and South America, as well as in South Africa there are quite a few thick-leafed representatives, and a small handful are from climates with cold winters.

Lewisia

Plants of the genus *Lewisia*, or bitterroots, are North American alpine succulents that are highly prized among rock garden enthusiasts everywhere. Cultivars of these species have become available in more garden centers in recent years. Not all *Lewisia* species are showy or easy to obtain, but those that are can be real attention getters, and all of them are interesting. Like other genera, this genus is not really understood by science, and the number of valid species is not agreed upon. *Lewisia* was named for Meriwether Lewis of the famed Lewis and Clark expedition, and was first brought to the attention of science at that time.

Not all *Lewisia* species can be considered cold hardy, but most are high-altitude alpines able to withstand long, cold winters. It is best to give these plants a northern exposure on a berm and to protect them from strong, afternoon sun. Drainage is critical to these plants, but they resent being overly dry during the growing season. Because lewisias are popular with rock garden enthusiasts, they are more likely to be available from rock garden plant specialists than from typical cactus and succulent nurseries. On occasion, some lewisias have even shown up in chain store garden departments. Almost everyone that I know with a cactus garden is growing at least a couple of these plants.

Lewisia brachycalyx (White Mountains bitterroot) grows in rocky soils in pine forests throughout northern Arizona, but is more plentiful in the eastern part of the state. The plant is typically four to five inches (10 to 13 cm) in diameter, with long, flat, dull green leaves arranged in loosely formed rosettes, on short stems. The single, inch-and-a-half (4-cm) wide flowers appear in late spring. They are white, or sometimes pink, with darker stripes through the petals, and they do not stand much above the foliage. In spring the plant needs regular watering, but soil should drain quickly. After flowering the plant is better able to cope with dry conditions.

Lewisia columbiana (Cascade bitterroot) is native to the Cascade mountains of Washington State and adjacent areas in Canada. The plant grows best in rocky soil with peat added, and in winter can be covered in deep snow for long periods. The fleshy leaves can be up to four inches (10 cm) long, making large rosettes. The flowers occur all summer and are small but plentiful, growing on stems up to a foot (30 cm) tall. The petals are white or light pink, with a darker pink midstripe. After spring flowering, the plant is best left on the dry side. Several named varieties of this species originate in the northwestern United States.

Lewisia brachycalyx (White Mountains bitterroot) in flower in the Barnett family's garden.

Lewisia cotyledon (showy bitterroot) is the official state flower of Montana, but has a large natural range that includes much of Idaho, Washington, Oregon, and northern California. In cultivation, it has become the most commonly available bitterroot. The trick to growing it successfully is to keep the crown of the plant in a layer of rock with rich soil about an inch (2.5 cm) below the surface. That way water never sits at the base of the rosette, but is available to the root system. In nature, this plant grows in crevices or fissures in rocks. It needs plenty of water when active, but can never sit in water. The evergreen leaves have smooth or ruffled edges and may be quite thick or barely succulent. The length of the leaves also varies considerably. The flowers are normally over half an inch (13 mm) across and can be an amazing variety of shades of orange to pink, or sometimes a blend of these colors. The plant flowers prolifically in spring and summer on six- to eight-inch (15- to 20-cm) tall, branching stems. There are many recognized varieties of this species. Some varieties from lower altitudes along the Pacific coast are not cold tolerant; however, several named hybrids and cultivars are worthy of space in any rock garden.

TOP LEFT AND RIGHT: Coral-colored and yellow-flowered plants of *Lewisia cotyledon* (showy bitterroot) in bloom in the author's garden.

BOTTOM: A brightly colored cultivar of *Lewisia cotyledon* (showy bitterroot) growing in Panayoti Kelaidis's garden.

Lewisia longipetala (narrow leaf bitterroot) 'Little Plum' flowering in Panayoti Kelaidis's garden.

Lewisia 'Edithae', one of several attractive hybrids, flowering in the author's garden.

Lewisia kelloggii (Kellogg's bitterroot) grows in the high Sierras of northern California into Idaho. It is not a common plant in nature or cultivation, but can sometimes be found in rock garden nurseries. The white or pinkish white flowers grow on short stems and are about an inch (2.5 cm) across. The bright green leaves can be rounded to strap-shaped and up to an inch and a half (4 cm) in length.

Lewisia leana (Lee's bitterroot) has a fat stem that can stand several inches above the soil, topped with an evergreen rosette of upward-pointing, blue-green, cylindrical leaves, which can be up to a couple of inches (5 cm) long. The flower petals vary from white to rose-colored, with red veins, and though the flowers are only about half an inch (13 mm) wide, they are numerous, on six- to eight-inch (15- to 20-cm) tall, branched stems.

Lewisia longipetala (syn. *L. pygmaea* subsp. *longipetala*) (narrow leaf bitterroot) can be found in nature from western Colorado, north through Montana into British Columbia, and west to around Truckee, California. This species has become a reasonably popular garden plant over the last few years. Several named cultivars have shown up in better garden centers: 'Little Plum' has clusters of rosy purple flowers with

a touch of orange, and 'Little Peach' has soft, peach-colored flowers. These plants bloom for long periods in the spring and sometimes again in the fall. The leaves are long and narrow, but thick and highly succulent. The plants form rosettes about six inches (15 cm) across and about four inches (10 cm) tall.

Lewisia nevadensis (Sierra bitterroot) has a large natural range that includes moist, gravelly situations at high altitudes in Oregon, California, Idaho, Montana, Nevada, Wyoming, and Colorado. The plant is leafless, except for a brief period in spring, and so is more interesting to collectors than it is to the average gardener. Think of leafless bitterroots as you would think of spring bulbs that disappear after flowering. The leaves are strap-shaped and can be over three inches (7.5 cm) long. The flower petals are white with green lines through them, and they vary slightly in length, giving the flowers a unique, lopsided appearance. Each flower is about an inch (2.5 cm) across and grows on a short stem.

Lewisia pygmaea (pygmy bitterroot), as the name indicates, is a miniature bitterroot. It grows at altitudes up to 12,500 feet (4,125 m) in many western states, including areas in Colorado. The rosy pink to purple flowers, with deep purple veins, are about three-quarters of an inch (2 cm) wide with petals that have serrated tips. The flowers are quite pretty when they are examined closely. One or more flowers grow on a short stem. The leaves are about two inches (5 cm) long and quite narrow. All of the several recognized varieties and subspecies of this species are cold tolerant.

Lewisia rediviva (deciduous bitterroot) is said to have been an important food source for Native Americans, who ate the roots. In nature, this species grows from California to Colorado and Wyoming. The flowers are large for the genus, sometimes close to two inches (5 cm) across, and grow on short stems. The petals are whitish to rich shades of pink. The leaves are strap-shaped, about an inch and a half (4 cm) long, and drop off after flowering. At that point, it is best to keep these plants on the dry side until spring.

Lewisia rediviva (deciduous bitterroot) flowering in early spring in the Barnett family's garden.

Lewisia sierrae (Sierra Nevada bitterroot) is a miniature and not as showy as some of its relatives, but nonetheless is showy and still worthy of a home in a trough or container, where it can be viewed closely. The dark green leaves are deciduous, about an inch and a half (4 cm) long, and are strap-shaped, with a groove in the center. The flowers develop on short, branched stems, and are white with pink patterns on the petals, but are less than half an inch (13 mm) across.

Lewisia tweedyi (Tweedy's bitterroot) is an evergreen crevice-dweller from Washington State and British Columbia. It makes large rosettes and can be quite showy. The leaves are fleshy and up to six inches (15 cm) long and an inch and a half (4 cm) wide. The flowers vary in color from salmon to white or yellow, and in size from two to two and a half inches (5 to 6 cm) across. One to three flowers are usually open at a time on short stems. In literature, this species is often cited as the showiest and hardest to grow of the genus. Sharp drainage is essential for cultivation of this bitterroot.

A flowering plant of *Lewisia tweedyi* (Tweedy's bitterroot) in Bill Adams's garden.

Talinum

The genus *Talinum* includes some succulent wildflowers that can add a unique charm to a garden or container. Like their well-known cousins the annual portulacas, or purslanes, the talinums produce flowers that are often brightly colored and that come in profusion for a long season. All of the following plants have juicy, succulent, cylindrical leaves. These plants perform well in full sun, even in poor soils. In autumn, most species die to the ground and do not show signs of life until midspring. *Talinum* is a large genus with species growing through almost all of the United States and elsewhere. Some are attractive, but seed too readily to be considered good garden plants. Taxonomists are now favoring the genus name *Phemeranthus* for these species. At least for the present it will be easier to find these plants for sale using the name *Talinum*.

Talinum brevifolium (syn. *Phemeranthus brevifolius*) (silver mound fame flower) can be found in nature from Texas into northern Arizona and Utah. The plant makes a dense mat of silvery foliage that is about an inch (2.5 cm) tall. The flowers, which grow on short, branching stems, range from soft to intense shades of pink, and are well over an inch (2.5 cm) across. This can be a very pretty plant, especially when it is used in multiples between small, decorative rocks.

Talinum calycinum (syn. *Phemeranthus calycinus*) (rock rose) is a very attractive wildflower native to the Great Plains, where it can be found in rock outcrops. The plant can grow quickly to a foot (30 cm) tall after breaking dormancy in the spring, becoming round, open, and bushlike, with long, green, cylindrical, succulent leaves. Through the summer an abundance of inch (2.5-cm) wide, lipstick-colored flowers open in the heat of day on tall, wiry, branching stems.

TOP:
Talinum brevifolium (silver mound fame flower) blooming in Panayoti Kelaidis's garden.

BOTTOM:
Talinum calycinum (rock rose), in the author's garden, blooms almost all summer.

The plant can seed around prolifically if conditions are moist, but in the right situation that can be a plus. This species attracts attention all summer long, even when the hot, dry conditions start to limit the number of flowers in xeric gardens.

Talinum okanoganense (syn. *Phemeranthus sediformis, T. sediforme*) (rose flower sedum) from eastern Washington State makes a gray-green mat about two inches (5 cm) tall. The flowers are white, but sometimes with a hint of pink, and they appear on branching stems from middle to late summer. Plants of the species are not easy to find in nurseries.

Talinum pulchellum (syn. *Phemeranthus pulchellum*) (sand hill fame flower) grows in rocky, sandy soils from West Texas to Arizona. It blooms for most of the summer, with small, pink flowers that do not reach above the tufts of green foliage.

Talinum spinescens (syn. *Phemeranthus spinescens*) (spiny fame flower) is the only *Talinum* species discussed here that does not lose its stem in winter. But it does drop its leaves late in summer, leaving a small spine where each leaf was. It is the small spine that gives the plant its name. The two-inch (5-cm) tall, bun-shaped plant has short, tightly crowded, silver-green leaves. The flowers are bright pink and about three-quarters of an inch (2 cm) across, on thin, wiry branches. In nature, these plants can be found in parts of Washington and Oregon. This ornamental species is slow growing and can be well-utilized in containers.

Talinum spinescens (spiny fame flower) blooming in a trough in Bill Adams's garden.

Cacti growing
with a
variety of
succulents
from
cold-winter
regions of
the world.

COMPANION
PLANTS

t is certainly not necessary to grow cacti and other New World succulents in a garden separate from other types of plant life. In fact, it is not even desirable. Without a doubt, gardens can be attractive and enjoyable with only cacti and succulents in them—although I would have to add an ornate rock or two to feel like I had completed the job—but the inclusion of other dryland plants, especially in larger landscapes, creates a more textural and natural environment.

Many wildflowers and grasses, as well as small trees and shrubs, will add color and contrast to cacti and succulent gardens, not to mention that these additions attract birds and butterflies. Some of the most overlooked plants in dry gardens as a whole are the spring-flowering bulbs that need little water and extend the flowering season by weeks. In nature, succulent plants do not normally grow in situations that isolate them from other kinds of plant life, so adding plants other than cacti and succulents helps to create a more natural-looking garden. Keep in mind that thin-leaved, nonsucculent xerophytes have to develop deep root systems to become drought tolerant. This means that generous amounts of water may be necessary the first growing season.

Wildflowers are becoming more commonly available in good garden centers, and the seed for these plants can be found quite easily. It seems like the ornamental grasses have become so popular over the last few years that they must be mandatory in all gardens. Without a doubt, they add movement in the breeze, besides textural beauty and a wild, natural quality to any garden setting. Small trees and shrubs can add height and create microclimates, such as shade, and protection from wind. Several slow-growing or dwarf conifers can add charm, as well as unique, esthetic qualities, and thrive in dry conditions.

The following list of suggested plants barely touches on some of the more easily obtainable species that make good companion plants to cacti and succulents in dry gardens. Further research, such as visiting local garden centers or demonstration gardens, will help you to find the right plants for your garden.

Wildflowers

Dryland gardeners need not feel limited to the following wildflowers, but rather should view the list as representing some of the more readily available species that have done well for me. Any wildflower that survives in dry situations and is not overly aggressive can be suitable for cactus garden culture. There are hundreds of desirable wildflowers that will be right at home in this type of garden and this is merely a limited number of suggestions.

Achillea species, or yarrows, are readily available almost anywhere plants are sold. The flowers are quite small, but grow tightly packed in flat clusters. Flower color is primarily white or shades of yellow or reds. The foliage is typically feathery and varies from silvery to green. Yarrows vary dramatically in size: some are ground huggers no more than an inch (2.5 cm) tall, and others are over three feet (90 cm) in height. Some of these plants spread rapidly by underground runners and can be invasive enough to quickly take over a garden. For that reason, this group sometimes gets a bad reputation among gardeners. Many of these plants however, remain controllable as clumps, or spread with less vigor and can make a valuable addition to a dry garden. All of the species in this group are considered to be deer resistant.

Some species of **Agastache**, known as hummingbird mints or hyssops, are somewhat drought tolerant, and new varieties are introduced every season. These plants

Cacti and succulents blended with wildflowers at Kendrick Lake Park in Lakewood, Colorado, are highly attractive, yet need less irrigation than most public gardens.

have strongly scented foliage and are generally left alone by grazing animals. Most plants bloom in autumn, and many unique colors are available. The flowers are somewhat tubular, on upright stalks, and will attract hummingbirds. If these plants are included in a cactus garden, it is important to know that they will need water in the fall, after cacti should be left dry. In many garden centers in the western states, these plants outsell the more traditional autumn favorites, such as mums and asters.

In dry shade or part sun, many **Aquilegia** species, which are known to gardeners and wildflower lovers as columbines, can be valuable garden plants. If a garden has a berm or large boulders, there almost always is a shady, north side, and the numerous choices in this group really should be considered. A vast array of species and named cultivars are available in worthwhile garden centers. These plants can be found in countless sizes and with flower colors in various shades of red, blue, yellow, or white. More often flowers are bicolored. If many different kinds of columbines are grown together, they will hybridize, and it can be fun to see the results when volunteer plants show up in the garden.

Asclepias species are the plants on which monarch butterflies lay their eggs. As wildflowers, these species are known as milkweeds or butterfly weeds. Some of them are native to dry regions and make good choices for a cactus garden. *Asclepias tuberosa* is the most popular and available of these species in cultivation. Its flowering period lasts through most of the summer. The flowers are orange and appear in tight clusters at the top of the stem. The thin, narrow leaves are dark green, and the plants are upright, to about two or three feet (60 to 90 cm) tall. Occasionally, a few other *Asclepias* species become available, such as *A. asperula* with unbelievably bicolored flowers, and *A. speciosa*, which grows several feet tall and is topped with bunches of fragrant, pink flowers. The genus *Asclepias* is in the same family as the genus *Hoya*, which comprises the always-popular houseplants known as wax plants. The flower clusters of the two genera have the same basic form.

The chocolate flower, known scientifically as **Berlandiera lyrata**, has yellow flowers that look a bit like small sunflowers, but smell like a cup of cocoa in the morning. The plant blooms early in the day, all through the summer, and makes a great conversation starter in the garden. The seed-heads that follow the flowers are disc-shaped. The plants are sprawling and come back from huge taproots year after year. They are particularly attractive hanging over large rocks or boulders. Once the chocolate flower has been established in the garden, additional water is not needed, except during the hottest, driest times. This species is a great choice for hot, sunny spots that cook many, traditional garden plants. The seed sprouts easily, and small plants spread through the garden if they are not controlled.

At least one species of the genus **Callirhoe** has become a standard in xeric gardens. Almost any garden center carries *C. involucrata*, also known as purple poppy mallow or wine cup. This

Cacti and agaves in one of Lola Nafziger's rock gardens with *Berlandiera lyrata* (chocolate flower) blooming in the rear.

plant blooms all summer, with hot, pinkish purple, poppy-like flowers, as the common name implies. By the middle of summer the plant is large and can be striking when it is draped over an edge. *Callirhoe alcaeoides* 'Logan Calhoun' has white flowers. Another species that is gaining popularity is *C. digitata*, with magenta flowers. These plants have the same basic, spreading style of growth. Any of these species can be left dry when they have settled in, even in full sun. The leaves will wilt and look miserable when they are without water, but the flowers will continue to open normally.

Many, but not all **Campanula** species, or bellflowers, have low water requirements and bloom for long periods of time. There are many small plants in this group that are ideal for rock gardens or cactus gardens, and they are readily available in the nursery trade. Garden centers that specialize in rock garden plants will have the more interesting species here. Many of the popular species in this genus spread too quickly to be included in gardens where space is limited.

Centranthus ruber, commonly known as Jupiter's beard or valerian, blooms well for long periods of the summer if the plants are deadheaded. The plant needs very little water and can become invasive by tiny, dandelion-type seeds if conditions are moist. The small, trumpet-shaped flowers are typically reddish, but a white-flowering form can be found in many garden centers. The flower size and shape are the same in either case, and they appear in clusters at the tips of stems. Typically, these plants are two to three feet (60 to 90 cm) tall, with glossy, green foliage. Deer and rabbits tend to leave Jupiter's beard unmolested.

Coreopsis species are familiar plants also known as tickseed by wildflower enthusiasts and gardeners alike. The plants have daisylike flowers that vary in size and flower color. Drought-tolerant species have flowers primarily in shades of yellow. The pink- and red-flowering species need richer soil and a little more water. Some of these plants bloom for the entire summer, making them useful in full sun in a dry garden. Yellow- or gold-blooming xeric species include *C. auriculata*, *C. grandiflora*, *C. lanceolata*, and *C. verticillata*. All of these species have named cultivars that vary in color shade and plant size.

The hardy iceplants are known to science as species of the genus **Delosperma**. Some of these plants are among the most striking groundcovers that exist. Several of these succulent species are somewhat xeric and tolerant of extreme cold. The intensely, brightly colored flowers bloom for much of the growing season. Many iceplants are quick to make large mats that cover their slower-growing neighbors, but others can be placed in tight quarters and will behave. Among the fast-growing types are *D. cooperi*, with bright purple flowers throughout the summer, and its cultivar 'Kelaidis' (Mesa Verde™), with knockout, salmon-colored flowers; *D. nubigenum*, a very low growing plant with yellow flowers in early spring; and *D.* 'John Proffitt' (Table Mountain™), with hot purple flowers.

The best of the medium-fast spreaders is *Delosperma dyeri*, a newer introduction with outstanding multicolored flowers that are predominantly a rich shade of orange. Slower-growing iceplants that are suitable for cactus gardens may need some extra water. Among these slow-growing types are *D. basuticum*, which blooms in early spring or even late winter, and its two cultivars, 'White Nugget' and 'Gold Nugget', depending on the flower color. My wife says that a person should have sunglasses on to look at this one, as the flower colors are so bright. The other slow-growing species that is becoming more readily available is *D. sphalmanthoides*, which makes tight clusters of cylindrical leaves and is covered

Delosperma and *Dianthus* flowers surround a blooming *Escobaria minima* (Nellie's pincushion) in the author's garden.

in spring by purple flowers. Gardeners have Panayoti Kelaidis to thank for the popularity of the cold-hardy iceplants. The few plants mentioned here just touch the surface of useful *Delosperma* species that can be found.

There are a large number of incredible **Dianthus** species, which gardeners know as pinks. Some of these are outstanding dry garden plants. The foliage generally is green, but often is an attractive glaucous color. The flowers are mostly shades of red or pink, but can also be white or even yellow. Many of these plants make neat, rounded mounds that remain attractive in the winter. In this huge group of plants are many species that can make exceptional contributions to dry gardens. Nurseries that specialize in rock garden plants sometimes have a number of suitable species, but even some of the more common species, such as *D. amurensis*, *D. deltoides*, *D. freynii*, and *D. subacaulis*, can be top-notch performers in a xeric garden, if conditions are not overly dry.

Diascia integerrima, the Coral Canyon twinspur, produces an amazing number of salmon-colored, trumpet-shaped flowers at the tops of stems. In a sunny position the plant blooms through the summer and can be expected to keep blooming well into autumn, after frosts have halted the growing season for most perennials. This twinspur readily adapts to the gritty soil that most cold-hardy succulents require. Generally, the plant is about a foot (30 cm) tall, but it may be slightly more or less, depending on available moisture and soil type.

Sources for rock garden plants often have an assortment of **Eriogonum** species that are suitable for cactus gardens. As wildflowers, these are often referred to as buckwheats or sulfur flowers. Some of these species make low, almost flat mats of neat foliage that will always get attention when planted with cacti. The flowers in this group are mostly shades of yellow, but as they fade they may turn orange or red. The foliage varies from species to species, but the leaves are typically rounded and may be green to silver in color and are sometimes velvety. Several varieties of *E. umbellatum* have foliage that turns reddish in the cooler months, adding a great deal of winter interest.

Eschscholzia species, known as California or Mexican poppies, make a perfect addition to any dry garden. These well-known annuals have lacy, gray-green foliage and reseed reliably in a garden year after year. Each season, these plants produce large, brightly colored, poppylike flowers from late spring until hard freezes in the fall. Several flower colors

A berm with California poppies (*Eschscholzia californica*) and a variety of cacti makes a beautiful low-maintenance garden.

have been bred for sale in the plant trade, but over many seasons they all revert to shades of orange. It can be expected that California poppies will naturalize in most gardens, adding color and texture in the process. The flowers of these plants close in the late afternoon as the cactus flowers do.

Indian blanket flowers, or **Gaillardia** species, are familiar to most gardeners and wildflower lovers. These readily available garden perennials and annuals come in many sizes and flower colors. Plants bloom all summer, even in very dry situations. These are not long-lived perennials, but if seed is not removed, the plants reproduce and spread through the garden on their own. The flowers of the volunteers are not likely to be exactly the same as those of the parent plant. The daisy-shaped blossoms come in various shades of orange and yellow, or sometimes red. Garden centers carry several unique, named, cultivated forms of these plants that vary in height from about eight to twenty-four inches (20 to 60 cm).

Gardeners and wildflower lovers know **Gaura lindheimeri** by the name whirling butterflies. Through most of the summer, the plant produces fresh flowers at the end of long, wispy stems. All the cultivars of this species that I have tried tend to look best in gritty, nutrient-poor soils, and all are quite drought tolerant. New cultivars with various leaf colors seem to be showing up in garden centers each season. Leaf color varies from dark green to reddish purple, depending on the cultivar. Several variegated cultivars also can be found. The flowers are white or some shade of pink, and the thin stalks move about in even the lightest breeze.

Kniphofia species have been popular garden perennials forever and are well known to most gardeners as red-hot pokers. Many more species of these aloe relatives are becoming available in the trade. Red-hot pokers are outstanding plants when flowering, with showy, tall, red, yellow, or orange spikes that last for weeks. To get the best from these plants, it is necessary to place them where they receive long hours of strong sunlight. They also may require occasional irrigation. *Kniphofia uvaria* has been a garden favorite for generations and has several named cultivars that can be found in any half-decent garden center. In recent years *K. caulescens*, *K. hirsuta*, and *K. triangularis* have been found reliably hardy in cold climates. More species will be found hardy as there is growing interest in this group.

Liatris punctata, one of the drought-tolerant gayfeather species, is often found growing with cacti in nature. This highly attractive wildflower has short, lavender flower-stalks in late summer. At that time of the year, most xeric perennial flowers seem to be yellow. Too much water or too many nutrients in the soil create tall plants that tend to flop over. These plants are best in full sun, but still flower when given a half day. The leaves are long and thin, and the feathery seed-heads retain a bit of color after flowers have faded, adding some fall and early winter interest. These plants have unbelievably huge tuberous roots when they are mature.

Melampodium leucanthum is a common western wild-flower with the image-invoking common name blackfoot daisy. This very drought tolerant plant makes compact mounds of dark green foliage and is almost ever blooming. From spring until hard frost the plant is covered with inch (2.5-cm) wide, white flowers. The plant performs best in the same poor, gravelly soil in which most cacti thrive. Blackfoot daisy is one of the best plants for dry gardens, but unfortunately is not readily available, except from nurseries that specialize in wildflowers.

Few garden perennials flower for long periods in dry situations as dependably as Faassen's catmint, or **Nepeta ×faassenii**, a plant not to be confused with the closely related catnip, or *N. cataria*. I have watched cats nibble catmint. Several catmint cultivars have become popular dry-garden standards, such as 'Six Hills Giant', 'Walker's Low', and 'White Wonder', with names that pretty much tell what to expect. These plants flower vigorously in early to midsummer and then again in late summer and autumn if they are sheared. The flowers of most cultivars are pretty bluish lavender, and the foliage is composed of small, rounded, strongly scented, gray-green leaves. In time, this plant spreads through a garden by seed and can be quite invasive.

Many **Oenothera** species, or evening primroses, have low water needs and are well suited to cacti and succulent gardens. Most of these plants have a long blooming season, with nice-sized flowers that open in the evening, and some have attractive foliage. Several species are well suited to dry situations, but especially *O. caespitosa*, with large, white flowers arising from the center of interesting rosettes. Another outstanding species is *O. macrocarpa* subsp. *fremontii*, with soft, yellow flowers and glossy foliage. Some very pretty, named cultivars and hybrids are becoming more readily available in mainstream garden centers.

Two cultivars of **Osteospermum barberiae** var. *compactum* are becoming popular with gardeners who recognize them by the name African sun daisies. In nature, var. *compactum* is found in the high mountains of South Africa. Both 'Purple Mountain', with dark purple flowers, and 'Lavender Mist' are cold hardy and somewhat drought tolerant. The flowers are attractive and abundant in spring, then sporadic through the rest of the growing season. The foliage remains looking nice well into the winter, and plants begin new growth early in spring. Shearing plants in late winter makes them more attractive. The plants form low-growing mounds of deep green foliage with abundant flowers that are about three inches (7.5 cm) across. Grazing animals generally do not like these plants.

No genus of wildflowers can rival **Penstemon** for the number of highly attractive, drought-tolerant species. If you are not familiar with penstemons and you have any interest in gardening with xeric plants, it will be worth your effort to investigate them. Some of the flowers in shades of blue are breathtaking, but there are also red-, pink-, white-, and yellow-flowering species. So many penstemons have attractive qualities that the better garden centers are increasing their selections every season. This genus includes a large number of miniature plants, as well as plants up to four or five feet (1.2 to 1.5 m) tall. Some penstemons bloom at any time throughout the summer. All of them have a low crown of evergreen foliage that remains through the winter, and even the foliage can be quite eye-catching in some species. I would grow *P. alamosensis* for its metallic foliage alone, but the brick-red flowers are gorgeous. Some of the more readily available species with reddish flowers include *P. barbatus*, *P. cardinalis*, *P. eatonii*, *P. pinifolius*, and *P. rostriflorus*. Blue-flowering species such as *P. hallii*, *P. linarioides*, *P. mensarum*, *P. nitidus*, and *P. strictus* will always get attention in the garden. Species with pink flowers are also abundant, like *P. grandiflorus* and *P. palmeri*, as well as some named cultivars

Many *Penstemon* species and other wildflowers grow with a large variety of cacti and woody lilies in the Barnett family's garden.

of *P. barbatus* and *P. superbus*. Thankfully, many of the best *Penstemon* species are from areas that have long periods of cold weather and thus they are dependably hardy. Most of these plants look their best with limited amounts of moisture; plants that receive too much water or grow in nutrient-rich soil will grow too tall and the flower-stalks will flop over. Robert Nold has written an excellent book on this genus which I recommend to anyone interested in water-thrifty gardens.

Salvia species, also known as sages, include some interesting plants, several of which tolerate dry situations. Gardeners have long praised sages for their deer resistance and long flowering period. Several popular cultivars of *S. nemorosa*, such as 'May Night' and "East Friesland" ('Ostfriesland'), are among the most used garden perennials. Some species, such as *S. argentea*, have interesting, large leaves, covered with fine, silvery hair. Certain cultivars of *S. greggii*, called the Texas red sage or autumn sage, even though it also blooms in summer, are cold tolerant and are valued for an abundance of showy flowers in various shades of red. *Salvia pachyphylla*, known as the Mojave sage, is a striking plant with silver-gray foliage and eye-catching flowers. It is becoming a popular garden plant of particular value in cacti and succulent gardens due to its drought tolerance and its outstanding, large, blue flowers with reddish bracts. Many other *Salvia* species can be utilized in xeric gardens.

Some of the tansies, or **Tanacetum** species, are popular garden perennials with somewhat low-water needs. The most familiar garden perennial in this group is *T. coccineum*, or painted daisy, a species valued for its large, brightly colored flowers that come in many colors. Also well known to gardeners is feverfew, or *T. parthenium*, which is covered for much of the summer with large numbers of small, white flowers. More recently, *T. densum* var. *amani*, or partridge feather tansy, has become popular in dry gardens. In time, I would be terribly surprised if it did not become a garden standard due to its outstanding, feathery, silver foliage, which stays attractive through winter.

Some of the many **Thymus** species, commonly referred to as thymes, have gained popularity for their ability to withstand foot traffic when placed between the stepping-stones in a garden path. Used in this way, thymes are an appealing presence in any garden but are especially nice in a dry garden, where they give the impression of lushness. Any of the cultivars of *T. praecox* are well suited to this purpose, as are all the low-growing types no matter what species. Several cultivars of *T. citriodorus* handle light foot traffic, but also can be used effectively on a rock-covered berm. As a group, thymes makes nice, rounded plants from six to twelve inches (15 to 30 cm) tall with tiny, scented leaves in a variety of colors, depending on the cultivar. When any species, variety, or cultivar of thyme has been established, it needs little supplemental water. There are many more plants in this group that could be valuable in a cactus garden. Few animals will graze on thymes.

Many **Townsendia** species are popular with wildflower growers and are sometimes available from rock garden specialists. The plants produce aster-type flowers that are huge when compared to the plant size. The flowers are white or very soft shades of lavender-blue, pink, or even yellow. Some of these plants are among the first to flower each year in my garden, but it is not unusual to see sporadic flowering after summer rains, all through the season. Most species are not long lived, but they are likely to naturalize in a garden. Although the plants themselves are normally less than six inches (15 cm) across, they can easily catch attention in the garden. The narrow leaves are somewhat strap-shaped and form low mounds or mats. Any species makes a worthwhile addition to any type of rock garden, but is especially nice with cacti and other slow-growing or small plants.

Every growing season brings at least one or two new speedwells, or **Veronica** species, to the attention of the garden world. Many of the low-growing plants are drought tolerant and provide weeks of brightly colored flowers. They can also tolerate a limited amount of foot traffic and thus can be used between stepping-stones, like the low-growing thymes. Species such as *V. austriaca*, *V. liwanensis*, *V. oltensis*, and *V. pectinata* can make outstanding contributions to a dry garden. Most of these plants will be covered for weeks by an unforgettable display of bright blue flowers. The upright veronicas such as *V. spicata* require more water than that available in a dry garden.

Cacti and a number of wildflowers grow in a corner of the author's garden with almost no water other than what falls naturally.

Late in the season, **Zauschneria** species attract hummingbirds with a succession of tubular, reddish orange flowers that continue until hard freezes occur. Several kinds of these plants, including some named cultivars, can be found in better garden centers. *Zauschneria californica* and *Z. garrettii* are low growing and look especially nice spilling over rocks. Less cold tolerant and more shrublike, *Z. arizonica* gets about three feet (90 cm) tall in my garden, where it has been growing for more than ten years. When established, these plants can survive dry conditions in gritty soil and full sun. The general advice is to plant these species early in the growing season and water them well the first summer.

Grasses

Grasses are some of the most valuable plants when it comes to creating natural-looking gardens. Most of the popular ornamental grasses need regular irrigation and are not suited to dry, gravelly soils, such as that in cactus and succulent gardens. However, some attractive grasses can add textural value in dry situations. The following is a partial list of grasses with low water requirements that will adapt to gritty soils. All of these species have interesting floral qualities or seed-heads, and most of them remain attractive well into the winter.

The type of soil and the availability of water have a huge influence on the ultimate size that grasses become in the garden, meaning that a grass used in a cactus garden may not reach the description on the garden center label. Grasses are still worthwhile in the xeric garden as they add movement in the breeze and a natural quality that cannot be achieved by anything else. They are still gaining in popularity, and new introductions are offered constantly. Many other grasses not mentioned here could be added to a dry garden. Most of the tall pampas-type grasses are outstanding, but they need more water than is generally beneficial for dry plantings. If there is a desire to include plants that need more moisture, it is always possible to run drips to individual plants without watering the whole garden.

Grasses and wildflowers are natural and attractive companions for cacti in the garden.

All the species described here do best in full sun. One of the reasons that grasses have become so popular has to be the lack of maintenance that they require. Once a year they should be sheared to a few inches from the ground, before they begin to grow in late winter. Many of these species provide winter interest in the garden until the weight of snow takes its toll on them.

Andropogon saccharoides, the silver bluestem grass, makes upright clumps close to three feet (90 cm) tall, with airy, silvery white seed-heads above the foliage in late summer into fall. The big bluestem grass, *A. gerardii*, grows to over four feet (1.2 m) tall and two feet (60 cm) wide, and begins flowering earlier than silver bluestem grass. The flower heads of both species have a purple cast and are quite eye-catching, especially in a light breeze. Any grass in this genus adapts to dry conditions, and at least a half a dozen other members of this group, including named cultivars, are common in cultivation. Plants need to be watered deeply and often during the first season, until they have settled in. In late fall these grasses will turn from green to shades of red and orange.

The sideoats grama grass, or **Bouteloua curtipendula**, has thin, soft, bluish green blades, forming upright tufts usually less than two feet (60 cm) tall. In late summer, flower-stalks carry orange- and green-colored flowers, all facing the same direction, which gives the plant its common name. *Bouteloua gracilis*, known as blue grama grass, is much like *B. curtipendula* but is more rounded and has odd, curly, tan-colored flowers. It also begins to flower much earlier in the season than *B. curtipendula* and continues flowering into late summer. Named cultivars of these species can be found in garden centers. Any grass in this genus is able to grow in dry situations.

The most recognizable ornamental grass to most gardeners has to be the **Calamagrostis ×acutiflora 'Karl Foerster'**, a cultivar of the feather reed grass. This four- to five-foot (1.2- to 1.5-m) tall, deep green, clumping grass has a neat, erect growth habit. The straw-colored, plumelike flower-spikes stand well above the foliage. Another popular cultivar is **C. ×acutiflora 'Overdam',** about a foot (30 cm) shorter, with white bands edging the leaf and with pink flowers. *Calamagrostis* 'Avalanche' is another well-known cultivar. It, too, is similar to 'Karl Foerster' but again shorter and it has a white stripe running lengthwise through the center of the leaf. All these plants tolerate dry conditions when they are established, but do look best when they receive at least moderate water during dry spells. I have seen all three grasses in chain store garden departments. One more species in this genus is gaining popularity with gardeners and that is *C. brachytricha*. It too is slightly smaller and has a rose cast in the flowers.

Eragrostis trichodes, or sand love grass, is one of the more spectacular, clumping, garden grasses that adapts to dry conditions. It is worth looking around for it. The medium to deep green, narrow leaves have a graceful arching habit and stand about two feet (60 cm) tall. The flower-stalks are purplish at first glance and have an open, airy quality; they are about a foot (30 cm) taller than the foliage. The clumps bend outward in an arching manner when they reach maturity. *Eragrostis elliotii* is just as drought tolerant as *E. trichodes* and very attractive, but is not quite as cold hardy; it has blue-green foliage and may reach up to four feet (1.2 m) in height.

One of the more popular small garden grasses for dry situations is **Festuca glauca**, or blue fescue. It forms symmetrical tufts of blue-gray foliage that are typically less than a foot (30 cm) high, with tan-colored flower heads that are a few inches taller. The most popular named cultivar of this grass is 'Elijah Blue'. It is slightly smaller than is typical of blue fescue, but does have a uniform, silvery blue color through the growing season and is easy to acquire as it is sold in garden centers everywhere. In time, blue fescues, which are popular in rock gardens, die in the center and become less than attractive. The blue fescue in my garden seeds readily, and I move small seedlings to where I want them and remove old plants. The many named cultivars of this species vary only slightly to my eye.

One of the all-around-best ornamental grasses for dry gardens is *Helictotrichon sempervirens*, commonly called blue oat or blue avena grass. It is very drought tolerant when established, but needs deep irrigation the first season. This grass makes two- to three-foot (60- to 90-cm) tall, balanced clumps of evergreen, rich, silvery blue foliage that cascades evenly in all directions. The straw-colored flowers stand well above the foliage. By midsummer the seed-heads are mature and look enough like oats to give the plant its common name. This popular grass can be found at almost any garden center.

The regal mist muhly grass, *Muhlenbergia capillaris*, is a fast-growing grass with narrow, green blades that form large clumps. This species requires as much sun as possible to ensure the amazing floral display that makes this grass so worthwhile. The plant makes a bold silhouette when it is flowering in the garden and may be up to four feet (1.2 m) tall and wide. Late in summer, tiny, pink flowers become numerous on delicate, airy spikes. They are simply incredible when the sun strikes them from an angle. This grass needs good drainage and is well suited to the gritty soils that cacti and other dryland plants like best.

Nassella tenuissima (syn. *Stipa tenuissima*) is commonly called the Mexican feather grass. It forms two- to three-foot (60- to 90-cm) tall, upright clumps with green leaves arching outward near the top. The leaves are about as thick as thread and move in the slightest breeze. The flowers and seed-heads are straw-colored and contrast nicely with the bright green foliage. This is a pretty species but can become a weed in even slightly moist situations. Gardeners are known to comb the seed-heads to remove seed before it falls, a practice that works well. A few other members of the genus have become available and are also attractive, such as *N. capillata* and *N. viridula* (green feather grass).

Many popular forms of **Panicum virgatum**, switch grass, provide an interesting quality in a cactus garden. Some cultivars of this variable species are quite tall in moist conditions and could be used as focal points in rich garden soil. 'Dallas Blues' can reach a height of six feet (1.8 m) and 'Prairie Wind' can be considerably taller, but both are generally less spectacular in a dry garden. They have bluish blades and pink flower plumes, and are capable of adapting to dry situations after the first season. 'Prairie Sky', which is strong blue, and 'Heavy Metal', with steel-blue foliage, are not quite as tall, but have the same erect growth form. The other favorite cultivar of this species is 'Shenandoah', with reddish blades in the summer that turn cranberry in the fall. There are at least another dozen named cultivars of this species.

The genus **Pennisetum** includes several species with low water needs when they are established, but most of them are sold as annuals in colder climates. These species are commonly referred to as fountain grasses due to the graceful, arching habit of the foliage. Several popular grasses in this genus are easy to find wherever plants are sold. The most well-known and reliable perennial species in zone 5 (-20°F or -28°C) is *P. alopecuroides*, which in its typical form has tall, silvery plumes with a purple cast. Several named cultivars have silvery white flower-stalks and vary in size, from less than a foot (30 cm) tall in the case of 'Little Bunny' and the variegated 'Little Honey', to three feet (90 cm) in the popular cultivar known as 'Hameln'. Variety *viridescens* has plumes that are close to black. Another species that is becoming more common in the garden trade is *P. orientale*, an upright grass that can reach three feet (90 cm) tall and produce feathery plumes that turn from white to pink as they mature.

Little blue stem grass, or **Schizachyrium scoparium**, is interesting to watch as it changes from soft, gray-green in spring to blue in summer, reddish purple in fall, and reddish brown in winter. This species has a couple of named cultivars that are commonly encountered in garden centers. The most popular is 'Blaze', with straw-colored flower-stalks, but there are others with a tint of pink in the foliage or a touch of rust in the flowers. Any form of this species will make an upright clump of thin leaves that may grow to a little over three feet (90 cm) tall and two feet (60 cm) wide. This very drought tolerant species looks best in soils that drain quickly, making it quite suitable for cacti and succulent gardens.

Sorghastrum nutans, long known by the common name Indian grass, has dark green to silvery blue-green foliage. The leaf blades are broad and somewhat flat. This species can grow to be an impressive, six-foot (1.8-m) tall, four-foot (1.2-m) wide grass, in rich soil with moisture. Though it is generally much smaller when it is kept dry, it is still quite attractive. The yellow flowers appear at the tips of wiry branches on airy stalks and are very pretty when examined closely. This grass is very ornamental and turns yellow, then reddish in the fall. It adapts to dry, nutrient-poor soils, but needs full sun to flower well.

Xeric Trees and Shrubs

Including the right small tree or shrub can add a great deal of interest to any garden. Many large, ornate, woody plants make excellent companions to succulents in a dry garden. If shrubs and trees are included on cactus berms, it may be necessary to do some occasional pruning. Most woody plants look best when they are trimmed in winter. The species listed here are adaptable to dry situations and gritty soils, but the list is no way intended to be complete.

Some species in the genus **Amelanchier**, known as serviceberries, can become nice, tall shrubs in dry situations. *Amelanchier utahensis* is a water-thrifty, rounded shrub to over ten feet (3 m) tall and wide. *Amelanchier alnifolia* has the same full, rounded look, but is not quite as large. These plants take well to pruning and can be kept to a desired shape and size. In spring, they produce numerous clusters of fragrant, white flowers before the unique, velvety, white leaves appear. Dark blue berries are abundant from midsummer until birds and squirrels find them. In autumn, the foliage turns a very attractive yellow and orange.

Without a doubt, one of the best small shrubs for any xeric garden is the leadplant, or **Amorpha canescens**. It has thin, woody stems that are not crowded, giving an open appearance, and grows

Xeric trees and shrubs as well as cacti and woody lilies fill the Dryland Mesa Garden at Denver Botanic Gardens.

to about four feet (1.2 m) tall and a couple of feet (60 cm) across. This little bush has delicate, thin, fernlike, gray-green leaves and stunning, violet-blue flower-spikes in summer. The leadplant is one of the last shrubs to leaf out in the spring, and that would be its only fault. A larger relative, *A. fruticosa*, known as false indigo, is often over six feet (1.8 m) tall and two or three times as wide. False indigo is a thick, sprawling shrub that needs some room. It is a very attractive species with fine, divided leaves. In midsummer, false indigo makes an outstanding show with dazzling, purple flowers. Both species need dry, gritty soils and are best in full days of sun.

Manzanitas are attractive, small, broadleaf evergreen trees and shrubs. Many of the larger species are popular with gardeners in milder climates, but there are some attractive species for higher elevations with cold winters. These ornate, woody plants are members of the genus **Arctostaphylus**. Several cold-hardy cultivars have made their way into garden centers over the last few years, and all of them are valuable in dry gardens. The most commonly encountered manzanita is *A. ×coloradoensis* (panchito manzanita), which is slightly over a foot (30 cm) tall. This very cold hardy, broadleaf evergreen has twisted, reddish stems and a spreading growth habit. The flowers hang from the stems in winter and are followed by red berries. At the coldest time of the year, these are among the most attractive plants that can be grown in climates with harsh winters. Manzanitas need to be watered deeply for the first season, before the soil is dry, but established plants need no care to remain attractive.

The genus **Aronia** includes some useful shrubs for dry gardens. Gardeners know them as chokeberry bushes. The most popular of these species are *A. arbutifolia* and *A. melanocarpa*, which mature at about eight feet (2.4 m) tall. A showy, miniature cultivar called *A. melanocarpa* 'Iroquois

Beauty' only grows to about three feet (90 cm). The leaves have a polished, shiny look and turn a brilliant, shade of red in fall. The flowers are white in spring, and the fruits are dark purple in late summer. All of the plants in this group sucker and create problems if they are placed too close to smaller or slower growing species in the garden.

Artemisia includes some of the most desirable, woody plants that can be included any kind of garden. These are well known as sagebrushes. Although most of them are small shrubs, *A. frigida*, the fringed sage, is a low-growing species with feathery, gray foliage that only becomes woody near the crown. It is less like a shrub than the rest of the species, but if sheared back occasionally, it is a wonderful plant for the garden. *Artemisia tridentata* is a tall, open, broadleaf evergreen shrub that can quickly grow to over ten feet (3 m) tall and look like an ancient desert dweller. It is a very desirable cactus garden shrub with stringy, silvery gray foliage. The other popular plants in this group are small, woody bushes or sub-shrubs, all of which have white, felt-covered foliage and are dependable garden plants. They are especially valued in areas where deer grazing is a problem. *Artemisia schmidtiana*, the silver mound, and *A.* 'Powis Castle' are well known. In recent years, *A. stelleriana*, the silver brocade, and *A. ludoviciana* 'Valerie Finnis' have become quite popular, as has *A. versicolor*, the sea foam sage, which has exceptional textural qualities. This is only a few of the *Artemisia* species that are cultivated, and there are others that would make good company for cacti.

Some **Atriplex** species can be found in quality garden centers. These are native to the western drylands, where they are known as saltbushes. The most widely grown member of the group is *A. canescens*, four-winged saltbush, which gets its name from the shape of the seedpods. This full, small, rounded shrub is generally not over three feet (90 cm) tall and has small, narrow, gray leaves. One other species that can be found from time to time is *A. confertifolia*, which makes a round shrub one to three feet (30 to 90 cm) tall and wide. The small, rounded, silver leaves remain through a good part of the winter. Both species thrive in the driest, nutrient-poor soil. The flowers are not likely to draw much attention in either species.

Several forms of **Berberis thunbergii**, or barberries, are often used in more traditional types of landscaping, but are suited to cactus and succulent gardens as well. All cultivars of this species have low water needs once they are established; however, they are touchy about being left too dry the first season. The most popular forms of these dense bushes are grown primarily for their brightly colored foliage, which ranges from crimson to rich shades of yellow on wiry, thorn-covered branches. 'Golden Nugget', with orange foliage in spring, and 'Crimson Pygmy', with bright purplish red leaves, may be less than two feet (60 cm) tall, but most of the named cultivars are larger and may be up to five or six feet (1.5 or 1.8 m) tall and wide. This species is considered invasive in some climates. These shrubs have small, but showy, reddish purple leaves. Barberries are easily obtainable plants and some type can be found in almost any garden center.

Some **Caragana** species are native to dry, windy climates with cold winters. These incredibly tough plants are known as peashrubs, due their flowers and seedpods looking like those of peas. Several species and named cultivars can be found in garden centers, and they vary from three to twenty feet (90 cm to 6 m) in height. The fernlike foliage varies from green to silver. Even in dry gardens, peashrubs can be expected to flower prolifically and that is the reason they are grown. The most commonly encountered peashrub is *C. microphylla*, a yellow-flowering species with several named cultivars.

Another popular species is *C. rosea*, with showy, red and yellow flowers, but several other species can be found in garden centers. Peashrubs bloom in late spring or early summer.

Caryopteris ×clandonensis is a standard landscape bush with several forms, all referred to as blue spireas. You might know some of these popular plants by names such as 'Blue Mist', 'Dark Knight', or 'First Choice', but there are many more. Blue spireas make perfectly round bushes that grow up to four feet (1.2 m) tall and wide, with small, thin, dull green leaves. Some cultivars are much smaller. The plants produce abundant clusters of feathery, blue flowers at the tips of stems for weeks in summer. When established, these are surprisingly drought tolerant shrubs, but are more attractive if they are sheared back in winter. At one time I was skeptical about these shrubs doing well in dry gardens, but they have proved themselves to be quite adaptable.

The mountain mahoganies, which are broadleaf semi-evergreen shrubs with an erect growth habit, can be valuable additions to a dry garden, especially the two varieties of **Cercocarpus ledifolius**. Variety *ledifolius* is treelike and can grow to over twenty feet (6 m) tall. The thick, deep green, narrow foliage makes an excellent garden backdrop. Next to the manzanitas and desert hollies, this is one of the best-looking broadleaf evergreens that will flourish in dry situations. In winter, it is hard to beat these small trees when it comes to keeping the garden green. The other variety of this species, known as var. *intricatus*, is much smaller and may be mature at five feet (1.5 m). It can be an outstanding choice on small berms with cacti and woody lilies. Another commonly available species in this group is *C. montanus*, which is a more spreading type shrub, with dull green, semideciduous foliage. At maturity, the plant is about eight feet (2.4 m) tall and wide. Any of these shrubs take well to being shaped.

A woody plant that has gained some rightful popularity in the last few years is **Chamaebatiara millefolium**, an interesting member of the rose family known as the fernbush. This shrub is native to the high drylands throughout the western United States and flourishes in the driest situations when established. It is not picky about soil, as long as it drains well. Without additional water, the fernbush is usually no more than a three- to five-foot (90- to 150-cm), rounded, evergreen shrub with gray-green, soft, fernlike foliage. If conditions are moist and soil is rich, the plant can be larger. In spring, pyramid-shaped clusters of small, white flowers appear at the tips of the branches.

Several cultivars of **Chilopsis linearis**, or desert willows, can be found in garden centers. It seems like more named cultivars appear out of nowhere each new growing season. The rate of growth, the length of the leaf, and the size and color of the flowers vary significantly among the cultivars. Generally, these are open trees that can mature at over twenty feet (6 m) tall and have the look of willows, but with clusters of large, attractive flowers at the tips of the stems. Desert willows are some of the last trees to leaf out in spring. At that time they sometimes have to be trimmed at the tips of braches, where there is some winter dieback. When these small trees are established, they can easily get by on natural rainfall, but will grow more quickly if they are watered during dry spells.

Rabbitbrush, or **Chrysothamnus nauseosus**, is starting to become somewhat common in cultivation. This dense, rounded shrub is covered with yellow flowers in late summer. Gardeners value it for its drought tolerance and cold hardiness, as well as its resistance to deer browsing. Rabbitbrush can often be found growing with cacti in nature. Three varieties are commercially available. The two taller ones, var. *albicaulis*, with gray-green foliage, and var. *graveolens*, with deep green leaves, may be up to six feet (1.8 m) tall and wide. The smaller variety has showier, silvery foliage and is seldom more than four feet (1.2 m) tall; it is known as var. *nauseosus*, or dwarf rabbit brush.

Among the eye-catching shrubs that work well in dry gardens are the many species, hybrids, and cultivars of the genus **Cytisus**. These shrubs have always been favorites with gardeners and are commonly known as brooms. In spring, brooms are covered with brightly colored flowers that may be from yellow to red, depending on the species or cultivar. Various types range quite broadly in size and shape, but are all less than six feet (1.8 m) tall. In the heat of summer, these plants drop all their tiny leaves, but remain attractive as they have evergreen stems that hold their color year-round. Most garden centers have a selection of these plants in early spring when they are flowering. Among the popular, yellow-flowering types are *C. ×praecox* 'Allgold', *C.* 'Moonlight', and *C. purgans* 'Spanish Gold'. Favorite, red-flowering brooms include *C.* 'Burkwoodii' and *C.* 'Lena'.

Several **Ephedra** species can make attractive additions to a cactus garden. As a group, these plants are commonly referred to as joint firs, but the Great Basin plants are well known as Mormon tea. These plants are interesting in that they are ancient life forms that are more closely related to conifers than to flowering plants. Species range from miniature to several feet tall and wide. They all have large numbers of thin, green or blue, tangled, cylindrical stems that retain their color through much of the year. Two of the most dependable species for dry gardens are *E. equisetina*, with soft blue stems, and *E. viridis*, with deep green stems. These are particularly nice when they are tumbling over large rocks or boulders. Also there are several dwarf species that are perfect for containers or rock gardens.

Fallugia paradoxa, also known as the Apache plume, is a member of the rose family. This interesting shrub is native to the southwestern United States. It requires little water for survival, but grows more quickly if it is given some additional moisture during the driest periods in summer. The plant becomes a five- or six-foot (1.5- or 1.8-m) tall, rounded shrub, with many, thin, twisted branches carrying small, light green leaves. Small, white flowers appear through the summer and look like those of a wild rose. It is the eye-catching, large, feathery seed-heads covering the stems that catch attention and give the plant its common name. Apache plume is a full shrub with a soft appearance that can make it exceptionally effective when used as a garden backdrop.

The New Mexico privet, or ***Forestiera neomexicana***, is a small tree or bush to a little more than ten feet (3 m) tall, with light bark and small, green leaves. With proper pruning, it can be a very pretty tree. In this species, plants may be male or female. Females have dark blue berries if pollination occurs. The plants have become common in landscapes in Colorado; when they are cut at the top of the stem, they become thick shrubs, and when side branches are removed, the plants grow taller and become more like a small tree. The New Mexico privet grows more quickly under dry conditions than can be expected of most species.

The genus ***Mahonia*** is familiar to many gardeners due to the popularity of *M. aquifolium*, the Oregon grape holly, a shade-loving shrub that is tolerant of dry soils. In a garden full of cacti and woody lilies, two other mahonias are exceptional: *M. haematocarpa* and *M. fremontii*. Both species, called desert hollies, have bluish evergreen foliage that takes on reddish tones in winter. Although *M. fremontii* is deeper blue, when kept trimmed both species are highly attractive. Their foliage has a strong resemblance to hollies, with needlelike projections from several points on the leaves. In time, these can become magnificent, dense trees that are several feet across and tall. Loads of reddish purple berries against the blue foliage in late summer are quite attractive. The shrubs look best when they are pruned or shaped, and can be useful in situations where space is limited, but not close to walkways where the stiff, needle-sharp points on the leaves can be painful to encounter.

In an effective use of a cactus with shrubs, *Cylindropuntia imbricata* (tree cholla) grows in front of a hot wall in Lola Nafziger's garden. Behind the cholla are *Perovskia atriplicifolia* (Russian sage) and a *Buddleja* sp. (butterfly bush), both more commonly planted garden shrubs.

Without a doubt, the most popular xeric shrub in western gardens is **Perovskia atriplicifolia**, or Russian sage. Under dry conditions, most forms of this species are less than four or five feet (1.2 or 1.5 m) tall and wide. In rich soil, with regular irrigation they can easily be twice that size. The plant makes a neat, rounded shrub, if cut back and shaped in winter. The small, soft, gray leaves create a strong contrast to the numerous clusters of frilly, blue flowers at the tips of the stems. Russian sage has become a standard garden feature where deer grazing is a problem, and many named cultivars are available.

Physocarpus opulifolius, known as ninebark, has many named cultivars that make handsome garden plants. These plants vary slightly in size and shape, but all have

textured leaves in a variety of colors. When established, they have an impressive ability to withstand dry conditions. In spring, flat clusters of white flowers stand out against the strong foliage colors. As ninebarks age, thin layers of bark peel from the stems to expose contrasting colors and give the plant its common name.

Most **Prunus** species are drought tolerant and can be useful in dry gardens. Some of these shrubs and trees sucker aggressively into thickets that become hard to control. Two examples are *P. virginiana*, or chokecherry, and *P. americana*, or American plum, either of which could make a good screen or backdrop for a garden but needs room. The species that I recommend is *P. besseyi*, western sand cherry. In dry gardens this rounded shrub is likely to never exceed six feet (1.8 m) tall and wide. The oval leaves are pale green, almost gray, and become orange or red in fall. In early spring the plant is covered with white flowers and in late summer with dark purple, cherrylike fruits.

Several cold-tolerant species of **Quercus**, or oaks, have low water needs. Most of these are too large for the average garden. *Quercus gambelii*, or Gambel's oak, thrives in poor soils with no extra water, but be aware that it spreads aggressively by underground stems. A better choice is *Q. turbinella*, a thick, upright shrub that matures at about twelve feet (3.6 m) tall. The leaves are blue-green and have pointed lobes, like holly leaves. There are other small oaks that could be good choices for dry gardens. Before planting an oak, be sure it is not the suckering type if it placed near slower-growing species. Most oaks provide good autumn color.

Many **Rhamnus** species, known as buckthorns, have low water needs and are tolerant of most soils that drain well. The most widely available species in horticulture is *R. frangula*, sometimes referred to as fernleaf buckthorn. Several of its named cultivars are grown commercially. All of them are narrow, upright trees about ten feet (3 m) tall. The deep green leaves are long and narrow. More *Rhamnus* species are being offered by some of the largest plant producers in the country, and they are becoming more common. Many of the buckthorns are from regions of extreme cold and are useful in mountain communities.

Almost all **Rhus** species, which are called sumacs, thrive in dry conditions when they are established. This well-known group of small trees has many species and cultivars for dry gardens. Some sumacs sucker aggressively and are hard to contain, but others, like *R. trilobata*, are controllable and make excellent additions to a dry garden. I do not recommend *R. trilobata* to anyone who is shy about pruning, but it can be shaped quite easily. This species produces male flowers on some plants and female flowers on others, and both have to be growing together to produce red berries. There are several drought-tolerant shrubs in this genus, but make sure that suckering types are placed wisely.

Currants and gooseberries are members of the genus **Ribes** with fragrant flowers in spring, and they attract wildlife in summer with a profusion of berries. Many species and named cultivars can be found in nurseries. Sizes vary, but most are rounded shrubs less than six feet (1.8 m) tall and across. These are very cold tolerant shrubs and most can be grown in zone 4 (-30°F or -35°C). *Ribes alpinum* has glossy, dark green foliage and insignificant flowers. *Ribes aureum* is showier, especially in flower, with small, strongly scented, yellow blossoms. The foliage is shiny green in summer and turns a brilliant red in fall. *Ribes cereum* is a little smaller than most in this group and has glossy, gray-green leaves and red berries. *Ribes odoratum* has fragrant, yellow flowers and a touch of blue in the foliage. *Ribes sanguineum* has red flowers and deep green leaves.

Gooseberries, such as *R. hirtellum*, have many cascading branches covered with drab green foliage and can look quite nice when placed in an elevated position between large boulders. The flowers are self-fertile in many of these species, meaning that only one plant must be present to produce fruit.

Robinia neomexicana, or the New Mexico locust, forms a dense thicket up to twenty feet (6 m) tall but is much smaller in dry conditions. The thorn-covered branches carry dull green, deciduous leaves. The thorns are ferocious and deserve respect, even in a garden filled with cacti and dagger-tipped woody lilies. The New Mexico locust is quite showy in bloom, with clusters of bright pink, pealike flowers in late spring and early summer. It is a good shrub to create a screen, but is not easily controlled when it starts to spread by suckering. It is tolerant of poor soil and dry conditions.

Many **Rosa** species, or roses, are drought tolerant once they are established, particularly the wild types. The roses that could be included in a cactus garden are not the fancy tea or floribunda types, but rather the roses with small, single flowers that in most cases are some shade of pink. Most of these roses sucker prolifically and should not be placed near slower-growing species. Bob Nold has high praises for *R. stellata* from the Grand Canyon area with medium, pink flowers, in his fun-to-read book *High and Dry*. I have not tried that one, but it sounds nice. I have grown *R. woodsii* and *R. gymnocarpa* and think they have their place in a dry garden. The only other rose I have growing in my cactus garden is a plant that a friend brought from his family's garden in Italy. I do not what species it is, but it has metallic blue-green leaves and small, pink flowers and never needs water. Some of the carpet type roses and the miniatures are surprisingly drought tolerant.

After suggesting so many woody shrubs, I recommend limiting the number of these species to a few. If space is available, use multiples of the same species for the most natural effect. Too many species growing together tends to create a jumbled look, but at the same time, including some of these species adds to the appeal of most dry gardens. Also, many of these shrubs provide fruit and flowers that attract birds and butterflies to the garden. Trees and shrubs can add height, texture, and color. They also help to create that natural, high-desert appeal, like cacti and woody lilies growing among scattered shrubs and trees in nature.

Tall pines (*Pinus*) make an effective backdrop to the Conrad family's garden.

SOURCES FOR PLANTS

Many garden centers offer a selection of cacti, succulents, and other xeric plants for sale, but if yours does not, here are some websites that I have found to be reliable and offer quality plants.

coldhardycactus.com is an easy-to-navigate website with photos and information on a variety of cacti as well as yuccas and agaves that are proven to grow in climates with cold winters. This site is an excellent source for many of the named cultivars of prickly pears and chollas, but also has a large selection of other cacti including *Coryphantha*, *Echinocereus*, *Escobaria*, and *Pediocactus* species, with new species offered from time to time.

highcountrygardens.com is a leading mail-order nursery specializing in drought-tolerant perennials. It also has a good selection of cold-hardy succulents, cacti, yuccas, and agaves, as well as cold-hardy South African plants. This site is full of helpful information and photos and is very user friendly.

laporteavenuenursery.com has an amazing selection of rock garden plants including some excellent wildflower companions to cacti and other succulents. A few cacti as well as other succulents such as *Lewisia* species are among the offerings here, but the number of well-grown western wildflowers that can adapt to dry situations is quite impressive.

mesagarden.com is a well-organized site offering a massive selection of both tender and cold-hardy cacti, as well as succulent plants and seed. This site does not show photos of plants, but does have good information that includes temperature limitations and an abundance of hard-to-find species at reasonable prices. The nursery specializes in North and South American cacti, as well as cold-hardy South African succulents and other succulent plants and seed, such as yuccas and agaves. It is one of the oldest mail-order nurseries in the United States specializing in cacti and succulents and is world famous for its seed selection.

milestogo.com offers an interesting assortment of succulents, including many rare and hard-to-find cacti. The site is well organized and easy to use.

riogrande-cacti.com has an easy-to-use site with nice photos and a good amount of information. The nursery grows mostly North American cacti, but has a variety of other plants, such as South African mesembs or iceplants as well as yuccas and agaves, at reasonable prices.

sunscapes.net is a mail-order nursery that specializes in rare, rock garden plants, including a number of interesting succulents, such as *Talinum* and *Dudleya cymosa* var. *pumila*, along with some cacti, many iceplants, and other South African garden species, which are naturals for dry gardens. This is also a great source for many western wildflowers that are adaptable to dry gardens. The site has an abundance of photos and good information, and it is easy to use.

timberlinegardens.com has a huge selection of perennials, including a large number of succulents and drought-tolerant species. Although it does not have many photos, it does have an abundance of plants at reasonable prices and much good information.

yuccado.com primarily deals in tropical and subtropical plants, but does offer a few of the cold-hardy yuccas and agaves, as well as some cacti. The site has lots of nice photos and is easy to use.

BIBLIOGRAPHY

Anderson, Edward F., *The Cactus Family*, Timber Press, 2001.

Anderson, Miles, *The Ultimate Book of Cacti and Succulents*, Hermes House, 2003.

Barthlott, Wilhelm, *Cacti: Botanical Aspects, Descriptions, and Cultivation*, Stanley Thornes, 1979.

Bartrúm, Douglas, *Growing Cacti and Succulents*, Hippocrene Books, 1975.

Beaston, Bill R., "Pediocacti in the Pacific Northwest," *Cactus and Succulent Journal* (U.S.) 65 (3), 1993.

Benson, Lyman, *The Cacti of the United States and Canada*, Stanford University Press, 1982.

Bickel, Darl G., "Winter-Hardy Cacti, Part 1," *Cactus and Succulent Journal* (U.S.) 68 (1), 1996.

Blum, Wolfgang, Michael Lange, Werner Rischer, and Jürgen Rutow, *Echinocereus: Monographie*, W. Blum et al., 1998.

Boissevain, Charles H., and Carol Davidson, *Colorado Cacti: An Illustrated Guide Describing All of the Native Colorado Cacti*, Abbey Garden Press, 1940.

Borg, John, *Cacti: A Gardener's Handbook for Their Identification and Cultivation*, 4th ed., Blanford Press, 1976.

Brethauer, Bruce, *Cactus in the Snow: A Guide to Growing Hardy Cacti in the Wet and Frozen North*, B. Brethauer, 2000.

Britton, Nathaniel L., and Joseph N. Rose, *The Cactaceae*, 4 vols. Dover Publications, reprint of the 1937 ed. as 2 vols., 1963.

Champie, Clark, *Cacti and Succulents of El Paso*, Abbey Garden Press, 1974.

Champie, Clark, "Discovery of a New Variant of *Cylindropuntia leptocaulis*," *Cactus and Succulent Journal* (U.S.) 75 (6), 2003.

Chidamian, Claude, *The Book of Cacti and Other Succulents*, Timber Press, reprint of the 1958 ed., 1984.

Colorado Native Plant Society, *Rare Plants of Colorado*, 2d ed., Falcon Press, 1997.

Craig, Robert T., *The Mammillaria Handbook*, Lofthouse, reprint of the 1945 ed., 1984.

Cullmann, Willy, Erich Götz, and Gerhard Gröner, *The Encyclopedia of Cacti*, Timber Press, 1986.

Dawson, E. Yale, *The Cacti of California*, University of California Press, [1966], 1975.

Dicht, Reto F., and Adrian D. Luthy, *Coryphantha: Cacti of Mexico and Southern USA*, Springer Books, 2005.

Donnell, Mark S., M.D., "*Sclerocactus*: Personal Observations," *Cactus and Succulent Journal* (U.S.) 55 (3), 1983.

Dringman, Dixie, "*Pediocactus* in the Hills Near Wenatchee," *The Cactus File* 2 (8), February 1996.

Dortort, Fred, "*Pediocactus*: The Not-So-Plain 'Cactus of the Plains'," parts 1 & 2, *Cactus and Succulent Journal* (U.S.) 71 (5 & 6), 1999.

Dortort, Fred, "The Canyon Conundrum," *Cactus and Succulent Journal* (U.S.) 75 (6), 2003.

Duke, Gary L., "Natural *Echinocereus* Hybrids of Otero County, New Mexico," parts 1 & 2, *Cactus and Succulent Journal* (U.S.) 75 (5& 6), 2003.

Earle, W. Hubert, *Cacti of the Southwest*, Rancho Arroyo Books, rev. ed., 1980.

Elliott, Roy C., *The Genus Lewisia*, Alpine Garden Society, 2d ed., 1978.

Evans, Douglas B., *Cactuses of Big Bend National Park*, University of Texas Press, 1998.

Fearn, Brian, and Leslie Pearcy, *The Genus Rebutia, 1895–1981*, Abbey Brook Cactus Nursery, 1981.

Ferguson, David J., "*Opuntia chisosensis,*" *Cactus and Succulent Journal* (U.S.) 58 (3), 1986.

Ferguson, David J., "*Opuntia macrocentra* and *Opuntia chlorotica,*" *Cactus and Succulent Journal* (U.S.) 60 (4), 1988.

Ferguson, David J., "Revision of the U.S. Members of the *Echinocereus triglochidiatus* Group," *British Cactus and Succulent Journal* 61 (5), 1989.

Fischer, Pierre C., "The Varieties of *Coryphantha vivipara,*" *Cactus and Succulent Journal* (U.S.) 52 (1), 1980.

Fischer, Pierre C., "*Echinocereus triglochidiatus* var. *toroweapensis,*" *Cactus and Succulent Journal* (U.S.) 63 (4), 1991.

Gentry, Howard Scott, *Agaves of Continental North America*, University of Arizona Press, 1982.

Glass, Charles, and Robert Foster, "*Toumeya* a *Sclerocactus?*" *Cactus and Succulent Journal* (U.S.) 56 (2), 1984.

Graf, Alfred B., *Exotica: Pictorial Cyclopedia of Exotic Plants from Tropical and Near-Tropic Regions*, 10th ed., Roehrs, 1990.

Griffin, Kelly J., "*Dudleya cymosa,*" *Cactus and Succulent Journal* (U.S.) 76 (5), 2004.

Haage, Walther, *Cacti and Succulents: A Practical Handbook*, Studio Vista, 1978.

Haenni, Rod, "Travels in the Southwest," *Cactus and Succulent Journal* (U.S.) 57 (34), 1985.

Hannon, Dylan, "*Manfreda* and Its Allies," *Cactus and Succulent Journal* (U.S.) 74 (5), 2002.

Heil, Kenneth, Barry Armstrong, and David Schleser, "A Review of the Genus *Pediocactus*," *Cactus and Succulent Journal* (U.S.) 53 (1), 1981.

Heil, Kenneth, and Steven Brack, "The Cacti of Big Bend National Park," *Cactus and Succulent Journal* (U.S.) 60 (1), 1988.

Heil, Kenneth, and Steven Brack, "The Cacti of Carlsbad Caverns National Park," *Cactus and Succulent Journal* (U.S.) 57 (3), 1985.

Heil, Kenneth, and Steven Brack, "The Cacti of Guadalupe National Park," *Cactus and Succulent Journal* (U.S.) 58 (4), 1986.

Heil, Kenneth, and Steven Brack, "The Cacti of White Sands National Monument," *Cactus and Succulent Journal* (U.S.) 58 (2), 1986.

Heil, Kenneth, and J. Mark Porter, "*Sclerocactus*: A Revision," *Haseltonia* 2, 1994.

Hochstätter, Fritz, *Pediocactus and Sclerocactus*, F. Hochstätter, 1989.

Hochstätter, Fritz, *Yucca*, 3 vols., F. Hochstätter, 2000–2004.

Houghton, Arthur D., "Genus *Pterocactus* Schumann," *Cactus and Succulent Journal* (U.S.) 57 (1), 1984.

Innes, Clive, *Alpines: The Illustrated Dictionary*, Timber Press, 1995.

Innes, Clive, *The Handbook of Cacti and Succulents*, Chartwell Books, 1988.

Innes, Clive, *Cacti*, rev. ed., Cassell Publishing, 1992.

Innes, Clive, and Charles Glass, *The Illustrated Encyclopedia of Cacti*, Chartwell Books, 2001.

Irish, Mary, "Growing Agaves in Cold Climates," *Cactus and Succulent Journal* (U.S.) 74 (4), 2002.

Irish, Mary, and Gary Irish, *Agaves, Yuccas, and Related Plants: A Gardener's Guide*, Timber Press, 2000.

Jankalski, Stephen M., *Cold-Hardy Cactus and Succulent Checklist*, S. M. Jankalski, 1990.

Kershaw, Linda, Andy MacKinnon, and Jim Pojar, *Plants of the Rocky Mountains*, Lone Pine Publishing, 1998.

Kiesling, Roberto, *Cactus de la Patagonia*, Colecion Cientifica Del Inta, 1988.

Kiesling, Roberto, "Cold-Resistant Cacti of Argentina," *Cactus and Succulent Journal* (U.S.) 58 (1), 1987.

Lamb, Brian M. *Letts Guide to Cacti of the World*, Charles Letts Publishing, 1991.

Leuenberger, Beat Ernst, "Observations on *Maihuenia* (Cactaceae) in Argentina and Chile," parts 1 & 2, *Cactus and Succulent Journal* (U.S.) 64 (2 and 3), 1992.

Lozano, Rogelio, and William Reid, "Claret Cup Cactus at White Sands National Monument," *Cactus and Succulent Journal* (U.S.) 54 (5), 1982.

Mabe, Rex E., *Gardening with Cactus*, Potpourri Press, 1989.

Mace, Tony, *Notocactus: A Review of the Genus*, 3d ed., Editors of the *Notocactus* Group, 1980.

Maddox, Ed, "*Homalocephala texensis*: Texas Horse Crippler," *Cactus and Succulent Journal* (U.S.) 58 (5), 1986.

Maddox, Ed, and Charles Glass, "Unique Cacti Unique to Texas," *Cactus and Succulent Journal* (U.S.) 63 (1), 1991.

Mellen, Georganne, "The *Echinocereus fendleri* Controversy," *Cactus and Succulent Journal* (U.S.) 63 (4), 1991.

Mineo, Baldassare, *Rock Garden Plants*, Timber Press, 1999.

Mitich, Larry, "The Minuscule *Coryphantha minima*," *Cactus and Succulent Journal* (U.S.) 73 (3), 2001.

Mitich, Larry, "*Echinocereus lloydii*," *Cactus and Succulent Journal* (U.S.) 73 (1), 2001.

Mitich, Larry, "*Sclerocactus mariposensis*," *Cactus and Succulent Journal* (U.S.) 73 (6), 2001.

Mosco, Alessandro, "Hardy Succulents: Cultivation Notes," *Cactus and Co.* 10 (2), 2002.

Nicholls, Graham, *Alpine Plants of North America*, Timber Press, 2002.

Nold, Robert, *High and Dry: Gardening with Cold-Hardy Dryland Plants*, Timber Press, 2008.

Nold, Robert, *Penstemons*, Timber Press, 1999.

Parfitt, Bruce D., "New Nomenclature Combinations in the *Opuntia polyacantha* Complex," *Cactus and Succulent Journal* (U.S.) 70 (4), 1998.

Pilbeam, John, *Cacti for the Connoisseur: A Guide for Growers and Collectors*, Timber Press, 1987.

Pilbeam, John, *Mammillaria: A Collector's Guide*, Universe Books, 1980.

Pilbeam, John, "Breathless in New Mexico," *The Cactus File* 1 (11), 1993.

Pizzetti, Mariella, *Simon and Schuster's Guide to Cacti and Succulents*, translated by Stanley Schuler, Simon and Schuster, 1985.

Powell, A. Michael, "Third-Generation Experimental Hybrids in the *Echinocereus ×lloydii* Complex," *Haseltonia* 6, 1998.

Powell, A. Michael, and James F. Weedin, *Cacti of the Trans-Pecos and Adjacent Areas*, Texas Tech University Press, 2004.

Putnam, E. W., *Gymnocalyciums: A Guide for Growers*, National Cactus and Succulent Society of Great Britain, 1978.

Raun, Gerald G., "Distribution and Density of *Coryphantha hesteri* in the Big Bend Region of Texas," *Cactus and Succulent Journal* (U.S.) 68 (3), 1996.

Raun, Gerald G., "*Echinomastus* in the Trans-Pecos Region of Texas," *Cactus and Succulent Journal* (U.S.) 69 (3), 1997.

Reeves, Bob, "*Toumeya papyracantha*: What and Where Next?" *Cactus and Succulent Journal* (U.S.) 66 (4), 1994.

Rowley, Gordon, *A History of Succulent Plants*, Strawberry Press, 1977.

Rowley, Gordon, *The Illustrated Encyclopedia of Succulents, Cacti, and Cactus-like Plants*, Leisure Books, 1978.

Rowley, Gordon, "Girolamo Molon and His 'Lost' *Yucca* Book," *Cactus and Succulent Journal* (U.S.) 81 (5), 2009.

Schifferdecker, Robert C., "Observations of a 'Kansas Pincushion' *Coryphantha missouriensis*," *Cactus and Succulent Journal* (U.S.) 53 (3), 1981.

Schifferdecker, Robert C., "*Opuntia macrorhiza* Engelmann: The Bigroot Prickly Pear of the Great Plains Grasslands," *Cactus and Succulent Journal* (U.S.) 58 (2), 1986.

Smith, Colin, *Yuccas: Giants Among the Lilies*, National Council for the Conservation of Plants and Gardens of Great Britain, 2004.

Speirs, Dale, "The Opuntias of Alberta, Canada," *Cactus and Succulent Journal* (U.S.) 61 (5), 1989.

Starr, Greg, "*Agave ovatifolia*: The Whale's Tongue Agave," *Cactus and Succulent Journal* (U.S.) 76 (6), 2004.

Stephenson, Ray, *Sedum: Cultivated Stonecrops*, Timber Press, 1994.

Ullrich, Bernd, "Open-Air Cultivation of Agaves in Southwestern Germany," *Cactus and Succulent Journal* (U.S.) 63 (6), 1991.

Weniger, Del, *Cacti of Texas and Neighboring States: A Field Guide*, University of Texas Press, [1984], 1988.

Wieprecht, Jean, "Winter-Hardy Cacti," parts 1 & 2, *Cactus and Succulent Journal* (U.S.) 55 (6), 1983, and 56 (1), 1984.

Worthington, Richard, "Observations on the Flowering of Cacti from the Vicinity of El Paso, Texas," *Cactus and Succulent Journal* (U.S.) 58 (5), 1986.

PHOTOGRAPHY CREDITS

All photos by the author unless otherwise noted below.

Bill Adams/sunscapes.net: pages 109 bottom; 110 bottom; 128; 134 bottom; 135 top; 148 top; 253; 255.

Don Barnett: pages 21; 61 left; 124 top; 127 bottom; 168 top; 216 bottom; 249; 252; 270.

Donnie Barnett: pages 110 top; 112 top & bottom; 117 bottom right; 121 top; 123; 132 bottom; 137 top; 139 bottom; 142 bottom; 147; 148 bottom; 149; 152; 165; 175 top & bottom; 176 bottom; 177 top & bottom; 178; 180; 185 top & bottom; 186 top & bottom; 187 left & right; 188 top & bottom; 189 top & bottom; 190; 195; 236 top.

Ann Chance: pages 132 top; 163 top.

Greg Foreman: pages 215 bottom; 236 bottom; 260.

Kelly Grummons/coldhardycactus.com: pages 19; 81 top; 86 top & bottom; 87 top & bottom; 88 bottom; 90 top; 91 bottom; 95 top & bottom; 97 bottom right; 98 top & bottom; 99 left top, right middle, bottom; 129 bottom; 137 bottom; 193 bottom; 203; 213; 223; 230 top.

Ben Heitman: pages 74; 227 top; 239.

Panayoti Kelaidis: pages 40; 44; 56; 57; 70; 90 bottom; 91 top; 92 top; 97 bottom left; 117 bottom left; 120 top; 122; 133 bottom; 174; 179 top & bottom; 196; 226; 232 top & bottom; 234 top left; 250 bottom; 251 left; 254 top; 266.

Steve Miles: pages 31; p. 46; 58; 100; 102; 105; 118 bottom; 126 bottom; 127 top; 136 bottom; 172.

Zach Tice: pages 50–52; 54; 59; 80 bottom; 89 top; 96 bottom; 201; 210 top & bottom; 221 top; 228 bottom; 234 top right & bottom; 235; 244; 250 top left; 280.

INDEX

backfilling a planting hole, 49
Bailey's hedgehog. See *Echinocereus baileyi*
banana yucca. See *Yucca baccata*
barberry. See *Berberis thunbergii*
Barnett family garden, 20, 147, 270
    cacti in, 124, 152, 165, 168
    coryphanthas/escobarias in, 110, 112, 115, 117, 120, 121
    echinocereus in, 127, 131, 137, 138, 139, 142
    echinomastus in, 147, 148, 149
    oddball cacti in, 194, 195
    pediocactus in, 175, 176, 177, 178, 180
    sclerocactus in, 185, 186, 187, 188, 189, 190
    succulents in, 210, 216, 234, 249, 252
beaked yucca. See *Yucca rostrata*
Beaucarnea recurvata, 238
beaver tail. See *Opuntia basilaris*
beehive cactus. See *Escobaria vivipara*
beetles, 60–61, 100
bellflower. See *Campanula*
Berberis thunbergii, 283
    'Crimson Pygmy', 283
    'Golden Nugget', 283
Bergeranthus jamesii, 139
Berlandiera lyrata, 262
berm preparation, 46–49
big bluestem grass. See *Andropogon gerardii*
big needle pincushion. See *Coryphantha macromeris*
birds, 236, 258, 261, 273, 280, 292
bitterroot. See *Lewisia*
black chin cactus. See *Gymnocalycium gibbosum* var. *nigrum*
blackfoot daisy. See *Melampodium leucanthum*
blue avena grass. See *Helictotrichon sempervirens*

blue barrel. See *Echinocactus horizonthalonius*
blue fescue. See *Festuca glauca*
blue grama grass. See *Boutelous gracilis*
blue oat grass. See *Helictotrichon sempervirens*
blue spirea. See *Caryopteris* ×*clandonensis*
Bouteloua curtipendula, 275
Bouteloua gracilis, 275
Boyce Thompson's hedgehog. See *Echinocereus boyce-thompsonii*
bristly suncup. See *Notocactus submammulosus*
brittle prickly pear. See *Opuntia fragilis*
broom. See *Cytisus*
Bruch's chin cactus. See *Gymnocalycium bruchii*
buckthorn. See *Rhamnus*
buckhorn cholla. See *Cylindropuntia acanthocarpa*
buckwheat. See *Eriogonum*
Buddleja, 288
bunch ball claret cup. See *Echinocereus coccineus*
butterflies, 258, 261, 292
butterfly bush. See *Buddleja*
butterfly weed. See *Asclepias*
button cactus. See *Epithelantha micromeris*

Cactaceae, 72, 73, 152
cactus beetle, black longhorn, 61, 125
cactus beetle, tiny, 61
cactus bug, 60
Calamagrostis ×*acutiflora* 'Karl Foerster', 276
Calamagrostis ×*acutiflora* 'Overdam', 276
Calamagrostis 'Avalanche', 276
Calamagrostis brachytricha, 276